"Doing ACT raises common, predictable challenges. In almost every case they are best overcome by stepping into the ACT model and its foundations with your head, your hands, and your heart. This gentle but wise book shows how to do that—and on all three of those levels. It is indeed *Advanced Acceptance and Commitment Therapy*—not because it applies only to those who are advanced, but because it teaches you how to advance. You don't have to *be* an ACT expert to buy it, read it, and benefit from it—but if you buy it and read it, I guarantee that you will be much more expert in the ACT work you do."

> —**Steven C. Hayes, PhD**, cofounder of Acceptance and Commitment Therapy (ACT)

"It's rare that I read a textbook that's so good, I don't merely want to recommend it, I want to actually *rave* about it—in a very loud voice! *Advanced Acceptance and Commitment Therapy* is such a book: a truly superb advanced-level textbook for the ACT practitioner who already has a handle on the basics, but now wants to evolve a more fluid, flexible, and effective style of ACT. I confess to having frequent pangs of envy as I read this book (which I devoured cover to cover in the space of one week) and many thoughts such as, *I wish I'd written this.* It's easy to read, extremely engaging (in parts, laugh-out-loud funny), and incredibly practical. Even highly experienced ACT practitioners will get a lot from this book. I certainly learned new things from reading it, and I'll bet good money that you will too! ... So if you're ready to move from the beginner level 'ACT-ish therapy' to genuine, high-powered ACT, then rush out and get this book *now*!"

> —**Russ Harris**, author of *The Happiness Trap* and *Getting Unstuck in ACT*

"As I read *Advanced Acceptance and Commitment Therapy*, I kept turning to my personal knowledge of Darrah Westrup and her incredible ability to communicate, in writing, her gifted therapeutic experience and understanding of ACT. I know Darrah as both a colleague and a friend, and this book shines a bright light on her amazing talent and facility with the intervention. Readers will be engaged from the opening pages regarding theory and processes, through the thoughtful and seasoned application of ACT, all the way to its invitation to continue the ACT journey at the book's close. She brings to this volume not only a digestible, considered, and at times humorous read, that every therapist, not just those using ACT, will find invaluable, but also a personal sense of herself that is kind, grounded, and compassionate. Thank you, Darrah, for this beautiful contribution to the ACT community and therapist community at large."

> —**Robyn D. Walser, PhD**, associate director of dissemination and training at the National Center for PTSD, director at TL Consultation Services, and assistant clinical professor at the University of California, Berkeley

"*Advanced Acceptance and Commitment Therapy* is an invaluable resource for every therapist who doesn't just want to do good ACT but great ACT. Easy to read and very practical, this book succeeds at linking concrete skills to deep philosophical and behavioral principles underlying the ACT model. The numerous clinical vignettes are commented with great precision and clarity, and show how to activate key processes through natural interactions, beyond traditional exercises."

—**Matthieu Villatte, PhD**, research scientist at the Evidence-Based Practice Institute, Seattle; ACBS-recognized ACT trainer; and associate editor of the *Journal of Contextual Behavioral Science*

Advanced Acceptance & Commitment Therapy

The Experienced Practitioner's Guide to Optimizing Delivery

DARRAH WESTRUP, PhD

New Harbinger Publications, Inc.

Publisher's Note

Distributed in Canada by Raincoast Books

Copyright © 2014 by Darrah Westrup
        New Harbinger Publications, Inc.
        5674 Shattuck Avenue
        Oakland, CA 94609
        www.newharbinger.com

Cover design by Amy Shoup
Acquired by Catharine Meyers
Edited by Susan LaCroix
Indexed by James Minkin

Library of Congress Cataloging-in-Publication Data

Westrup, Darrah.
  Advanced acceptance and commitment therapy : the experienced practitioner's guide to optimizing delivery / Darrah Westrup, PhD.
     pages cm
  Summary: "In Advanced Acceptance and Commitment Therapy, a licensed clinical psychologist and renowned ACT expert presents the first advanced ACT book for use in client sessions. Inside, readers will hone their understanding of the core processes behind ACT and learn practical strategies for moving past common barriers that can present during therapy, such as over-identifying with clients or difficulty putting theory into practice"-- Provided by publisher.
  Includes bibliographical references and index.
  ISBN 978-1-60882-649-0 (paperback) -- ISBN 978-1-60882-650-6 (pdf e-book) -- ISBN 978-1-60882-651-3 (epub) 1. Acceptance and commitment therapy. I. Title.
  RC489.C62W47 2014
  616.89'1425--dc23
                         2014006466

Printed in the United States of America

16   15   14

10 9 8 7 6 5 4 3 2 1   First printing

Contents

PART 1
Getting Oriented

PART 2
Tricky Little Pieces and Common Missteps

PART 3
Some Finer Points

Acknowledgments

I would like to thank my patient copy editor, Susan LaCroix, and the rest of the folks at New Harbinger for being so consistently great to work with. Thank you, Tammy Hoier and Mike Todt, for your support and feedback, crucial "Chloe coverage," and the gift of the perfect writing space at the perfect time. I owe the eagle-eyed Matthieu Villatte a huge thanks for his generosity, time, and wisdom. I feel the need to acknowledge Steven Hayes's big brain and all the other big brains that have contributed to this technology. How extraordinary to have developed something with so much potential to improve the human condition! I give a heartfelt thanks to my forbearing husband and daughter for those precious weekends, evenings, and untold other sacrifices. You give me the gift of being present and in the business of active loving every day. Finally, I wish to thank all the consultees, trainees, and supervisees with whom I've had the great fortune to travel, and who are in large part responsible for any wisdom contained in these pages.

INTRODUCTION

Where It All Begins

This is my sixth attempt to introduce this book. Since previous efforts to ease into my purpose here while also avoiding discomfort have failed, I'll just be direct with why I felt there was room for a book of this sort. It has been my observation (starting with my own history) that there can be a real gap between being trained in or otherwise learning about Acceptance and Commitment Therapy (ACT) and doing it effectively. If you have worked with ACT you may have experienced this as well. In fact, that may be one of the reasons you have picked up this book. There are a couple of things that stand out for me about this gap. One concerns the degree of departure many ACT therapists make from the model, despite the proliferation of ACT trainings and a wealth of excellent ACT texts and learning materials. So while there is no shortage of information on how to conduct ACT with fidelity, I have observed that what actually happens in real-world sessions is often something quite different. This has important theoretical implications, but it is the practical consequences that will be examined most closely in this book. The other aspect that seems important is the commonalities in the struggles many therapists have with ACT. There are certain areas where providers tend to flounder, and typical difficulties and missteps that seem to be made by nearly everyone at some point or another. That's actually good news, for if particular pitfalls are that predictable then certainly they can be talked about and worked on.

It took me a few years to move from learning about the therapy to putting it into practice. Although I had previously completed a two-day ACT workshop run by Steven Hayes, and had read various ACT texts and even completed an ACT-related dissertation back in '97, something had prevented me from actually implementing the therapy. I can best describe this as a vague yet pervasive fear that I might do something wrong. Not only was I unsure of how to proceed, I was pretty sure I would not know what I was doing much of the time. Turns out I was right. In my subsequent work as a training supervisor and ACT consultant, I have found my experience to be a natural and essentially unavoidable one for therapists working with ACT, and that this is about more than learning something new. The fact that ACT is so firmly rooted in a coherent and fleshed-out theory—that it was built from the ground up as the clinical derivative of established behavioral principles—means that there is a distinct model in ACT that is either being followed or not. And just because it's elegant doesn't mean it's easy. The fundamental tenets of ACT directly oppose ideas supported by our culture (and our own minds), making it very easy for therapists to purposefully or inadvertently depart from the model to varying degrees. This departure poses a theoretical dilemma, because unless you are conducting ACT in a way that is consistent with the principles upon which it is based, you are contradicting the entire model. Clinically speaking, conducting ACT in this way hamstrings the therapy. Or rather, the greater the congruence with the model, the more powerful the therapy will be.

Discomfort shows up again as I make such sweeping statements. I am emboldened, however, by my experience supervising numerous psychology interns, practicum students, and postdoctoral fellows in conducting ACT, which typically has involved direct observation and cofacilitation. I also work as an ACT consultant for various organizations and individuals, including serving as an expert ACT consultant for a nationwide rollout of ACT in Veterans Affairs. I have participated in this last project for the past five years. It involves working with groups of providers over a period of six months, listening to taped sessions and providing weekly feedback. This particular project has provided me a window into the experiences of seasoned providers as they conduct ACT over time with a variety of individuals. Needless to say, the project has significantly enhanced my own ACT skills. At last count I have reviewed and provided critical feedback on well over 1,000 ACT sessions. All together, these experiences have taught me a great deal about ACT and its challenges, and convinced me of the value of passing what I've learned on to others interested in this therapy. I certainly have had a chance to see what does and doesn't work.

My intention with this book is to be helpful at the clinical level, to offer substantive assistance with the common barriers and challenges encountered as therapists conduct the therapy with actual clients, and to help those working with ACT to optimize what the therapy offers. A major thrust of this book is that in order to do ACT well, therapists need to approach the therapy from the behavioral principles forming ACT. Doing so, of course, requires familiarity with those principles. (As we work with the various clinical issues discussed in this book, I'll sometimes refer to this stance as operating from within the ACT framework, or as looking at the therapy through an "ACT lens.") This is why we begin in part 1 by taking a look at theoretical underpinnings of ACT, as this is the place from which everything else flows. Similarly, the way in which sessions are structured, pacing, and the manner in which the therapist shows up in the room play a major part in how well (or not) the therapy will go, so we will explore these topics before moving on to specific components of the therapy. Part 2 tackles common difficulties encountered when therapists approach the main components of ACT—such as the role of language, creative hopelessness, and self-as-context—and will explore ways to work with some of the barriers that tend to show up over the course of the therapy. The last section, part 3, examines the more subtle issues that are no less significant in terms of their impact on ACT sessions.

It is important to note at this point that the clinical examples provided throughout the book are either fictitious or amalgams of various clinical scenarios and individuals I have encountered over the course of my supervisory, consulting, and personal clinical work. While my intent has been to capture "real life" examples of this therapy and its challenges, care has been taken that no particular individual or therapeutic situation can be identified. For example, when pulling out an actual snippet of dialogue in order to make a point, I have altered other information as a way to protect confidentiality.

I would like to add, before jumping in, that although the learning curve in ACT can sometimes seem steep, the slope can be short, or certainly shorter than it might seem when you're slogging up the steep part. Many of the common missteps, once rectified, help the rest of the therapy come together. In addition, as therapists our own experiences during this process offer up countless opportunities to apply and practice ACT principles in our own lives. These opportunities not only give us a deeper appreciation of the relevance of these principles but offer a firsthand account of what our clients are experiencing as well. Nonetheless, the challenges of conducting ACT well can be disheartening even to the most determined practitioner. It is my intention with this book to identify the areas where therapists tend to struggle, and then work with these in a way that will prove helpful to those traveling this particular journey.

It is at once humbling and exciting to think that at this moment someone is reading this sentence and contemplating whether there might be something of personal value in these pages. My hope is that there is, and that you will ultimately lay down this book feeling encouraged and inspired to take this powerful therapy as far as it can go. So let's get to it!

PART 1

Getting Oriented

CHAPTER 1

Let the Theory Guide the Way

Since this book is about optimizing ACT, it makes sense that almost immediately we bump up against the issue of fidelity. I've already been up front about my belief that fidelity to the model increases clinical effectiveness, as well as my observation that many therapists depart from the model to varying degrees. For most, this departure is not intentional. That is, many of the therapists with whom I have worked wholeheartedly buy into the importance of the ACT model, but for reasons we'll be exploring in these pages, they can struggle with translating ACT principles into what is going on in session. So even if the intention is to work consistently within the model, there seems to be no end to ways, large and small, that we can inadvertently do something inconsistent in session. Such moves are not always accidental. I have worked with many therapists who are simply less concerned with conducting ACT with fidelity, who might intentionally choose to move off the model here or there for various reasons. In many cases congruence with the theory behind ACT is just not viewed as being that clinically important.

One potential reason for this view is that ACT can be seen as dovetailing with a previously held philosophy or therapeutic orientation that has simply not required the sort of articulation we see in ACT. For example, therapists with backgrounds in mindfulness, narrative, or other acceptance-based approaches find many of the central ideas in ACT familiar and consistent with what they have already been doing—doing without the benefit of an evidence-based theoretical model. The difference in language used by the scientific and clinical domains of ACT has not helped. It's not just that there's a difference, but that the language differs so much in feel. Whereas an ACT therapist will speak to clients about "accepting what is" and "making choices according to deeply held values," the researcher might discuss "coming into contact with direct contingencies" or "verbally construed consequences that establish intrinsically reinforcing behavior." There is a warm and fuzzy feel to the language used in the therapy, whereas the language used in the science is necessarily technical and precise. Not particularly friendly, in other words. The bottom line is that without translation it isn't immediately clear how one domain pertains to the other, and the technical language can simply turn off therapists who were particularly drawn to the language of the therapy.

I have also found that sometimes therapists miss the fact that in ACT, the theory *is* the therapy. It is understandable but misleading to view the theory as being "behind" the therapy, as simply supporting or explaining the clinical piece. The discussion topics, exercises, and metaphors suggested in various ACT texts are used to advance core behavioral processes found to be central to psychological flexibility. These processes are the point, not all the technique. It is significant that this topic is addressed in virtually every ACT text, and yet many providers approach the topics, metaphors, and exercises (the technique of ACT) as *being* the point rather than *illustrating* the point (the processes of ACT). As we will be exploring, this approach has the effect in the therapy room of actually working against the very abilities you are hoping to develop in ACT.

To summarize, there is a perception by many therapists that the clinical and theoretical domains pertinent to ACT are bound only by ideas, that the theory matters chiefly at an academic level rather than having an active role in the therapy room. In fact, theory drives the entire intervention in ACT, whether or not the therapist would articulate the therapeutic process in this way. As we will be seeing in the pages to come, when it comes to clinical decision-making in ACT, the theory is the therapist's best friend.

DIVING IN

And now I face a couple of challenges: Based upon the numerous ACT therapists I have encountered, I imagine that readers of this book could include those who are highly familiar with the theory and science behind ACT, those with little familiarity and little interest, and of course everyone in between. So one challenge is to provide a useful orientation to the rest of this book while not turning anyone off or boring anyone to death. The second challenge concerns how far into detail to go with this material. ACT is 1) a culmination of a particular worldview and approach to science (functional contextualism), 2) a particular approach to behavior (radical behaviorism), and 3) a particular methodology (applied behavioral analysis) which, when applied to the processes of human thinking and language acquisition, resulted in 4) a particular theory (relational frame theory) that informs the therapy. As it stands today ACT is considered one clinical piece of a larger and rapidly expanding area of science with the specific aim of applying functional contextualism to behavior (contextual behavioral science). In short, the schools of thought and areas of study just mentioned have their own histories, objectives, and implications. Together they represent the evolution of a particular way of approaching human behavior that manifests in this therapy we call ACT. They are therefore each deserving of close examination, particularly in what is being put forth as an "advanced" text. However, their very depth and cogency make that unrealistic here for reasons of scope alone. This is a highly clinical book, and there is plenty to talk about using clinically directed language. What to do?

I have decided to approach this question as pragmatically as possible. That is, while any point of discussion in this next section could be taken further (in other words, could get more technical), I hope to stay at a level that translates fairly obviously to what we do in session. Although each of the areas of study listed above has contributed to the psychological model forming ACT, some principles and processes are particularly evident in the therapy room. As I work through some of the common barriers in ACT in this book, for example, we will see how increased clarity regarding these principles can optimize decision-making and help prevent common missteps. However, some additional context is needed to understand how principles derived from these areas of study fit together so that we approach the therapy in the way that we do—with fidelity, in other words. So how *do* the principles and processes fit together?

THE AIM OF ACT

Let's start with the overarching objective of ACT, which is to help clients develop psychological flexibility. In their seminal book, *Acceptance and Commitment Therapy: The Process and Practice of Mindful Change*, Steven Hayes, Kirk Strosahl, and Kelly Wilson offer the following definition: "Psychological flexibility can be defined as contacting the present moment as a conscious human being, fully and without needless defense—as it is and not what it says it is—and persisting with or changing behavior in the service of chosen values" (2012, pp. 96–97). A simple way to think about psychological flexibility is that it's the ability to respond to life in a workable way, a way that enables us to live vital, meaningful lives.

This question of workability is a fundamental aspect of the therapy. From understanding what the client is pursuing in therapy, to determining what to target, to deciding how to respond to something that occurs in session, we look to workability as our guide in ACT. Asking whether or not something is workable is asking about its function. That is, what function is a particular behavior serving in the client's life, in the particular situation being explored, even in this moment? How will a particular response on our part function in this session? These questions cannot be answered without considering the consequences of the behavior in question, both short- and long-term. In other words, the function of a specific behavior depends upon the context in which it occurs, specifically upon what follows the behavior. So in ACT we are very interested in function, which necessarily involves the relations between whatever behavior we are considering and its particular context.

In this pragmatic focus in ACT we can already see the respective influences of two of the four areas mentioned previously: a particular worldview and approach to science (functional contextualism), and a particular approach to the study of human behavior (radical behaviorism). Functional contextualism is a philosophy of science that views an event or act as inseparable from the context in which it is embedded. Since there is no way to examine anything completely separate from its context, there is no way to establish its inherent "truth" (or "reality" or "correctness"), as that is always going to be influenced by its context (which cannot be separated out from the event or act in question). The focus of functional contextualism is accordingly and pragmatically on prediction and control of events, rather than on attempting to uncover or establish their inherent truth or rightness. To a functional contextualist, "what's true is what works" (Hayes, Strosahl, & Wilson, 2012, p. 33). This philosophical approach to science is reflected in the influential school of psychology known as radical behaviorism. That is, radical behaviorism also recognizes that there is no way to uncover or prove the inherent trueness, or rightness, or correctness of something—in this case, behavior. It is context that determines how a behavior functions. Like functional contextualism, the focus is pragmatically on prediction and control, specifically the prediction and control of behavior toward a desired end. The point is that ACT's focus on workability, on the function of behavior as determined by context, is based upon these fundamental views of the world, of science, and of behavior.

There is another implication: what is *not* a focus in ACT. In ACT we do not approach client behavior (which is meant to include internal thoughts, feelings, and sensations as well as overt actions) as being inherently bad, or abnormal, or as a symptom of something that is inherently bad or abnormal. This again is because the normality or abnormality of something, its correctness or incorrectness as a "truth," cannot be established (because it cannot be separated from context and its influences). Working with the categories abnormal and normal is therefore not productive. So when considering a particular behavior in ACT (such as anxious thoughts or feelings, depressive mood, traumatic memories, or drinking alcohol) we do so from the pragmatic standpoint of how it is functioning for the client.

This pragmatic focus is quite different from many other "mental health" approaches. If we give up viewing behavior as inherently bad or abnormal, there is no need to attempt to fix, heal, or otherwise alter the actual behavior. In fact, if it is function (as determined by context) that determines workability, it would follow that targeting function, rather than behavior per se, would be a productive goal. This is one reason why, in ACT, we don't strive to fix or eliminate behaviors that other approaches might view as abnormal or unhealthy—such as anxious thoughts, intrusive trauma memories, depressive feelings, or urges to drink. Instead we focus on altering how they are functioning in our clients' lives. So not only have the philosophy and theory forming ACT influenced what we are ultimately shooting for; they directly guide how we go about getting there.

THE MEANS OF ACT

So far I have pointed to the focus on workability in ACT; how this focus necessarily involves an examination of how behaviors are functioning for clients; and the fact that this, in turn, means considering the context in which they occur. But how do we go about this? Once a behavior is determined to be unworkable, what do we do then? This is where the other two areas of study, applied behavioral analysis—specifically functional analysis—and behavioral learning principles, come in. (And, in this and the next few paragraphs, we will also have a perfect example of that disconcerting difference between the language used in the science and that used in the therapy room.)

Heading in fearlessly, when we talk about the functional analysis of behavior, we are referring to an examination of the relations between a particular unit of behavior and certain contextual variables that influence that behavior. We look at what was going on in the environment, the presence of which made the behavior more likely to occur (also called a setting event or antecedent), and what followed the behavior that made it more or less likely to occur again (the behavior's consequences). This terminology helps define the focus of study—meaning the behavior in question—which could be a small unit of behavior (for example, smoking), a smaller unit still (such as the act of inhaling), or a larger set of behaviors (such as coping strategies). Functional analysis of behavior also articulates the relations between that behavior and its antecedents and consequences. That was a mouthful! And yet it describes what we are continually doing as human beings. Whether we know it or not, we continually engage in functional analyses in our daily lives.

Everyday Ol' Functional Analyses

Imagine for a moment that you are sitting in a movie theater and a wad of paper hits your head. Your first response, after blinking, would be to determine what in the heck just happened. By that I don't really mean the what—you already know that: a wad of paper hit your head. You would be interested in the why. Not just the why at a descriptive level, as in "The paper hit my head because someone propelled it in a trajectory consistent with where my head was positioned," but why at a functional level: "What was the purpose of that wad of paper hitting my head?" And not only would you immediately seek the answer to that question in the current context (in other words, who threw that and why); you would almost as immediately be formulating an answer: "Oh, my friend Jane two rows back *saw me here* (the antecedent) and *threw* that (the behavior) to *get my attention* (the consequence)." Note that it was the result of her throwing the paper wad that determined its actual function for Jane. That is, if you hadn't felt the wad of paper and turned your head, her throwing it wouldn't have served the function of getting your attention. Also, if instead of Jane, it were a surly-looking teenager scowling at you who'd thrown the wad of paper, you might come up with a different analysis for the incident altogether. The point is that we are constantly engaging in functional analyses as a way to understand our world and form our responses to it.

As therapists, too, we automatically look to context to determine how to interpret client behavior. If my client informs me that he turned down a dinner invitation, for example, declining means very little in and of itself. It is the current and historical context that determines how I respond to this, and it is something I begin to take into consideration the moment I hear that he declined. If he experiences anxiety in social situations (antecedent) and declines (behavior) as a way to avoid the anxiety (consequence), yet wants to be more connected with others, I would respond one way. If he is in early recovery from alcohol abuse, and staying away from these sorts of situations increases the likelihood he stays sober, I would respond in another. Perhaps he has a history of avoiding social situations but on this particular evening had the flu. In each case the workability of the client's behavior rests upon how it is functioning for him, which in turn rests upon the consequences in the particular context we are examining. If we look only at the more immediate context, declining might be deemed workable because a consequence was tension relief. Looking at a larger context—say his social network—declining may not be so workable if it ultimately increases his isolation.

Everyday Ol' Learning Principles

In the scenario just described we immediately recognize there are important differences in the various ways a therapist could respond. We can even make educated guesses on which response would be best depending on the situation. But let's take a closer look. Why do we reject one possible response and select another? How do we know one will serve better than another depending upon the context? Because our own learning has taught us about learning. Just as our behavior, past and present, is the product of fundamental learning principles, we have learned how to utilize these principles to analyze and influence others. We have learned from experience, for example, that our responses form a consequence, that we can influence client behavior in this way, and that we can predict how our influence will impact (function for) the client.

Consider the following example: When your client takes a risk and hesitantly shares an experience of being raped that has been the source of much shame and suffering, you immediately consider how best to respond. That is, although you might find yourself feeling as though you want to avoid the topic, or perhaps thinking, "She never should have trusted that guy," you would likely refrain from expressing these thoughts and feelings because you can predict the way this might impact the therapy. In fact, a reasonably seasoned or skilled clinician would likely be formulating his response with awareness that he might do something that could increase the client's shame and secret-keeping (for example, reacting with disgust or offering a harsh judgment), as opposed to something that would make her more likely to share shameful experiences in future sessions (such as listening compassionately and validating her experience). There would be recognition that his responses could result in new learning. For example, the client might learn that she can share such a secret and remain safe, that she will not be rejected by the therapist (although her mind and even previous experience has told her otherwise), and that she can tolerate the experience of talking about it. In this sense the therapist recognizes that he might be able to alter how the experience of having been raped functions for the client. In fact, in ACT our aim would be to help the client relate to this rape and all it entails in a more workable way. We can think of the therapist here as having "common sense," or perhaps as being "perceptive." The bottom line is that when we consider how to respond to clients we are utilizing fundamental learning principles that describe how we humans learn to do what we do.

In the above example, I mentioned various ways you could respond to your client after she has shared something like this in session, and that each represented a different consequence with the potential for influencing the client's behavior in the future. This is an example of the process of *operant conditioning*—learning by consequences. If what you said or did, or even what you did *not* say or do, increased the likelihood that the client would share such a secret again, your response positively reinforced that action. For example, if simply being silent resulted in her sharing more of these sorts of things in session, your silence functioned as a reinforcer. If your response decreased the likelihood, it served as a punisher to her sharing.

Moving on, if your client were to tell you that she felt nauseated every time she saw someone who resembled the perpetrator, you would immediately understand why. That is, you would understand that in those instances the other, unknown individual was being associated with the perpetrator in such a way that your client was having the same visceral responses as she did at the time of the rape. Whether or not you would describe it in these terms, you are recognizing the principle of *respondent conditioning*—learning by association. In fact, it would probably make sense to you if she said that over time she had noticed this association process was growing. Now, even if someone only slightly resembles the perpetrator she feels nauseated, and sometimes just seeing a strange man, period, is enough to make her feel a little queasy. This represents yet another fundamental learning principle, technically termed *generalization*.

Finally, if the client were to tell you that she quickly removes herself from such situations I'm guessing you would not be surprised. You would understand that she does so in order to escape the unpleasant reactions she is having—a very typical, very human response. As you know, in ACT we call this *experiential avoidance*, and it is also a learned behavior. Not only would you anticipate that this avoidance might cause problems in her life, you would most likely understand that this sort of avoidant response helps maintain her fear around these types of situations.

I have been pointing out that the learning principles so fundamental to the ACT model are familiar principles that we use in our everyday lives and in the therapy room. This isn't intended as an intellectual exercise. Just as there are reasons for what we do and don't do in life, just as there is purpose behind any of the choices we make in the therapy room, there is clear intention behind what we do and don't do in ACT.

The same fundamental learning principles are at work in all these scenarios. In ACT, having an *awareness* of these principles is key because that awareness is what drives intention and clinical decision-making. In ACT we work at the level of these principles. More on that in a minute—it's time to pull in one more essential piece: relational frame theory (RFT), a more recent area of study.

WHAT ABOUT RFT?

My favorite *Far Side* cartoon is just a single drawing of two cows, clearly a married couple. The male cow is sitting in an armchair with a beer, watching TV, while the wife, in pearls and with wine glass in hand (hoof), stands gazing wistfully out a picture window. "Wendell," she declares, "I am not content." The absurdity in this one statement reflects much of what is illuminated in RFT. The notion that a cow would have that particular thought is absurd. The notion that a cow would experience this type of discontent (the grass is always greener) is absurd, and particularly funny given the metaphor "contented as a cow." But why is it absurd? How is it that we understand the situation depicted here is uniquely human? Come to think of it, why is it we humans suffer in these ways to begin with, especially since other species don't appear to be saddled with this stuff? Basic research into the study of thinking and language acquisition began to suggest answers. What's more, the processes illuminated in this work pointed to something that could be done.

Given its central role in ACT, I suspect there's not an ACT therapist out there who hasn't read or heard at least something about RFT. It is a fascinating (I think) and impressive area of study, and expanding rapidly in terms of its relevancy and application. In the following very selective overview I don't mean to assume readers are not familiar with RFT. If you are familiar with it, then I hope you will forgive both the review and the license I am giving myself to pull out certain principles and forgo others. If you are not familiar with RFT, however, then perhaps this overview will help forge a connection between this fifth area and the therapy, and spark an interest in learning more about this important area of work. Every piece of RFT matters in terms of helping to develop and refine what we know about language and cognition, which has direct implications for what we do in ACT and for how all of us might approach the business of being human.

I find background helpful, so here's a brief overview of how RFT came to be: Prior to the development of RFT we did not have a useful theoretical model for the behavior we call thinking. The lack of a model stood in the way of studying and better understanding this important aspect of being human. What began as a behavior analytic examination into how verbal rules guide human behavior (for example, how it is that the process of therapy—what a therapist says to a client—can actually result in behavior change) eventually expanded to a full-blown model of human language and cognition. As we learned more about how humans acquire language and how "languaging" consequently functions, we gained clarity regarding some powerful abilities particular to humans when it comes to behavior. We began to develop a new understanding of human pathology. Specifically, we began to understand how our relationship with language can result in behaviors that are not very workable. This understanding, in turn, pointed to the specific abilities needed to respond to life in a more workable way (enter psychological flexibility). Over the course of many years of study, core processes underlying language and cognition were articulated and given empirical support. Processes with significant implications ranging from how we build an identity to how it is that we can suffer from something we have never even actually experienced (or that we experienced long ago) were revealed. Ultimately a technology—ACT—was developed that provided a means to develop psychological flexibility. More than a way to respond to life "nonpathologically," this technology offered a way to help humans live in accordance with deeply held values such that "workable" meant living a vital, meaningful life.

Relational What?

Let's touch on some of these abilities humans have when it comes to language and then I'll move more specifically to the ACT model. The starting point is about the human ability to infer—to relate things to one another. Inferring is deceptively simple, but unique to humans, as it turns out. The most basic explanation of this process that I've encountered is simply this: When we learn that A = B, we also infer that B = A. We've learned a relation: *the same as*—or the relation of *coordination*, as termed in RFT. But it gets more meaningful quickly. That is, we humans have the ability to infer that if A = B, and B = C, then A = C (and C = A). We don't have to be directly taught that A is the same as C, and that C is the same as A; we are able to "derive that relation," as said in RFT. Unlike other species (as far as we can tell), we can relate things even if they don't share physical properties. The expression on my daughter's face when I tell her that the stuff on her plate is a "vegetable" compared with the expression I would see if I told her it's "candy" says it all. For her, the learning sequence probably goes something like this:

The icky stuff (A) is called "peas" (B). So icky stuff equals "peas;" A = B. Then she learns through further language acquisition that "peas" (B) are "vegetables" (C), so peas equal vegetables; B = C. She then *derives* that the icky stuff (A) is a "vegetable" and that vegetables equal icky stuff (A = C and C = A). As it happens, she had also experienced learning along the lines of this: Wonderful-tasting stuff equals "lollipop," "lollipop" equals "candy," "candy" equals wonderful-tasting stuff. Further, the fact that she ignores the vegetable but then asks for candy for dessert suggests she has learned some additional relations, such as that of *comparison* (candy tastes *better* than vegetables, candy is *preferable* to vegetables). And—here's where it gets really interesting—it's not just that she knows that peas equal vegetables and that lollipops equal candy; the *qualities* (icky, wonderful) of each get transformed along with the derived relation. That is, when she scrunches up her face as though eating this never-before-encountered vegetable would be an unspeakable horror, it's clear that her experience of peas has been attached to the word "vegetable" and hence this stuff on her plate. In RFT this process is called *transformation of stimulus functions*—that is, the way the stimuli (peas), or more specifically the taste of the peas, functions for my daughter (ick), is transformed to anything that falls within this class of things called vegetables. (By the way, the ability to recognize and place something as part of a class represents another type of derived relation, referred to as the inferred relation of *hierarchy*). In short, with language comes the ability to relate various things in this way, to relationally frame ("frame" used metaphorically, as in how frames contain things). It's not just that my daughter has learned something about vegetables and candy, but that she has learned something about what "the same as" means, and what "better than" or "worse than" means.

The sequence described above, while inconvenient for a parent, is a relatively benign example of what this ability brings. Languaging (via relational framing) can also bring much suffering. So, for example, one moment my daughter could be dancing with joy, reveling in the experience of moving to music. All it would take to devastate her would be the words "You are the worst dancer in your class." "Worse than" would have no meaning for her, however, without her having previously learned the relational frame of comparison. Because she has acquired language and the ability to relationally frame, she has learned that "bad" equals something negative, and that "worse" equals more bad. Thanks to a host of other types of relational frames and the transformation of stimulus functions, this notion of being the worst dancer and the shame and hurt associated with it could easily be related to anything framed as being in the same class as dancing, such as performing, athletics, public speaking, or being "out there" in any way. The result could well be that she avoids such opportunities the rest of her life. She will have formed a *relational network* around "worst dancer in class" that can easily be expanded but not erased. (In other words, history cannot be erased). Enter a particular type of framing called *deictic framing* (to be defined and discussed at length in chapter 9). Briefly, via deictic framing we learn to build a sense of identity. So for my daughter, her self-concept would now likely include "I am a bad dancer." By means of the ever-constant relational framing, her self-concept becomes part of a complex relational network and could easily come to include such things as "I am clumsy," "I am shameful," or even "I am not good enough." Her very selfhood has now been significantly impacted by that one phrase—which, when you think about it, technically just consists of a combination of sounds.

So relational framing explains a key difference between us and cows. It demonstrates, for example, how it is that we can compare our life experience to an ideal ("Wendell, I am not content" or "I am not a good dancer"). It also explains how it is that we respond positively or problematically to things we've never encountered, how something that happened years ago can continue to influence how we live our lives now, and how we can perceive ourselves as being fundamentally okay or not okay. Unlike other species, we don't have to directly experience something in order to have a relationship with it. I learned long ago that venom equals bad, and that a water moccasin equals venom, so water moccasins are definitively bad in my book, although hopefully I will go my entire life without encountering one. The relational networks we form around ourselves and our experiences also explain how we come to relate to historical events as though they are in the present. For example, development of relational networks explains how the rape experienced by the client described earlier could lead to an avoidance of men—or even of intimacy, more generally—more than a decade after the actual event.

So What?

Now that I've gone here, I'll tell you why I think understanding this stuff at a basic level matters when doing ACT. First, the model starts to make a whole lot of sense, and it is easier to keep the core processes front and center as we move through the therapy. Second, it is easier to keep from doing things that contradict the model if we understand how doing so undermines the psychological flexibility we are hoping to further. Third, we are less tempted to try to "fix" our clients via changing things like self-concept and other internal experiences because we understand language operations (relational frames and networks), and we understand why we must instead look to alter how such experiences function for clients. Fourth, we understand the focus on workability, and the importance of analyzing behavior in terms of its specific context. While I suggested earlier that we naturally employ behavioral learning principles in our lives, being aware of and able to articulate what it is that we are doing expands our options, sharpens our decision-making, and helps us sort out how to respond in challenging clinical situations.

RFT has made a powerful contribution to our understanding of human behavior. RFT demonstrates how it becomes easy to live in a virtual world of relational frames rather than contacting and responding to what is actually happening in the moment. It is the reason ACT targets language, specifically this sort of "verbal dominance." I have found that some clarity into the actual processes going on here enables me to better work with the language piece of ACT. For example, when we say that, "A thought is just a thought," we really mean it is just a thought; that is, it is a construction and its meaning has been relationally derived.

Familiarity with RFT is clinically helpful because in clarifying how our relationship with language can cause so much difficulty, we see that these difficulties are clearly a fundamental aspect of being human. That is, rather than just going along with the notion that in ACT we strive for a horizontal therapeutic relationship, familiarity with the theory helps us see that such a relationship is the only sensible position to take. (While our clients might be caught up with language and thinking in a way that is perhaps more obviously detrimental, we truly are in the same boat in terms of struggling with this stuff.) We can also see that rigidly holding on to the expert role represents our own form of attachment to a conceptualized self, and that this can actually promote behavior that costs our clients (for example, supporting an attachment to a one-down patient or "sick" role, or rule following for the sake of rule following).

Finally, for me, it has been profoundly important to understand at a technical level how we go about forming our relationship to the world and especially to ourselves. It is significant to consider that the notions we hold most close are actually derived, that they are essentially learned behavior. So much of what our clients seek is about being fundamentally okay. They want to know whether they are essentially good or not, lovable or not, healthy or not, savable or not. You and I might have our own words for this struggle. Not only can these basic questions never be answered in a way that can be proven (remember "truth" versus functional contextualism?); those very concepts are just more products of languaging. It all reminds me of some TV episode I saw once—I can't remember where—in which the hero was caught in a spell that made it seem as though he were trapped in leg irons. The only way to escape was to realize that the leg irons were an illusion; until then the chains held fast. I see ACT as a way to help clients see that their leg irons are an illusion, and RFT as demonstrating how the spell was cast.

THE CORE PROCESSES OF ACT

Since this is an advanced text, this next section assumes readers have some familiarity with the six core processes of ACT. I'll cover them briefly just to get oriented, and will take the opportunity to mention some aspects that are sometimes overlooked or misunderstood. This is intended only as an overview, as these points will be discussed more fully in the following chapters.

In the original ACT text, Hayes, Strosahl, and Wilson (1999) organized the processes into three highly related pairs that comprised three basic response styles: *open*, *centered*, and *engaged*. I find this conceptualization helpful, as it clearly links the processes targeted in ACT to the learning principles we've been reviewing. That is, the science behind ACT illuminated how easily human beings can develop unworkable ways to respond to our experiences. ACT is the clinical response, helping to develop ways of responding that help us move through life very differently. The following is a brief description of these response styles that, together, represent psychological flexibility.

Open Response Style (Defusion and Acceptance)

We hope to develop an open and willing response style as a more flexible alternative to being caught up in verbal content and the effort to escape or control uncomfortable internal experiences. *Defusion* is the ability to see thoughts as internal phenomena, as representing a behavioral process rather than literal truth. It is the ability to look *at* thoughts, rather than *from* thoughts. When this perspective changes, we alter the way in which the thoughts function for clients. This is not about changing the form of the thought itself. The thought is still there, but in seeing it for what it is, the relationship with that thought is altered. The thought functions differently because you have altered the context. A common misstep here is to use defusion as a control strategy—as a way to get rid of emotional pain that might accompany the thought, for example. There is a subtle but very important difference in using defusion as a way to hold a thought (and attendant feelings) differently, versus using it to try to change or eliminate that thought and any accompanying emotions. One is about altering function, the other about trying to fix—which in turn supports a very problematic verbal system. It is this sort of necessary distinction that is so aided by understanding the theoretical model in ACT.

Acceptance, as viewed in ACT, is the ability to actively embrace thoughts, feelings, and physical sensations, even very uncomfortable ones. "Willingness" is also used to denote this process; it's a term I often use, as it tends to be less loaded for clients and taps into the active nature of this process. A common misperception clients have about acceptance is that it is passive, that it's about giving up, and so forth. Far from it; acceptance is an intentional and powerful action. Acceptance is also not about a feeling. It is not the feeling of wanting, or whatever, but a stance to take. This is pointed out in virtually every ACT text, but the incessant pull to have discomfort be gone can make both clients and therapists fall back into thinking acceptance is going to somehow lessen discomfort.

Centered Response Style (Present Moment and Self-as-Context)

What we have learned about how humans get stuck tells us the importance of being centered in the moment and aware of life as an ongoing process. *Contact with the present moment* refers to the ability to be in the here and now. More than that, in ACT it is defined as consciously contacting the present moment *as it is,* meaning without buying (fusing with) ongoing evaluations, judgments, and so forth. Doing so allows us to be in direct contact with and observe the actual contingencies of our life (in other words, the ways in which our behavior does and doesn't work) in a way that creates flexibility rather than more suffering. Of course, "getting present" is actually an oxymoron. That is, if you are getting somewhere you are not there. Trying to technically get present, as if the present were a destination, is to pursue an ever-moving target. The moment you become aware of a thought, a sensation, a sound, and so on, that moment has already been replaced by the next. So getting present as viewed in ACT isn't about arriving someplace; rather, it's about the *process* of getting out of our heads (defusing) and bringing awareness to the stream of experience unfolding in our lives. That process of attention is quite selective, in that it can be directed to the flow of thoughts, to bodily sensations, to any portion of a particular ongoing stream of experiences (for example, "What came up for you just now when I asked about your daughter?" "Notice your breath," or "I feel like there is something being avoided here—do you sense that as well?"). In fact, the process of bringing attention to the present and determining what to home in on constitutes much of the clinical decision-making in ACT.

Self-as-context refers to the distinction between the self that experiences thoughts, feelings, and sensations, and the experiences themselves. Self-as-context is the most commonly used term for this domain, but it actually refers to just one of three types of self defined in ACT. That is, in ACT we build the ability to promote *self-as-process*, which is the ongoing noticing of unfolding thoughts, feelings, and sensations, as in "I am thinking X," or "I am worried about Y." We help clients detach from the *conceptualized self*, which refers to the self-identity that has been constructed from a series of categorizations and evaluations. (Recall the discussion of my daughter as the worst dancer.) Finally, we have what is actually meant by *self-as-context*. This refers to the experience of the self that has "always been there," that is distinct from and includes the thoughts, feelings, and sensations of the moment. It is the context in which those phenomena occur, but distinct from those phenomena. It has been referred to as the *observing* or *transcendent* self, but a more recent definition emphasizes self-as-context as a behavioral ability, as the process of flexible perspective taking (Hayes, 2011). I have found that self-as-context is the most elusive piece of ACT for therapists and clients, and I will be exploring it more deeply in chapter 9.

Engaged Response Style (Values Clarification and Committed Action)

Abilities in the previous two sections we have covered help us respond to what life hands us in a workable way. That is, instead of buying whatever our minds tell us, we are able to notice all that mental activity while getting present to our actual lives. Instead of waging a war with our thoughts and feelings, we hold them with interest, curiosity, and compassion. These abilities go a long way toward freeing us up from the more negative aspects of language and cognition. But it is the next dyad, values clarification and construction, and committed action, that brings vitality and meaning to our existence.

Values clarification, as used in ACT, refers to identifying how we want to be in the world. Valued living is seen as the ability to engage in a pattern of action that is in line with the values we hold in the different areas of our lives, such as parenting, partnership, work, citizenship, and so forth. The focus on values is a distinct feature of ACT. It brings the other processes together. That is, "it is only within the context of values that action, acceptance, and defusion come together into a sensible whole" (Hayes et al., 2012, p. 92).

Committed action is about making choices that are in line with identified values. Whereas there's no actual arriving at a given value, committed action is a series of goals that move the client in a valued direction. Eventually, in ACT, we are hoping to build ever larger patterns of valued (workable) action. I've noticed that while committed action is perhaps the most straightforward piece of the therapy—the easiest to explain, teach, or write about—it can be the most difficult to manifest behaviorally. Taking committed action is where we want clients to ultimately land. It is where "the rubber meets the road," and where all the other processes will be put into practice in the service of psychological flexibility.

PROBLEMS WITH THE PROCESSES

One problem I've noticed in my consulting and supervisory work is that all the references to "the six core processes" can make it seem as though they are things rather than abilities. Losing sight of this distinction can result in approaching the therapy as a collection of techniques. For example, acceptance and willingness is not a concept to teach to the client but rather a behavioral ability to foster. Another possible implication is that both therapist and client can fall into the idea that there is some destination in ACT, that once you "get" the six processes you arrive at psychological flexibility. This idea—that there is some happiness place out there that they can reach if they just acquire the right knowledge—is part of what gets clients stuck in the first place. In remembering that the core processes are ongoing behaviors, not things, we are reminded that abilities fall along a continuum and that abilities can be developed—all of which is more representative of what actually happens in therapy. Clients don't tend to suddenly become 100 percent willing or suddenly choose to take value-driven action 100 percent of the time. Rather, these abilities develop over time through applied practice, and will likely continue to ebb and flow as part of the business of living.

A second problem in emphasizing the six essential processes is that we can forget the degree to which these processes are interrelated. While a given process might highlight a particular functional dimension of behavior (such as being present or defusing), each process involves the others, and all are ongoing acts that together constitute another ongoing process: the expansion and contraction of psychological flexibility. The fact that the processes are interrelated in this way means that work on any one affects the others, and that there are going to be multiple ways to work with whatever is happening in session.

Just as these abilities combine to promote psychological flexibility, deficits in these areas can lead to real suffering. To summarize thirty years of applied research, the problem is that through languaging and cultural influences, we are essentially set up to respond to life in a way that is closed (rigid and avoidant), noncentered (fused with conceptualized selves, pasts, and futures) and disengaged (caught up in our virtual reality rather than engaging with our actual lives in rewarding ways). Because we are geared to avoid discomfort, we wage a fruitless battle with unwanted thoughts and feelings at the cost of living. Our desire to control and move away from internal discomfort is omnipresent and very problematic when it comes at the cost of vital living. Again and again, we fuse with what our minds are telling us rather than simply having what's there to be had internally and doing what works. Fortunately, we can learn new ways of approaching things, but it isn't easy. We need both verbal and experiential learning to help us hold our experiences differently—learning that is consistent and that doesn't support unworkable, reactive responses.

But Isn't All This a Strategy?

Well, sure. I have been posed this question from time to time, and it reveals an agenda that is not supported by the model. That is, embedded in the question is the idea that strategies are wrong or bad. Remembering that ACT is based upon a functional contextual account of behavior, there is no rightness or wrongness to having strategies, no verbal rule along the lines of "acceptance = good" and "control strategies = bad." It is about workability. Years of research have taught us that avoidance or suppression of unwanted thoughts and feelings can be problematic. We have learned that interventions geared toward altering the form or frequency of these internal experiences are not that effective and can actually add to the problem. Focusing on altering how unwanted internal experiences function for clients is offered as a more workable approach. It is certainly a strategy. That's a problem only if it becomes a problem for the client in some way.

It is important to remember also that unworkable behavior isn't necessarily about avoidance. That is, it could be that clients are behaving in ways that, while costly, are also rewarding (such as being right, or substance addiction). By furthering the core processes in ACT we help clients defuse from the content of their minds (for example, rigid self-concepts, or rules such as "I have to be right," or thoughts such as "It won't matter if I use just this one time") and get more present to the direct consequences of their behavior (such as distancing others, or not being able to fulfill daily responsibilities). The same language processes that can pose difficulties are used to increase the influence of values on clients' behavior, with the objective of making behavioral choices that are ultimately more workable and that lead to lives with vitality and meaning.

EITHER IN OR OUT

It is sometime in the fall of 2000, and Robyn Walser and I are conducting an ACT group for female veterans participating in a ninety-day residential treatment program for Post-Traumatic Stress Disorder (PTSD). For me, this represents *doing* ACT, at last, rather than just researching or reading about it. Robyn opens the session, and I listen carefully as she navigates the trickiness of gaining informed consent for a therapy that is hard to explain in advance. I sit back and observe as she skillfully presents the unworkability of the control agenda and the futility of trying to be "more, better, different." I take on the "man-in-the-hole" metaphor and find that I didn't understand it quite as well as I thought I did. I look invitingly at Robyn and she steps in and makes it all make sense. Soon after, someone in the group asks me a question I didn't expect; I look at Robyn expectantly. She handles it with ease. Later on, someone suggests this therapy is a waste of time. I look at Robyn....You get the idea. This tendency hung around for a while, too. "You say nothing's worked but I've been sober for fifteen years now!" (Look at Robyn.) "Why is the bus driver the only one who can drive the bus?" (Look at Robyn.) "So I'm supposed to just be okay with what happened?" (Look at Robyn.) And I might as well go ahead and confess that what seemed important in those moments was to conceal my own unknowing—to look as though I was simply being collaborative rather than unsure of what to do. And all this while earnestly hoping to help the group see that attempting to control unwanted thoughts and feelings is problematic and unnecessary!

There were several missteps here. One was to forget that the behavioral principles behind ACT applied to me as much as anyone else in the room, which meant I also missed the fact that I was fused with what my mind was telling me (not knowing = incompetence = bad). Another misstep was trying to address content rather than core ACT processes, and a third involved attempting to teach one thing (such as willingness) while *doing* the other (such as avoidance). All of these responses were moving away from the model, although I didn't realize that at the time. As we will see as we explore the therapy together in this book, these sorts of missteps are easy to make, and can usually be resolved by returning to the core principles of ACT and operating from there. However, it can be a real challenge for therapists to avoid these sorts of missteps and darn near impossible if they haven't fully bought into the theory in the first place.

I once worked with a supervisee who was up-front about having this sort of ambivalence prior to starting the therapy. This particular supervisee had a lot of training and experience in cognitive behavioral therapy, and explained that even though he understood the theory behind ACT he just wasn't "sold on the notion that it was always a bad idea to try to improve thinking that was clearly distorted." Fair enough. Rather than try to persuade him to have different thoughts about ACT, I talked with him about how his position could potentially affect the therapy, particularly in terms of sending mixed messages to the client. We agreed to move forward, with the supervisee holding his ambivalence lightly as he strove to remain consistent with the model while in session.

We found that a certain type of misstep tended to occur. As an example, my supervisee would do a nice job of setting up a cognitive defusion exercise or a self-as-context metaphor, but if you listened closely you would hear that the point being put forth, to help the client have a "different perspective," was actually about helping the client have a different (improved) thought process altogether, rather than learning to observe and simply experience whatever thoughts showed up. I think most of us can relate to feeling tempted to help our clients with thoughts that seem particularly "irrational" and needlessly painful, but if we allow ourselves to dip into content willy-nilly, tweaking this interpretation here and that conclusion there, we risk aligning with the very strategies that got the client stuck in the first place. What we are doing in such moments flies in the face of what ACT has to offer. However, these things can slip in despite our best efforts, and it is difficult to imagine being able to really stay the course if you aren't fully on board with the theory.

Back to my supervisee: While perfectly pleasant, the sessions also lacked that "ACT feel," the genuine connection, vitality, and authenticity that is present when ACT is done well. The consultee couldn't get himself "in the room" in an authentic way. He was attached to his own verbal rules rather than present to the interactions unfolding in sessions.

Ultimately, there is no half-in with ACT because being half-out contradicts the "in" part, not just theoretically but in terms of what happens during the course of therapy. The consequences of not understanding or not buying into the theoretical underpinnings of ACT range from being completely adrift in sessions—as though you are on a sailboat without a rudder, buffeted and blown about by the content of the moment—to directly contradicting and working against yourself, to conducting a sort of tepid, in-the-head therapy with little clinical oomph. All these struggles will be explored in subsequent sections of this book.

I have stressed the importance of understanding and buying into the theoretical underpinnings of ACT, which in turn determines how the therapy is approached, both overall and in each individual session. These ideas form a fundamental component of any ACT text. Most of the trainees and consultees I've worked with get these ideas; most agree they make sense. And yet there can still be a disconnect between understanding these precepts and keeping them front and center during the course of the therapy. It's actually very understandable—there is a lot of content to ACT, lots of ideas that need to be conveyed, lots of metaphors to cover, lots of exercises to explain and process. We get hooked into all that and our minds start handing us rules about how it all needs to be mastered. Before we know it we're caught up in the "what" rather than the "why." As I wrote this last sentence I became aware of an image flitting through my mind—that of a fish trying to snap up a shiny and particularly enticing lure. This is what my mind does with the things clients say in session—it wants to address (expertly, of course) what has been said, rather than focusing on the *function* of what was just said. It is important that the fish sees the lure for what it is and that someone is fishing.

QUICK TIPS FOR STAYING ON POINT

If you are thrown by something the client has introduced to the session, if you find yourself struggling because something didn't go as planned, or if there's something funky going on in the room, slow down and get present. I tend to rely on a few simple questions to help me orient to what is happening from the ACT framework: 1) What is happening in this moment and what function is it serving? 2) Does this move my client closer to or further away from her values? 3) What might be reinforcing this behavior—for example, is something being avoided? 4) In what ways does the client think internal thoughts or feelings are the problem? 5) In what ways is this costing my client? I have found that these questions keep me aligned with the model and point to which processes to target.

At those times when a client has come to session with a real conundrum or crisis (for example, his wife informed him she wants a divorce, he's been diagnosed with a chronic illness, or he was demoted at work), it is particularly tempting to engage with the client's view of the situation rather than continuing to look through that ACT lens. Asking yourself the following question will help guide you: "If this client had completed ACT and received an A+—that is, if he really understood and bought into the concepts and was applying them to his life—how would he respond to this situation?" This helps you orient to what, in terms of ACT, you are ultimately shooting for, and should also flush out where your client may still be stuck. You will find that this approach will help you refrain from focusing on how the situation needs to change, and instead focus on how the client can continue to move through the situation in a way that is in line with his values.

SUMMARY

This chapter is intended to serve as our starting point in exploring how to optimize ACT and work with its challenges. I've made no bones about the importance of fidelity to the model, having found over time that doing otherwise affects the therapy. In an effort to promote that fidelity, I have attempted to show that the theory in ACT is the therapy, and that the principles in the theory form the basis for how the therapy unfolds moment by moment. I've mentioned specific costs to approaching ACT differently, ranging from missing golden opportunities to work with clients in the here-and-now, to sessions being completely adrift. I imagine it is already clear to the reader that I am no stranger to moving off the model or various other missteps. Not surprisingly, such experiences have been the source of my greatest learning.

With this basic orientation to the therapy established, the remainder of the book addresses various issues that have stood out for me, both in my own practice and in my work with other ACT therapists. One thing that may not be clear at this point is the degree to which I love this stuff—all of it: the therapy, its challenges, and most of all, our ability to work on it, chew on it, experiment, and ultimately grow as therapists and human beings. I hope that enjoyment will be clear in this book. To be blunt, I hope you will share it with me in the pages to come. Onward!

CHAPTER 2

Starting Off Well and Staying the Course

In this chapter I will explore challenges related to starting and staying on track with ACT. One reason this can be so difficult is that our clients don't cooperate! They say and do any manner of things that easily pull us off course. Fortunately there are some basic strategies therapists can use to help themselves. Specifically, there are ways to approach ACT sessions that make it easier to work within the model, just as there are ways that make it all the more difficult. We'll explore these general approaches in this section, with some clinical examples that demonstrate how their differences roll out in the therapy room.

SESSION OBJECTIVES

Setting up the work requires the therapist to stay grounded in the aim and objectives of ACT. (See chapter 1.) Recall that the overall objective in ACT is to enhance psychological flexibility by moving clients toward open, centered, and engaged response styles. In-the-moment work is geared toward *decreasing* experiential avoidance, control agendas, and verbal dominance, and *increasing* willingness, contacting the present moment, defusion, self-as-context, values clarification, and committed action (the core processes of ACT). The therapist helps the client move toward these objectives by consistently looking through an ACT lens and considering the function of what is occurring.

THE IMPORTANCE OF STRUCTURE

I have often been told by therapists that at some point in their learning curve with ACT, they find themselves unexpectedly free and in-the-moment with their clients. Free and in-the-moment is not the same as operating without focus and intention. The in-the-moment feel to the therapy comes from working effectively with relevant ACT processes as they manifest in session, not because it's "anything goes." As we've seen, the objectives in ACT are clearly defined, as are the means of accomplishing these objectives. It is not treatment as usual, or treatment as usual with ACT concepts pulled in here or there. Being clear on this at the outset and establishing a consistent structure for sessions is a way to communicate that to clients (and serves as a reminder to therapists). ACT sessions are distinct because ACT is a distinct therapy.

Of course, making this clear at the outset doesn't mean that neither client nor therapist will struggle with approaching what comes up in session in an ACT-consistent way. The reason we need ACT in the first place is because other, often less workable ways of relating to our experiences, such as fusion and avoidance, are so pervasive and entrenched. It's just that this sort of clarity at the outset can make it easier to reorient when we are tempted to move away from the model.

A particular challenge can arise when the therapist has been providing another type of therapy to the client prior to doing ACT. This has been the case for many of my consultees who turned to ACT as a way to work with clients who did not respond to other therapies. In this situation it is important that the therapist and client discuss together what moving to this new approach entails. It is especially important to address differences in how the therapist will be responding to the client in session. Even when this step has been taken, however, there tends to be a strong and ongoing pull for both client and therapist to approach sessions in the way in which they are accustomed. Discussing this tendency in advance makes it easier to both recognize and adjust when this occurs.

Opening the Session

When I refer to structuring the session, I mean establishing it as an ACT session. One of the most important ways to do this is by starting off in a way that communicates that this is time set aside for ACT. How you begin sets the tone for the rest of the work. For example, I've seen therapists set themselves up for difficulty by opening sessions in a general, "anything goes" fashion. They might begin by asking an open-ended question such as "How are you doing?" or "How did your week go?" Most clients are quite ready to air their grievances or troubles of the week (I'm not intending to be disparaging here), and the therapist is left trying to figure out how to make all that content apply to what she had wanted to work on in the session.

An effective way to get firmly on track with ACT from the start of the session is to begin with a mindfulness exercise. Not only does this provide a practice opportunity for building mindfulness—obviously a key ability in ACT—but starting in this way sends the message that the next hour is going to be about this therapy called ACT. In addition, the *choice* to start with mindfulness experientially demonstrates much of what we are after in ACT. That is, most therapists and clients I know do not go about their day mindfully present. (I'm working on it.) It can feel just plain uncomfortable to *stop*, especially with all the compelling reasons to just keep moving on with our day. By choosing to stop and get present nonetheless, therapist and client engage in value-driven action, which pulls in the other core processes (such as acceptance, defusion, getting present, self-as-process, values, and committed action). You have made a choice to intentionally get present in the service of ACT.

Once the mindfulness exercise, and any processing of it, is completed, it can be effective to do a recap of the previous session. Here again, you are setting the stage for ACT, making it easier to approach the rest of the session from an ACT orientation. The recap also provides a natural opportunity to assess what your client's response was to the last session. Did the main points get across? Is the client stuck on something? What were the client's reactions to the session and what does that tell you in terms of moving forward? I personally do a recap at the beginning of nearly every session, briefly reviewing the journey the client and I have taken to that point.

A quick comment here: If you find that a client has little recollection of the previous session, just know that I have found that this response is not at all uncommon. The ideas in ACT go directly against those supported by our culture. To most clients, abilities such as mindfulness and acceptance are novel, downright foreign, and thus easily forgotten or even distorted between sessions. So we simply keep chipping away, reminding clients of the steps they have taken so far and revisiting key processes with new exercises and metaphors that will help things stick.

What doesn't work so well is to try to work ACT around what the client brings to sessions. There is an important difference between working with what shows up in the room and letting your client (and an unworkable agenda) drive the session. Some of the therapists with whom I have worked mistakenly think they have to choose between ACT and validating their clients, or feel it is disrespectful to "ignore" their clients' agendas. We will explore such concerns more fully in chapter 3, when we take a look at the specifics of style. I'll simply say here that the clinical utility of ACT is impeded when the therapist is in the position of following the client's lead while trying to squeeze in ACT if and when she can. When listening to these sorts of sessions conducted by consultees I usually get an image in my head of the therapist literally running after the client, frantically waving an ACT book.

STAYING ON THE PATH

I have been promoting session structure as a way to orient therapists and clients specifically to ACT. This is just an initial step in avoiding ACT-ish therapy. By ACT-ish therapy, I mean sessions in which ACT concepts might be touched upon here or there, but the principles are not being consistently followed, and abilities in the core processes are not being consistently fostered. I've mentioned my observation that such sessions fail to fully harness what ACT has to offer. Another, potentially greater problem is that in ACT-ish sessions much of what is happening actually contradicts the very processes you are hoping to further.

Stick with the Process

Earlier I stated that in ACT the theory is the therapist's best friend. What I mean is that the basic learning principles and processes of ACT will guide you again and again through the morass of stuff that occurs in session. When you are operating from the objectives and behavioral principles in ACT, it's as though you are looking at everything that happens in session (and in the client's daily life) through an ACT lens. As a particular behavior unfolds—say the client suddenly changes the topic—rather than staying at the level of content (the words being exchanged), you observe what is happening at a process level. Not only does this require getting present; you must also be able to defuse from your own verbal content. You then home in on the behavior that seems most relevant at the moment—changing the topic, in this case—and consider its function. As discussed, function is always going to involve a consideration of context: what was happening just prior and what are the behavior's consequences. This sort of functional analysis would lead you to an observation perhaps along the lines of the following: "The client *changed the topic* (behavior) just as we began to *talk about her relationship with her kids* (antecedent)....She may be *avoiding what this brings up* (consequence) for her." This observation, in turn, would point you to the potential processes in play, such as *experiential avoidance* and *fusion*, helping you to recognize that were you to stay at the level of content and go with the change in topic, you would risk reinforcing the avoidance. The client's intended purpose of the behavior (avoidance of painful material, let's suppose) would have been served, in other words, but at the same time a larger and problematic response pattern would have been reinforced. By continuing to view the session through that ACT lens, you are better able to identify the intended functions of the client's behavior, how the core processes are playing out, and how you might respond so that the client progresses in the therapy. The ability to identify these things will help you to remain ACT-consistent regardless of what your client brings to the session.

Here's an example: Let's say your client brings in something salient such as "I wasn't able to go to Thanksgiving dinner because I found out my brother-in-law is having an affair." It would be understandable to go straight to content and ask more about the situation with the brother-in-law, how your client found out about it, whether she told her sister, and so forth. However, in pursuing more content-level details around this situation, you are essentially aligning with the verbal content the client has already put forward, which is that her brother-in-law's actions (having an affair) dictate her behavior (going to dinner). In contrast, when you keep the core processes in the forefront, it is easier to sift through a statement like this to make sure you work with it in a way that is consistent with the model.

In the above example, *experiential avoidance* would be operating if the client decided not to go to the dinner in an effort to avoid discomfort, and *cognitive fusion* is there if she has bought what her mind is telling her about the situation (that she can't go because it would be too upsetting). Avoiding discomfort in this way would be considered problematic if it served to move the client away from her values. So *values* also pertain, and you could consider whether your client holds certain values around supporting her sister—values about marriage, commitment, family dinners, and so on. *Willingness* comes in there as well: is she willing to experience the thoughts, feelings, and physical sensations that show up around this situation? And *committed action* is where you are ultimately headed with a situation like this: given this scenario and all it brings up for your client, how might she respond in a way that reflects her values, and is she willing to have the internal experiences that come along with that course of action?

So it's not just that clinical opportunities are missed when we stay at the content level rather than working at the level of the processes. There is another cost. When we as therapists fuse with the client's verbal content in session, we can work against their developing psychological flexibility. This can happen incredibly quickly, as seen in the following example.

In this scenario the therapist and client have completed a mindfulness exercise ("leaves on a stream") and are talking it over:

Therapist: "What was that like for you?"

Client: "It was okay."

Therapist: "What do you mean by okay? What sorts of thoughts or feelings showed up for you?"

Client: "I was picturing the leaves but then started thinking about other things....It's been a crappy day—had a bad interaction with my mom this morning. She really gave me a hard time about dropping out this semester. She basically told me I have to move out of the house!"

Therapist: "She told you to move out?"

Client:	"Yeah! She said she's not going to support me if I'm just going to be sitting around."
Therapist:	"When does she want you to leave?"

Here again the therapist has been pulled into the content of what the client is saying (the interaction with his mother), rather than sticking with the processes she was targeting in the mindfulness exercise (*getting present, defusion, self-as-process*). The problem isn't the words themselves but how they function here. As soon as the therapist moves away from process and into content by asking the client, "When does she want you to leave?" she is working against the abilities she was hoping to advance in the session. More specifically, by asking for additional details around the thoughts that came up for her client during the exercise, she is reinforcing that verbal content. She is giving weight to his thoughts rather than helping him defuse from them. Rather than stick with helping the client learn to observe the flow of his thoughts, she gets pulled into them herself. This misstep is particularly common when content seems significant. Having to move out of his mother's house is certainly an important development for this client. But there are ways to work with this information that are more in line with the model. For example:

Therapist:	"What was that like for you?"
Client:	"It was okay."
Therapist:	"What do you mean by okay? What sorts of thoughts showed up for you?"
Client:	"I was picturing the leaves but then started thinking about other things....It's been a crappy day—had a bad interaction with my mom this morning. She really gave me a hard time about deciding not to finish school. She basically told me I have to move out of the house!"
Therapist:	"Wow, so some tough thoughts showed up! Did they take you downstream?"
Client:	"What do you mean?"
Therapist:	"When you found yourself thinking about the interaction with your mom during the exercise, were you on the riverbank noticing all the thoughts you have around it, or were you sort of lost in what happened this morning?"
Client:	"Oh, I was totally lost in it. I just can't believe she said that! She knows how stressful this semester has been—now what am I going to do?"

Therapist:	"I can hear the worry in your voice. Let's just work with this for a moment, though. Did you notice the thoughts you just had? 'She knows how stressful this has been' and 'Now what am I going to do?'"
Client:	"Yeah."
Therapist:	"What other thoughts show up with those?"
Client:	"She's totally not supportive—never has been, actually."
Therapist:	"So not supportive, never has been….What sorts of feelings come along with those thoughts? Like, what are you experiencing right in this moment?"

And so on. Now, just because the therapist is staying on track with helping the client learn to observe his experience, it does not mean the situation with his mother is going to be ignored. How they work with it will depend on where they are in the therapy, the key being that they will do so from within the ACT framework. Note that the therapist is not invalidating the client's situation by sticking with the process. In fact, she is attending to his experience—his thoughts and feelings around it—but by staying at the process level, she helps her client explore *self-as-process*. She doesn't align with the idea that his thoughts and feelings (or as he would probably argue, his mother's actions) run the show.

The first therapist-client exchange in the leaves-on-a-stream scenario was intended to show how even slight inconsistencies are not necessarily benign. A point I want to stress is that fidelity to the model in ACT is not about right and wrong, but rather about either advancing or working against certain behavioral abilities. As we have seen, it is extremely easy to move off the model. Even while engaged with an exercise geared toward furthering self-as-process, the therapist inadvertently plugged into the client's story and therefore supported verbal dominance.

Making Things More Difficult

When making a case to establish a clear structure for your sessions, I pointed out that we make it harder on ourselves when we let clients' habitual verbal processes (such as stories, history recounting, and reason giving) drive the session. We are then in a position of trying to make all that applicable *and* remain within the model *and* move things forward. I also provided some examples of how fusing with session content can mislead therapists into promoting ACT processes verbally while working against those same processes behaviorally. This is just one of many ways therapists can dip in and out of ACT and send clients contradictory messages.

Another way ACT-ish therapy can result is when the therapist does nothing with the content a client introduces. That is, he waits for the client to finish whatever she is saying before moving on with what he had planned to discuss. It's as though the therapist is saying, "Alrighty then, now back to ACT...." Usually this sort of move comes from the therapist not knowing how to work with what the client has introduced or simply being more intent on what was planned for the session than what is actually happening in the session. Both of these, in turn, can arise from approaching the therapy at the level of content rather than processes. As a result, the therapist will miss working with ACT processes in the here-and-now. Such sessions seem disjointed, as there is no common thread pulling ideas together. Finally, clients can experience these sessions as invalidating.

Sometimes the therapist will make a sort of lunge to get ACT in there, as though she's been at a loss and was just waiting for some sort of opening to talk about an ACT idea or exercise. As I said, there is an important difference between trying to squeeze in an ACT concept and working with whatever is happening in an ACT-consistent way. When you are working at the level of the processes, you are better able to translate functionally what is going on in a way that is genuine and that fits. In the following example scenario, the client, an eighteen-year-old male, has been complaining to his therapist about his relationship with his father.

> *Client:* "And—I don't know—my dad obviously thinks I'm a loser. Nothing I do is good enough. I'm just not the son he wanted.... He's on me all the time! I'm so sick of it. Like, why bother? We're never going to get along."

> *Therapist:* "Huh. This sounds like you're a computer and you've got all this programming around your dad—about how you're a loser, how you're not the son he wanted."

The therapist apparently wants to introduce an ACT metaphor called "two computers," but this exchange seems forced. (For those readers who are unfamiliar with it, two computers is a common metaphor targeting defusion. It helps clients to see the difference between looking *at* thoughts and looking *from* thoughts. In this metaphor, fusion is akin to sitting with your head actually buried in a computer monitor. In contrast, defusion is the ability to sit back and observe what is happening on the screen—a series of thoughts showing up, for example—while remaining aware that what you are seeing is text among more text.) Suddenly interjecting the metaphor here, however, doesn't quite work. Or rather, it might work, but it feels as though the therapist is putting a new idea on top of what the client shared, rather than approaching what was shared—and how that functions—at the process level. There are many ways to further defusion without being stuck on a particular intervention (such as the two computers metaphor, in this case). With this in mind, let's take another look.

> *Client:* "And—I don't know—my dad obviously thinks I'm a loser. Nothing I do is good enough. I'm just not the son he wanted.... He's on me all the time! I'm so sick of it. Like, why bother? We're never going to get along."

Looking at these statements through that ACT lens, we see cognitive fusion in the client's thoughts around his dad and their relationship. We also see fusion with a conceptualized self (for example, "not good enough"). In looking for function, we get a sense of the client giving up ("Why bother?") as a way to escape or avoid the pain of this experience. So work on defusing would be a good idea, as would building self-as-process and acceptance of his thoughts and feelings, in place of avoidance. The two computers metaphor does get at these processes, but we don't need to force it in. Rather, we can do in-the-moment work with what the client has offered. For example:

Therapist	(pausing to let the moment sink in a little): "What sorts of feelings come up for you around this? Like, what are you feeling right now when we're talking about it?" (*Here the therapist is undermining the avoidance by inviting the client to get present to his feelings around his father. She is also working on building the client's ability to access self-as-process.*)
Client	(heavy sigh): "I feel hopeless, I guess."
Therapist:	"And what is that like for you, feeling hopeless around this situation with your dad?"
Client:	"Sad! I feel sad. It really sucks!"
Therapist:	"Yeah." (*Sits with this a bit.*)
Client:	"It doesn't matter; I'm out of here in two months anyway."
Therapist:	"So that's one thought that comes up: 'I'm outta here.'"
Client:	"Yeah, thank God."
Therapist:	"Have you had that thought before?"
Client:	"Tons of times!"
Therapist:	"And yet the sadness is still there." (*The therapist is homing in on experiential avoidance. She is working on how "I'm out of here" might be functioning for the client. Not only would leaving home literally be an escape move, but the thought itself likely functions as a way to move away from emotional pain. That is, when the client experiences the sadness and hurt around his dad, he quickly tells himself, "I'm out of here." The therapist could have explored this avoidance mechanism explicitly with the client, but instead she chose to simply point to how this ultimately hasn't worked. The therapist is also promoting self-as-process, which will be important in helping the client learn to defuse and detach from the conceptualized self.*)

Client:	"Yeah, it is. I just wish our relationship was better. We just fall into this...thing."
Therapist:	"Yeah. I'm noticing that right now—are you? That you are in this 'thing' that you have with your dad?"
Client	*(sighs heavily):* "Yep."

(Both sit for a moment.)

Client:	"Yeah, it's always been that way with him."
Therapist:	"Is that one part of it too? I mean, have you had that thought before, that it's always been this way?"
Client:	"Oh yeah."
Therapist:	"It seems a little easier for you to talk about the thoughts you have around this than the feelings. I can hear feelings in what you're saying, but it seems like it's hard for you to go there."
Client	*(sits silently for a moment):* "It is hard. I guess I'm tired of feeling sad about this. It doesn't change anything."
Therapist:	"And does saying that to yourself change anything?"
Client	*(thinks this over):* "No, I guess not."
Therapist:	"So despite the various ways you've tried not to be affected by this, you still are. And it's clear there is a lot of stuff around it, a lot of painful feelings, and all sorts of thoughts—from "I'm a loser" to "I'm out of here" to "I wish we had a better relationship." *(The therapist is continuing with self-as-process.)*
Client:	"Yeah. Unfortunately that's true."

At this point the therapist has pulled out experiential avoidance as a strategy and has been repeatedly pointing to self-as-process as the client introduces various content. Now that these processes have been pulled out in the moment, it would likely work well to bring in a metaphor or exercise to advance these ideas using another modality (rather than relying on dialogue alone). For example, two computers would work well now, using the idea that the client has a "Dad button" that brings up a particular computer program. There are any number of exercises and metaphors that could be used. The point is that the therapist is offering them in response to what is happening in the room, rather than pushing aside or supplanting what is happening in order to insert an ACT metaphor or exercise.

One thing that becomes clear in this discussion is how ACT can be tricky. On one hand, we have a particular direction to head in this therapy, and a certain route to take. On the other hand, ignoring, overriding, or mishandling the content the client brings can work against the therapy. I have been suggesting ways to resolve this inherent difficulty. One is to explicitly make room in our ACT sessions to work directly on these processes; two, we watch for the processes as sessions unfold; and three, we use the processes themselves to work on content that arises.

PREPARATION IS GOOD, BUT BEING PRESENT IS BETTER!

I don't know about you, but there have been times I have just flown by the seat of my pants as a therapist—counting on my experience and basic clinical skills to see me through. Unless you are extremely facile with the processes, flying by the seat of your pants can land you on your you-know-what when it comes to ACT. I have found that putting some time into thinking about sessions beforehand can really help maximize the therapy. Before going any further, though, let me clarify that I am not promoting preparation in the service of being smooth. *Being prepared can help you get present to what's actually happening in the room with your client.* So this is not about developing a script or protocol that then steamrolls over everything else in session. Rather, it's about orienting yourself to the objectives and principles of ACT, knowing where your client stands in terms of the core clinical processes, and familiarizing yourself with ways to introduce and talk about key abilities. The idea is to take all that into the session with you, knowing that the present is going to trump everything else.

One of the funniest session tapes I've heard (and related here with my consultee's generous permission) is a great example of how a therapist can get caught up in "doing ACT" rather than using ACT principles to work with what is happening in session. This consultee and her client, a male veteran, had been attempting to do ACT in the middle of extensive construction going on at her worksite. With each session tape I could hear the construction coming closer and closer to my consultee's office, ultimately making it very hard to make out what she and her client were saying. This pattern culminated with a mindfulness exercise that was suddenly interrupted with what sounded like a jackhammer two inches from the tape recorder. (I later learned it was literally under their feet as the work went on in the room directly beneath them.) My favorite part (truly meant affectionately) was how both my consultee and the client earnestly tried to ignore the cacophony, attempting to focus solely on their breathing and "just being present." This is a rather endearing example of a therapist thinking she has to choose between ACT and what is happening, and the additional difficulty that brings to the therapy.

Planning for Sessions

Recently a consultee and I were discussing his first session with a new client and where to head next. My consultee asked whether, now that the client had completed the man-in-the-hole metaphor (a metaphor commonly used in an initial session to point out the futility of the control agenda), he should introduce the "95 percent versus 5 percent rule" in his next session. As some readers may know, this is a concept used to get at how understandable, yet fruitless, it is to try to control internal events. The main point is that because control works for 95 percent of things we interact with in life, we then try to apply it to "that other 5 percent—the stuff underneath the skin." My consultee's desire to know what metaphor might come next seems reasonable, don't you think? But it could also reflect a misplaced focus on technique rather than behavioral principles. Is this question coming from looking at his project manual or other ACT material and checking to see what is next in line? Is he doing a mental checklist of the metaphors he needs to be sure to cover? ("I did man-in-the-hole last week; what's up next?") Or is his question more process-based? ("Now that my client seems clear on how experiential avoidance has been functioning for him, is it time to move into further exploring the problems that come with misapplied control?") If the question is process-based, a more effective one might be "How might I best introduce the idea of 'control as the culprit?'" or "What exercises and metaphors will best illuminate this principle for this client?"

Notice how this last series of questions entails a consideration of what is actually happening in the therapy with the particular client. To determine whether it's time to move forward, you must assess where the client is in terms of the therapy overall. This assessment entails an ongoing consideration of where he stands in terms of the behavioral abilities targeted in ACT—which, by necessity, will include what is, and what has been, happening in the room. It would not be clinically effective to continue with whatever you had planned for the session if your client subsequently gives you conflicting information—if, for example, you had determined that it was time to move into values work and then your client suddenly revealed that he was still fused with the idea that reasons are causes.

Case Conceptualization

In planning sessions, it makes sense to begin with a grasp of how the client perceives his problem(s) and how that perception might be reframed from an ACT perspective. I will leave a detailed overview of how to assess and conceptualize cases to the several authors who have provided excellent information on this topic (Bach & Moran, 2008; Luoma, Hayes, & Walser, 2007; Walser & Westrup, 2007; Wilson & Dufrene, 2008). Worksheets such as the one developed by Luoma, Hayes, and Walser (2007) walk you through the thought process needed to understand your client within an ACT framework. What all these materials have in common is that they help therapists translate how clients perceive their difficulties to an ACT framework. They guide therapists in assessing clients' abilities in terms of the six core processes. I find a key contribution of these sorts of materials is that they help therapists focus on the processes at the outset of therapy. Ongoing use of these sorts of materials can help therapists defuse from the therapy, as it were. That is, sometimes we get *so* focused on what is currently happening that we forget to consider the larger picture: how is the therapy going overall?

An easy way to maintain perspective is to ask yourself the following questions before each session: "Where is my client still stuck?" and "What key ACT idea, if embraced, would be the game changer for this client?" It is important to carefully consider where you and your client are in terms of the ACT objectives (in other words, in terms of the client's abilities in respect to the core processes), so that you can determine where it would be fruitful to go next. Once this is clarified, you can consider which metaphors and experiential exercises you will need to have in your back pocket that will help demonstrate the abilities you wish to explore in the next session.

If you are thinking about pulling in a new metaphor or experiential exercise, you might want to rehearse it first—*not* for the purpose of appearing polished, but to make the words more available to you when you want them. I was surprised early on to discover how tricky it was to effectively introduce metaphors and experiential exercises. I would read an exercise or metaphor over; it would make perfect sense; and then I would find myself mutilating it in session. This problem is pretty solvable: practice! Run the directions to the exercises through and try the metaphors out loud a couple of times. You won't say it the exact same way with your client, nor do you need to. But this sort of run-through will put the words you will need within reach during the session and will also point out where you might get hung up. Just make sure you practice out loud—to your plants, if need be. In later chapters we will discuss specifics such as timing, pacing, and getting the most out of metaphors. The point to grasp here is the utility of spending some time prior to your session thinking about the overall picture and the next therapy hour.

Here's a session preparation summary:

1. Case conceptualization (using a worksheet if needed)

   a. How does the client view the problem?

   b. How would you translate that view into an ACT framework?

   c. What core ACT abilities will likely be most key for this client?

2. Where are you?

   a. What core ACT processes have you explicitly worked on so far?

   b. Where is the client in terms of those processes (comprehension, buy-in, application, barriers)?

   c. Does it make sense to move forward, or should you stick with the processes of the moment?

3. When moving on, what metaphor(s) will you use to further the client's ability with the particular process(es) you anticipate targeting?

4. What two experiential exercises will bring it home?

5. Practice.

6. Get present.

PRINCIPLES OVER PLANNING

The previous sections have been about putting yourself in the best possible place to conduct ACT. We've talked about ways to approach the client and prepare for sessions. We've talked about how to set a clear tone and structure for sessions, and the importance of working at the process level. All this preparation takes a backseat to being present, however. In other words, the preparation helps you and your clients get oriented in a certain direction. You carry the information you have gathered in your back pocket while attending to what is happening in the moment. There will be times when your client is completely hung up and you will spend the entire session reviewing a previously explored idea. There will also be times when it works well to simply recap and move forward to a new piece of the therapy. While being present is central to the ability to see what is happening, it will again be the principles of ACT that best guide how you respond.

But What About Crisis as Content?

One of the questions I get as a consultant concerns working with clients in crises. Therapists can struggle with being ACT-consistent in such moments, feeling at war with previous training or even requirements of their setting. ACT is well suited to work with clients in crisis, which makes sense when we consider the theory on which it is based. That is, basic learning principles and relational frame theory have taught us a great deal about how it is that humans can despair. Further, we come to understand that this type of suffering comes with the territory of being human. This level of understanding helps us respond to such situations in a way that is consistent with the therapy and also quite effective.

Scenario: The therapist and her female client are at the beginning of a session, and have just completed a mindfulness exercise.

Therapist	*(wrapping up the exercise):* "What did you notice during that exercise?"
Client	*(mumbling and looking very shut down):* "I don't know."

Therapist: "I'm not sure what you mean."

(*Client remains silent, looking at the floor.*)

Therapist   (*after waiting a bit*): "What's happening for you right now?"

(*Client is silent.*)

Therapist   (*waits*): "I'm not sure what to do here. It seems as though something important is going on." (*Waits, then continues.*) "My mind is giving me all sorts of stuff around this, worries about what you are thinking and so on, but I don't want to assume what's happening for you. Would you be willing to share what you're experiencing right now?"

Client   (*whispers*): "I don't want to be here."

Therapist: "So that's a thought you're having: 'I don't want to be here'?"

(*Client nods.*)

Therapist: "Can you tell me what feelings are coming along with that?"

Client: "I feel like dying."

Therapist   (*very gently, compassionately*): "You feel like dying." (*Pause.*) "That tells me there's a lot of despair going on right now."

(*Client is silent, continues to look at the floor.*)

Therapist: "And that thought about not being here....Are there thoughts about killing yourself? About taking yourself out of all this?"

(*Client nods.*)

Therapist   (*very compassionately*): "I am so glad you are letting me know about this, about what you are experiencing right now." (*Long pause.*) "And of course my mind is handing me stuff about it too—mostly, I'm just feeling a lot of concern for you right now."

(*Client is silent, just listening.*)

Therapist   (*another long pause, speaks slowly and gently*): "There's a struggle going on, too. On one hand, I want to somehow swoop in there and make this all okay, take away the pain and despair, the tough thoughts....But we know it doesn't work like that."

Client: "No, it doesn't."

Let's take a look at this: The therapist has stayed on track, immediately working with the language she is using to create some distance between the client and the suicidal thoughts and feelings she is experiencing. The therapist models self-as-process by sharing her own internal experiences. She encourages client disclosure (which entails willingness) by demonstrating her own willingness to self-disclose in a vulnerable way. She has not asked *why* the client is feeling this way. Whys are less important in this moment than helping the client access self-as-process (and ultimately self-as-context). Her first priority is to undermine her client's fusion with thoughts that her experience is intolerable and that killing herself is the answer.

There are numerous ways the therapist could work on defusion. For example, she could encourage her client to sit with her and simply have what's there to be had, then eventually make the point that they were both fully capable of tolerating the pain of the moment. She could do a physicalizing exercise, asking the client to visualize her pain and put it in front of her so that they can examine it together. She could do an experiential exercise that targets self-as-process and self-as-context, such as the label parade. [Note: In this exercise the client is asked what thought or feeling she is struggling with, and it is then written on an index card. The therapist gives the card to the client with some tape with which she can attach it to herself, while asking what thought or feeling comes up next. They proceed until the client has covered herself in cards—a graphic demonstration of self-as-process and self-as-context. See Walser and Westrup (2007) for a more detailed description of this exercise.]

Other ways to work with this client could be to introduce the "chessboard metaphor" (detailed in chapter 9), or to remind the client of this metaphor if they have already worked on it. She could bring in values as a way to help the client regain access to thoughts that aren't about ending it all. First, though, it seems that just slowing down, and leaning in to the moment with great compassion, is what is called for here. It would not be ACT-consistent to respond to this situation in an alarmist way, as suicidal thoughts and feelings are a common human experience. The therapist is not fusing with the client's thoughts, but is attending to them. While gently pointing out that these thoughts and feelings are yet another experience to be had, the therapist is treating this situation seriously. She is well placed to follow the guidelines many settings require in situations such as this. That is, she can complete a full risk assessment, develop a safety plan, and even move toward hospitalization, if need be.

Therapist: "One of the things I struggle with at times like this is needing to know you will be safe and also knowing this is part of being human. Life can be truly hard—it makes sense that our mind hands us stuff like 'If *this* is what my life is going to be like, *forget it!*'" (*Client nods; therapist continues.*) "And we've also worked on the idea that thoughts and feelings aren't actually in charge, that we don't even have to do battle with them; they come and go, while we remain constant. In fact, there may have been other times in your life when these sorts of thoughts and feelings were around. Is that the case?"

Client: "Yeah, a few times. But this is the worst. I'm just done."

Therapist: "Okay. And while, on one hand, I know that this is an experience you are having, and that you are more than, larger than even thoughts and feelings this painful, I also have a value around making sure you remain safe. It's time to talk about what we need to do, right now, to make sure you are safe."

I wanted to include an example like this because it illustrates how therapists don't have to choose between what their clinical judgment is telling them (this person is at risk) and being ACT-consistent. Again, it's not about choosing between ACT and something else, or fitting ACT into something elso, so much as looking at what is unfolding through an ACT lens.

SUMMARY

In this chapter I have focused on two broad strategies for optimizing ACT. One is to start in a way that clearly marks the therapy as being about ACT. The other is to consistently approach session content by staying clear about where the therapy is in respect to the core processes of ACT. I am aware that I have been quite repetitious with that refrain. That is because nearly every ACT therapist with whom I have worked frequently moves off of process and into content despite their best intentions. This tendency simply speaks to the strength of languaging. Fortunately, with time and practice we build our ability to recognize and work with the processes in play.

I have stressed preparation as a way to keep the ACT lens before us. This lens helps us determine *what* processes are key for this client generally, *where* in the six processes the client is working and developing competencies, *when* to stay or move on, and *how* (such as which exercises and metaphors might serve skill development). I've suggested practicing delivering metaphors and exercises to increase effectiveness in the therapy room. Finally, I pointed out that looking through that ACT lens can keep therapists from being consumed by the content of a client crisis. Rather than try to fix the client's experience, the therapist uses ACT processes to highlight what is happening for the client and move forward to a safe resolution. Next, we move to a topic area that can make all the difference in how effective these strategies are: therapist style.

CHAPTER 3

Style Matters

Those observing an ACT session for the first time often remark on its distinct feel. The way the therapist is "being" in the room, how the therapist relates to the client and responds to what arises in session, can be a real departure for those trained in other models. In this section we will explore therapist style from an ACT perspective, including ways in which therapists intentionally or inadvertently depart from the model and what this means in terms of clinical effectiveness.

INDIVIDUALITY, BUT NOT AT THE COST OF FIDELITY

ACT has evolved, gained flesh, and remained vital as therapists contribute their own unique style and ideas to the work. Some of my favorite metaphors and ways of explaining things have come from consultees or trainees, who found themselves increasingly able to work with the basic processes of ACT in creative ways that spoke to them and their clients. Evolving in such a way is a major strength of a process-based—versus technique-based—model of therapy. As I've said, there is no one "right" way to do ACT. As long as the identified core processes are being advanced, ACT is taking place, leaving lots of room for individuality and treatment tailoring. At the same time, the therapist can embody a style that actually contradicts the model and impedes the therapy. Again, the style isn't "wrong" because of some verbal rule (such as "This is not how it was done in the book"). Rather, the issue is a functional one: is how you're being with the client furthering psychological flexibility, or does it contradict the very processes that you are hoping to develop? It would be disingenuous, however, to suggest that there isn't a better or worse way to deliver the therapy. After listening to hundreds of sessions I can say with good conscience that there is a powerful difference between those sessions where the therapist is relating with the client in a way that is consistent with ACT theory and those wherein something else is happening. For one thing, there is a certain quality to sessions conducted by therapists who have personally embraced the principles forming ACT. They have heart, and there is often an electric sort of hum—or feel—to them that comes, I believe, from authentic connection between two human beings in the here and now. It has been my experience that the clinical potential of the therapeutic relationship is more fully optimized when the therapist not only conducts ACT with fidelity but embraces the model at a personal level.

It's Okay to Be Directive

I mentioned in an earlier chapter that a common misstep is when therapists end up conducting a sort of hybrid therapy, where the intervention is best described as treatment as usual with a bit of ACT pulled in here and there. One of the oft-reported reasons for this approach is that the therapist is hesitant to drive or direct the therapy. There seems to be a rule embraced by many therapists that states they must prioritize what the client wishes to do in session—that doing otherwise is not respectful or will upset the client in some way (which should be avoided). We can respect where the client wishes to go *and* take her in a direction that meets multiple needs. That is, "respect equals not interfering," or conversely, "not going where the client wishes to go equals disrespect" are examples of relational framing that bear closer examination. It can be helpful to step back and look at these and similar rules I have heard from various trainees and consultees over time:

Leading discussion = dictating = not caring about client's perspective = bad

Interrupting = discourteous = not caring = bad

Not going with the client's agenda = invalidating = not caring = bad

Having an agenda (the therapist) = not respecting or caring about the client's wants = bad

No doubt we could come up with others. But hopefully just pulling these few out in this way provokes a questioning process. For instance, you would likely agree that leading a discussion about a particular topic doesn't mean you don't care about the client. What about situations where "supporting" the client would mean joining her in the notion that she is helpless? As another example, a concern I hear surprisingly often is that it is wrong for therapists to pursue a defined agenda with a client. For one thing, I think we always have at least some agenda. At the very least, we have an idea of what our clients need and how to get there—that is part of why we have put ourselves in the position of being their mental health care provider. But I do think the concern that lies behind these sorts of rules is an important one, in that it behooves us to be mindful of exploiting, unduly manipulating, disempowering, or otherwise negatively impacting our clients via the therapeutic process. It is important to see that we can hold that concern—or value, if you will—in one hand while giving ourselves permission to firmly be in the room with our clients on the other. I think it's okay to own that we do indeed have an agenda that we think (or at least hope) will be helpful to our client. While the tenets of ACT hold that the therapist, as a fellow human being, has the same sorts of struggles as the client, it is still the therapist who has familiarity with this particular therapy. It can be useful to be straightforward about this, especially if you (or your clients) are struggling with the idea of following a particular agenda. Here's an example of placing this paradox—that despite swimming in the same soup as the client you still have something to offer as therapist—on the table:

Therapist	(in a compassionate, human-to-human manner): "You know, I can hear how important this is, how much you have been struggling. And while I don't know what it's like to be in your shoes, I have my own struggles—that's part of being human. But I do have something to offer you, an approach that I believe may help you get unstuck. One way to say it is that there's a very particular journey I'd like to take with you—one that isn't about doing more of the same."

Notice there's no message about there being one right way to do things. The therapist isn't holding himself up as the expert "fixer," but rather as a fellow human being who has information that might be useful. As an ACT therapist, you are simply offering a different way to work with being human based on a theory you hold as to what might be keeping clients stuck. With your clients' permission, you will be taking them through a distinct process designed to help them move forward in their lives. This process may require you to be directive at times, in the sense of identifying, guiding, refocusing, and choosing what to emphasize and when. Just as in any therapy, what your client chooses to do with the information gained along the way is entirely up to her. Here's another example of how to work with concerns about having an ACT agenda when your client presents with another:

Therapist:	"This is one of those times when I need to ask your permission to refocus us a bit."
Client:	"Oh! That's okay—I was sort of running at the mouth there."
Therapist:	"That's not the thought I was having, actually. I think that what you were saying matters—it's taken up a big part of your life and is certainly on your mind. It's more about wanting to make sure we move forward in here because I think this therapy has something to offer you. In fact, the point of this therapy is to help you with situations like the one you just described, but maybe not in the way that you might expect. At any rate, my concern is that if we don't stay on track a bit more, we won't get there."

Client:	"Shoot away, Doc!"
Therapist	*(pauses):* "Huh. I just had a worry come up with that comment. On the one hand it struck me as funny; on the other I found myself worrying that now I've put myself in the expert role here, like, 'I'm the doctor; you're the patient.'"
Client:	"You think too much."
Therapist	*(laughing):* "For sure. But it is important for us both to remember that we are in the same boat when it comes to this stuff. This is about how we humans tend to get stuck. And it's also important for you to know that even if I steer us in a certain direction, I do care about what you have to say."
Client:	"Got it. And I never felt like you didn't."
Therapist:	"Cool. So one thing we could do is review where we've been so far in terms of this therapy, and then take a look at control. By that I mean control as a strategy to not have what we have inside the skin. We might even be able to look to see where control might come into play in the situation you were just describing."
Client:	"Sounds good."

The point of this example is to demonstrate how therapists can hold firmly onto values around respect, compassion, and caring while also providing direction for the therapy. It also highlights, right at the end, one of the decision points we face countless times as therapy unfolds. That is, one way to work with the content a client brings into session is to reframe it according to the core ACT processes, to look at it through that ACT lens mentioned in the beginning of this book. As it applies here, the therapist would be listening for relevant core processes (such as experiential avoidance, defusion, or conceptualized self) and determining how best to work with these. In this example, the therapist noted that the client had become stuck in telling a story, and asked the client to return to the present and engage with the therapist. Here, core processes (present-moment awareness, willingness) are experientially—versus explicitly—in play. The therapist models acceptance and defusion ("I had a worry," "the thought I was having") and implies having values around the therapy. (Taken as a whole, the therapist's responses demonstrate willingness to take action in the service of his values.) The last couple of statements made by the therapist suggest they will then take that new material—in this example, control as problematic—and reexamine what the client had been discussing from that perspective.

So "being directive" in session clearly involves guiding and refocusing at times, but by no means is it steamrolling over the client's concerns. Care is taken to demonstrate consideration for the client by both verbal and nonverbal behaviors. Liberal use of the present moment (as in "What is happening in this moment with my client?" "What are we doing in this moment?" "What am I experiencing?") will help you find ways to both honor your value to treat your client with kindness and keep the therapy progressing.

ACTUAL, NOT THEORETICAL, EQUALITY

Just about all the ACT providers I've worked with have been quick to say that they understand they are "in the same boat" as their clients. That is, they understand that the behavioral processes informing ACT apply to human beings in general, and that they, too, have many of the same sorts of struggles as do their clients. Many seem to understand the role of verbal dominance in psychopathology, and how remaining fused with rules around being the expert or with labels such as "client with PTSD" is incongruent with the model and can work against the psychological flexibility we are hoping to develop. Most have seemed on board with the notion that being stuck might not be so much about a particular diagnosis as it is about the difficulties of being a verbal being. Nonetheless when I listen to, or observe, actual sessions, the "fellow human being" part is often missing. There is a pervasive tendency to keep the focus solely on the client, to remain staunchly in the expert role rather than getting more personally in the room. And yet it is when the therapist steps out of the therapist/expert role and meets the client at a more equal and authentic level that the full power of ACT is accessed.

I have explored this issue at length with numerous ACT providers. Many who are new to the therapy tell me frankly that they are struggling enough to just convey the main ideas of ACT to their clients—putting themselves in the room as well simply seems out of reach. When we look at this struggle more closely, it is often the case that the provider is feeling intensely incompetent and working hard to conceal that uncertainty from himself and most definitely from his clients. I suspect new ACT providers do not have the corner on this one. Here are some common relational frames that present as reasons therapists give for not being more authentic in their therapy sessions:

Not knowing = incompetence = bad

Hesitating = not knowing = incompetence = bad

Pausing to think = hesitating = not knowing = incompetence = bad

Fumbling = not knowing = incompetence = bad

Are any of these familiar to you? I've known most of them at one point or another. Here are some more:

Feeling uncomfortable with the material = incompetence

Confidence = competence = success

Not feeling confident = not knowing = failure

Self-disclosure = regular person = nonexpert = fraud = bad

You might add to this list; it's kind of fun. Let me just say that never in my personal work with clients or with consultees or supervisees have I seen a therapist lose credibility by owning his own uncertainty, fallibility, or downright confusion. We providers seem to be the ones putting such expectations on ourselves, thinking that it is our "expertise" that matters. I believe it is our humanity that clients connect to most. I should take care to add, however, that we are going to have trouble if we try to get rid of this desire for competence. The desire for certainty, for composure, for feeling competent, is here to stay. The trick is to have it for what it is, not what it says it is. It has been tremendously exciting to watch a consultee or supervisee venture out of that armchair comfort zone and begin to explore genuine connection with her clients. Yes, you must be thoughtful. Yes, you can go too far in one direction: If you find yourself involved in a story as to why your children made you late to work this morning and your client is giving you a "Why are you telling me this?" look, then it's time to ask yourself the same question. But better to be out in the room with the client, where the possibility for genuine, authentic connection exists, than safely in your therapist chair.

Self-Disclosure as Clinical Tool

The primary way to behaviorally demonstrate therapist/client equality is with thoughtful self-disclosure. By this I refer to the sharing of personal experiences, including thoughts and feelings going on in the moment, as a means to further the therapy. In working with providers on this issue, I have observed two main barriers to using self-disclosure in session. (For the purposes of this discussion I am leaving out therapies where such omissions are theory-driven, such as in classic psychoanalysis.) One is previous training that dictates that therapists refrain from self-disclosure due to concerns around "maintaining appropriate boundaries." In my own training regarding this issue, the idea was that if the therapist stepped too far out of the therapist role by sharing personal information, the therapeutic relationship would somehow deteriorate. There were ethical concerns regarding dual role (such as that the therapist would somehow become not just therapist but also a friend, or more) and that the client would subsequently be exploited or otherwise injured. As mentioned in the earlier discussion about being directive, we can honor these concerns without needing to rigidly hold on to global rules about therapist behavior. Over time it has seemed to me that many providers hold this line more because it is a rule than because it is the most effective stance to take at a given clinical moment. Operating behind a clearly defined, black-and-white line is simply easier than working within the grayer area of self-disclosure. Once you step out from behind that line you must think about things such as what to disclose, how much to disclose, the potential impact of that disclosure, and so on. In ACT, however, self-disclosure is an important means to move the client forward in some way. In exploring this terrain I have found the following to be a helpful questioning process:

1. Is what I'm thinking about sharing for me or for the client? If it's purely or even mostly to fulfill my own needs, time to pass.

2. Is what I'm thinking about saying going to further things? Will it clarify an idea, or model a certain skill, or directly demonstrate that I am in the same boat as the client? If not, time to pass.

3. Is there a potential drawback to sharing this? For example, might this disclosure shift the focus to me or bring up other content that will stand in the way of what I am hoping to highlight? If so, it may be best to pass.

The barrier that might be even more at the heart of things concerns vulnerability. When my consultees or supervisees and I explore missed opportunities to authentically connect with the client as a fellow human being, it often comes down to a comfort issue. As long as the focus remains firmly on the client, the therapist's own experience remains private and out of reach. It is important to note that various definitions of the word "vulnerable" stress being *open*, such as "open to censure or criticism, assailable" (http://www.thefreedictionary.com) or "capable of being wounded or hurt...." (http://dictionary.reference.com). When you put yourself in the room, authentically sharing your experience, you have opened yourself; you are assailable because you can be impacted by the client's response to what you shared. I have been struck by the degree to which therapists fear authentically sharing themselves with clients. Even when the thing to be shared seems perfectly harmless, the discomfort of being vulnerable in this way can be intense. Yet I can't stress how much thoughtful sharing of your experience enhances the work. Here again we have the opportunity to actively demonstrate our awareness of being in the same soup as our clients. There is an inherent vulnerability in the client role—just coming to therapy is an acknowledgment of wanting or needing another's help. By claiming our own vulnerability in this process we demonstrate willingness and join our clients in the most powerful of ways.

GETTING IN THE ROOM

The simplest way to get in the therapy room as a person rather than simply as a therapist is to use words that convey what you are currently experiencing. That is, you make a statement about what's going on with you in that moment (a thought, feeling, or sensation), rather than restricting yourself to asking a question or making an observation about the client.

Scenario 1: The therapist notices that the client has a confused expression, and wonders whether the client understood what she was saying.

EXAMPLE 1.

Therapist: "You seem confused. Is what I'm saying making sense to you?"

EXAMPLE 2.

Therapist: "I just noticed that I'm worrying about whether I'm making any sense. What's going on for you?"

In the second example the therapist has simply included her experience. Even though the difference is quite slight, there's much more going on here. "I just noticed (*modeling present-moment, defusion*) that I'm worrying about whether I'm making any sense (*defusion; self-as-context; being authentic, vulnerable, and equally human*). What's going on for you (*furthering being present and willingness*)?"

Scenario 2: The therapist and client have been working on values, and the client has balked when asked to come up with concrete goals around establishing friendships.

EXAMPLE 1.

Therapist: "You just said you don't care about making friends, but I remember that was one of the first things you mentioned when we started out."

Client: "Well, I don't know. Sometimes I want friends, but sometimes I don't want the hassle. I'm more of a loner anyway."

Therapist: "So you are having the thought that you're a loner, because making friends seems like too much hassle?"

And therapy goes on from here. For comparison, let's look at the same scenario with the therapist getting in there on a more personal level:

EXAMPLE 2.

Therapist (*after client balks when asked to come up with concrete goals around establishing friendships*): "Hmmm. I'm not quite sure what to do with this." (*Pauses.*)

Client (*waits, then*): "What do you mean?"

Therapist: "Let me stop and think a moment because *I want to get clear* (*long pause*). Well, there's a lot going on. *I'm noticing that I want* to point out that earlier on you were pretty clear about wanting to have more friends, so *one thought I'm having*, a question really, is whether you are avoiding something right now by saying that you don't care about friendship. But *I'm also realizing* that I might be putting my own value on you. That is, *I happen to believe* that your life would be enhanced if you had more meaningful relationships, but *I'm realizing* that might be my value, not yours."

In this exchange we can almost imagine the client coming back with "Well, I *do* want more meaningful relationships, but…" There is an opening there. The therapist essentially modeled being authentically present to what was happening, creating an opening for the client to do the same.

In the second exchange, the therapist's authentic use of her experience in the moment helped her avoid a potential barrier with her client (such as a power struggle or debate over whether or not the client wants to develop friendships) and also furthered the therapy. The therapist used present-moment awareness and willingness to work with something potentially difficult. This approach can also enhance positive developments in session. Said another way, I have noticed at times that therapists' tendency to leave themselves out—sticking with offering observations, interpretations, or questions about the client—can actually diminish the good stuff that also happens in session.

Scenario 3: The client suddenly announces near the end of a session that she has decided to make an extremely bold move and contact her daughter, whom she'd given up for adoption nearly thirty years ago.

EXAMPLE 1:

Client: "…and then I just got on that online service and there she was! There was my daughter….She'd been looking for me." (*Begins to cry.*)

Therapist: "That must have been so amazing to see her there! What was that like for you?"

Client: "I couldn't believe it! I was scared, but I e-mailed her and she wrote me right back. We've been exchanging e-mails and even talked on the phone—we're making plans to meet each other in person."

Therapist: "That was a bold move."

Client: "Yeah, I still can't believe it."

Therapist: "You chose to make that move even though you've had fear around it for thirty years."

Client:	"Yeah."

Nothing untoward here. However, let's explore an alternative:

EXAMPLE 2:

Client:	"…and then I just got on that online service and there she was! There was my daughter…. She'd been looking for me." (*Begins to cry.*)

(Therapist is silent but listens attentively. Specifically, she uses nonverbal behaviors such as facial expression and body position to convey absolute absorption and recognition of the importance of what the client is saying. The client begins to cry harder, then releases and really begins to sob. The therapist remains silent, making it clear by her demeanor that there is plenty of room in the session for the client's emotion.)

Therapist	(*as the client begins to quiet*): "I am really moved by what you are telling me."
Client	(*through fresh tears*): "I know. This has been my whole life."
Therapist:	"I am so moved, and so impressed by you, and so very excited for you and your daughter."
Client	(*absolutely lit up*): "Thank you! Thanks for helping me get here. I can't *believe* it!"

Hopefully you can see the difference I am talking about here. One response is fine; in the other, where the therapist meets the client and connects at an authentic, emotional level, the exchange is far more vital. In ACT we are continually on the lookout for experiential avoidance, out of recognition of how costly the control agenda can be. We look for opportunities to demonstrate that it is possible to notice and hold whatever is there, pleasant or unpleasant. For many, strong emotion of any kind is uncomfortable. We fear and avoid "being a mess" and then wonder why life has become flat. In this session the therapist did not settle for simply acknowledging the positive step the client had made. Rather, she leaned fully in to the experience, reveling in its richness and helping her client do the same.

SHARING AS CONTRIBUTION

Earlier I mentioned that when navigating through whether or not to share something personal with your client it is important to determine its intended function. What purpose do you think sharing this particular experience or story will serve? What purpose do you want it to serve? For example, not infrequently I catch myself just before I am about to share a funny story or comment and realize it's probably not the best thing to do. That is, while sometimes this seems to be about just wanting to have fun, sometimes it's an avoidance move—a quick step off of some affect going on in the session, for example. Too often (judges my mind), it is about pleasing or being liked by the client. Getting clear on my intended purpose helps me determine whether to make that comment or tell that story or whether to sit on the impulse. In most cases it simply isn't needed and could prevent something else important from happening. The humor takes up space, in other words. At other times a bit of humor or irreverence functions to undermine language in a way that benefits the client. Being present enough to engage in the questioning process is the key.

I absolutely am in favor of sharing examples from our personal lives if the intent is to move the client forward. Authentic sharing of yourself is a gift, and a powerful one at that. As pointed out in numerous examples throughout this book, this way of relating to clients offers a rich modeling opportunity. It provides a way to authentically connect and demonstrate willingness, and it underscores that you, too, are a human being who struggles. This is an important message for clients, many of whom are highly fused with conceptualized selves that are "abnormal" or "lesser than." This sort of self-disclosure is also an effective learning tool, as it is often easier for clients to grasp something "out there" (referring here to the therapist's life) when they are highly fused with their own stuff.

It is important to emphasize that you can step into this sometimes-disconcerting territory while firmly honoring your sense of propriety and values around self-care. Just because I share how the passengers-on-the-bus metaphor helped me work with my fear of playing music in public doesn't mean I'll also share how my husband and I celebrated my first bluegrass performance! You get to decide how far you go with this. Nonetheless, defusing from verbal rules about client/therapist boundaries and stepping over that established line can be unsettling work. Having full awareness of the values that drive this sort of move does not save me from the experience of vulnerability and uncertainty that often come along. That is why self-disclosure used in this way is a gift—the therapist chooses to move into uncomfortable or new terrain because it will help the client move forward in some way.

THE GIFT OF TRANSPARENCY

When you take yourself out of having to be the confident, knowing expert, you free yourself to use your experience in the session as a clinical tool. It is about being transparent in session, about being overt about what you are doing, rather than trying to operate like the Wizard of Oz behind his curtain. One of my consultees said it brilliantly: "I had an epiphany in my last session. I was trying to figure out how to do something; there was this thing I wanted my client to see; and I suddenly had this realization that I could just be open about that. I saw that I'd been approaching the therapy like a card game, holding my hand close to the chest and carefully strategizing which cards to lay down. I now understand that with ACT I can simply lay out my hand in front of my client and work on it together." Further exploration of this powerful realization reflected several of the ideas we have explored in this chapter. For example, the consultee had been approaching ACT as being about technique—that is, as if he needed to say the right thing, or use the correct metaphor or exercise (play the right card, in other words) in order to get a desired effect with the client. Tucked into this idea is the notion that there is a Truth to be had, that if you can just play the right cards you will win—the client will see and understand what she should be seeing and understanding. I love this metaphor because it gets at that subtle, pernicious tendency to think that ACT is the "right" way to be living. It shows how the therapy can easily become a card game we are hoping to win. ACT does not propose to be the answer to life, so much as an alternative to how we hold and work with our cards. Going with this metaphor, when we lay our cards down alongside our clients' and study them together, we have moved away from the idea of winning and begun to focus on how we both are playing the game. To continue with my consultee, he also identified wanting to control feelings of incompetence and uncertainty by appearing clever and together—to play a smart game, in other words. In choosing transparency over cleverness, he demonstrated willingness to have what he had, undermined the idea that there was some right answer to establish, and lived his values around how he wants to be working with his clients in ACT.

Putting It All Out There

It is important to note again that transparency is an important aspect of the horizontal client-therapist relationship inherent in the ACT model. Therapists moving to a more transparent style often report feeling freed up in session and more able to move the therapy forward. Another way to examine this difference is to look at how non-transparency might be functioning in session. For example, for therapists who report feeling stuck or lost during a therapy session, it has often been the case that they have been in an internal struggle over how to respond to something, such as trying to decide whether to go with "Intervention A" or "Intervention B," or "Response A" or "Response B." When we examine this struggle closely, it is often apparent that the therapist is operating with the notion that there is a right answer or right response that he must uncover, and that something bad will happen if he makes the wrong decision. The therapist is often privately trying to discern which course of action will result in the least negative consequences. Getting caught in the content of this debate supports verbal dominance and often a control agenda, and it puts the therapist in a bind that is not necessary. It would be more ACT-consistent to get present to, and defuse from, this internal debate—to consider how it may be functioning in the session, and then choose willingness and valued action over control or avoidance. Transparency with clients regarding what is happening facilitates this shift and provides a great modeling opportunity. In the following examples, I attempt to demonstrate this sort of inclusive transparency—in other words, that it doesn't have to be either/or. I first present seemingly contradictory options or thoughts a therapist might be having, and then follow with an example of a transparent, ACT-consistent response.

EXAMPLE 1:

The therapist, after listening to a client complain about some perceived wrong, has the following thought (we'll call it Option A): I need to listen and support what my client is saying or she will feel invalidated.

She is also having another thought that, on the surface, may seem contradictory (Option B): My client is really holding onto the victim role and I don't want to reinforce something that keeps her stuck.

As described above, it is consistent with the model to bring such a dilemma directly in the room in a way that advances ACT processes:

Therapist: "I'm feeling sort of stuck. I feel pulled to agree with what you're saying about this, as though in order to feel supported you need me to agree with your point of view. But that would mean agreeing that you're helpless in this situation, and I just can't get on board with that one."

This example response reflects many of the topics discussed in this chapter. The therapist becomes present to what is happening and demonstrates her willingness to have what is there to be had, including being vulnerable with the client. Rather than privately trying to come up with the right answer, she is being transparent about her dilemma and putting her concern—that the client is fused with being helpless—right out there on the table.

EXAMPLE 2:

Thought A: *I would really like to know more about that painful event the client doesn't want to talk about.*

Thought B: *I need to respect that the client doesn't want to go there.*

ACT-consistent and transparent response:

Therapist: "I'm pausing because I'm not sure where to go next. It seems you don't want to talk about this, and I want to be respectful of that. At the same time, we know that avoiding these sorts of things hasn't worked too well. I think there's another way to go here, one that will open things up for you, but the only way we'll get to see is if we head in there. Would you be willing to tell me more about what your experience with this thing has been?"

EXAMPLE 3:

Thought A: *I had planned to do this metaphor today.*

Thought B: *I don't think this metaphor is going so well.*

ACT-consistent and transparent response:

Therapist   (interrupting himself): "I'm wondering if this metaphor is making any sense to you. I'm feeling sort of stuck with it myself."

Client: "No, not really."

Therapist: "Let's bag it, then. There's another way to talk about this...."

The following scenario, shared with permission, is an example of how being in the room authentically can be a game changer. The consultee was new to ACT and feeling pretty iffy about some of the concepts. On top of that, he was working with a very challenging client. Truly, my own jaw would clench when listening to their sessions, the fellow was so darn contrary. Clinically speaking, this client had a very negative conceptualized self—not good enough, not lovable, stupid. He was so fused with his thoughts that he was unable to actively listen, and so avoidant of his feelings of insecurity and vulnerability that every move he made was to self-protect. My consultee couldn't open his mouth without the client deciding (often erroneously) where the therapist was headed and assuming an oppositional stance to make sure he was not tricked or manipulated in some way. The exchange in question took place during a session in which my consultee had been attempting to introduce the idea of self-as-context.

Therapist   (after completing a thorough "Observer You" exercise): "So what did you notice?"

Client: "What do you mean?"

Therapist: "I'm wondering what you experienced during that exercise."

Client: "It didn't really make sense to me."

Therapist: "Which part?"

Client: "That whole thing about the—what do you call it? The continual you."

Therapist: "The continuous you?"

Client:	"Yeah, that makes no sense. I'm not continuous. I'm just here."
Therapist:	"Were you able to pick out other points in time, like where you were this morning, what you were doing last week…?"
Client:	"Of course. I could remember some times. But that whole thing about observing—of course I'm observing. How could I not be observing?"
Therapist	(*a little stymied*): "Um. Well, the point of this exercise is to see that you've been there all along."
Client:	"Of course I'm there all along! Where else would I be?"

(*Long pause.*)

Therapist:	"There's a you there, a self, that's larger than the experience."
Client	(*clearly exasperated*): "You see? That makes no sense. I don't know what that means. What do you mean by the Self?"
Therapist:	"Um…"
Client:	"Are you talking about the soul?"
Therapist	(*flustered*): "Uh, let's see….Well, yeah, I guess some people would call it that."
Client	(*truly fed up*): "So the soul is watching? I don't know what you're talking about here. I just don't get what you mean by the Self."
Therapist	(*throwing up his hands*): "I don't either, dadgummit!"

(*Silence.*)

This taped exchange, which nearly made me fall off my chair laughing, was the turning point in the therapy. Because after this long silence, full of mutual surprise and shared exasperation, the therapist and client began a dialogue, human to human, about what-in-the-heck this self thing was. It took a couple more sessions, but you can imagine how powerful it was when they ultimately got clear. More importantly, the client saw that there was no need to defend against this fellow human being who was not only similarly confused but willing to share his confusion (in other words, be vulnerable). From that point forward there was a marked change in the dynamic between this therapist and his client. Sure, the tendency for the client to control made regular appearances: mutual frustration came and went. But from that point on, their relationship was primarily one of collaboration.

NURTURING OR ENABLING

One of the therapist "styles" I've seen that can be inconsistent with the ACT model is that of being a mother or father figure. By this I mean the therapist is assuming a sort of parental role, caretaking the client in the guise of being helpful and nurturing. If you look to see how "nurturing" is formally defined, you will find two definitions most prominent: one emphasizing support of another's *development,* the other being more about *protection.* This is a useful distinction to consider when it comes to your own therapeutic stance. If you would describe yourself as nurturing with your clients, would you say this is in the service of moving them toward the life they want to be living? Or is it in the service of protecting them? And if the latter, what are you protecting them from? If you are protecting them from their own pain (anxiety, reactions to the therapy, tough thoughts, memories, and so forth), you are buying into the notion that (1) pain is not tolerable, (2) the client is fragile and can be destroyed by pain, (3) pain must be ameliorated in order for the client to be okay, and (4) as the therapist you are somehow stronger (wiser, less damaged) and able to fix the client's internal experience. All these notions fly in the face of the ACT model. In ACT we aim for compassion— for encouragement and kindness, surely—while at the same time working against the idea that clients need fixing.

SUPPORT DOES NOT MEAN ALIGNING

Another, related misstep I have observed is when the provider, in an effort to demonstrate understanding and support, actually strengthens the client's cognitive fusion. For example:

Client:	"I'm so fed up with my boss. He has never once told me I am doing a good job; in fact, he jumps at the chance to point out any little thing I do wrong. Even when I go above and beyond, it's like it's nothing."
Therapist:	"Like he's taking you for granted."
Client:	"Exactly! I might as well not bother."
Therapist:	"Have you tried to talk to him about being so critical?"
Client:	"He doesn't care what I think."
Therapist:	"Doesn't sound like a very good boss."
Client:	"No, he sucks."

This quick exchange is problematic from an ACT perspective because as a whole, it functions as a validation not of the client, but of what the client's mind is handing him. I have found it helpful to ask myself what I would be aligning with if I supported what the client is saying content-wise. Would I be supporting what the client ultimately wants from his life, or a thought process that, while compelling at the surface level—our minds just love right/wrong scenarios—actually ensnares him? Let's take a look at each of the therapist's responses:

Client:	"I'm so fed up with my boss. He has never once told me I am doing a good job; in fact, he jumps at the chance to point out any little thing I do wrong. Even when I go above and beyond, it's like it's nothing."
Therapist:	"Like he's taking you for granted." (*The therapist is pulled into the content—his response could be perceived as agreeing with the client's take on things.*)
Client:	"Exactly! I might as well not bother."
Therapist:	"Have you tried to talk to him about being so critical?" (*The therapist is again pulled into content, has fused with the client's evaluation of his boss, and is engaged in problem-solving aimed at fixing the boss.*)
Client:	"He doesn't care what I think."
Therapist:	"Doesn't sound like a very good boss." (*The therapist is again joining in the client's cognitive fusion and aligning with the idea that "the problem" is his boss.*)
Client:	"No, he sucks." (*At this point the client may feel understood and "supported," but is in no better position life-wise than when this exchange began. If anything, he is more firmly entrenched in the idea that his work life is, and will remain, terrible because of his boss's attitude.*)

Again, you don't have to choose between furthering the therapy and demonstrating that you understand and care about what your client is saying. You can go the following route instead:

Client:	"I'm so fed up with my boss. He has never once told me I am doing a good job; in fact, he jumps at the chance to point out any little thing I do wrong. Even when I go above and beyond, it's like it's nothing."
Therapist	(*nodding in understanding*): "I can see this whole work thing is pretty upsetting."
Client:	"Yeah! I've just had it!"

Therapist:	"So one of the thoughts you have around this is 'I've had it,' like, 'I'm done.'"
Client:	"Yeah."
Therapist:	"What sort of feelings show up? Seems like frustration is there…."
Client:	"Frustration, anger…I mean, what happens if I really do lose my job?"
Therapist:	"So frustration, anger, you have thoughts about losing your job…. What emotion comes up with that one, with thoughts about losing your job?"
Client:	"Fear."
Therapist:	"Yeah, I would think! Even now, as we're talking about this, does fear show up?"
Client:	"Yes, fear, and anger too. I don't need this."
Therapist:	"So that's another thought your mind just handed you: 'I don't need this.'"
Client:	"Yes."
Therapist:	"What do you do at work when these sorts of thoughts and feelings show up? I ask because I've noticed that you have always seemed to work hard at your job."
Client:	"Yeah, I just try to do my job and not worry about what he thinks. But he's such a jerk!"
Therapist:	"That's pretty amazing. Even though your experience of your boss is that he doesn't notice or care about the work you do, *you* care enough to do it right."
Client:	"Yep. I'm just not comfortable putting my name on crappy work."
Therapist:	"So let's look at this carefully, because it's a big deal. You have a value around work. You value doing good work, and you have put that value ahead of the thoughts and feelings you have about your boss. Even though he does his thing and you have your reactions to it, you make sure you do a good job."
Client:	"I guess that's right."
Therapist:	"It looks to me like it's you, not your boss, who decides how you are at work."
Client:	"Yeah!"

The point of this section was to address a common misstep, where therapists, in an effort to be supportive of their clients, actually work against the therapy. Hopefully it is evident that there is no loss of empathy or caring in this last exchange. This example dialogue also highlights the point emphasized at the beginning of this book, which is that in order to conduct the therapy well, one must operate from the basic principles of ACT. The key is to continually look for and work with the processes in play. This approach often involves reframing what has occurred or been said in a way that highlights those core processes. In contrast to the first example, the second exchange moved the conversation from being about the client's employer and the notion that the employer needs to change to establishing the client as the Experiencer who is capable of making valued choices. The therapist and client remain on course with the processes targeted in ACT and are poised to do some meaningful work on an important issue in the client's life. Let's look at this exchange again:

Client: "I'm so fed up with my boss. He has never once told me I am doing a good job; in fact, he jumps at the chance to point out any little thing I do wrong. Even when I go above and beyond, it's like it's nothing."

Therapist (*nodding in understanding*): "I can see this whole work thing is pretty upsetting." (*The therapist validates the client's distress while refraining from agreeing with his thought process.*)

Client: "Yeah! I've just had it!"

Therapist: "So one of the thoughts you have around this is, 'I've had it,' like, 'I'm done.' (*The therapist demonstrates understanding while targeting cognitive defusion. Note that although the therapist adds the statement "I'm done" to demonstrate understanding, this is more a redundancy than the introduction of new content.*)

Client: "Yeah."

Therapist: "What sort of feelings show up? Seems like frustration is there...." (*The therapist is working against experiential avoidance, represented by the client's tendency to complain and blame others—staying in the "head" rather than accessing the difficult emotions present in a situation like this—while building the client's awareness of self-as-process.*)

Client: "Frustration, anger...I mean, what happens if I really do lose my job?"

Therapist: "So frustration, anger, you have thoughts about losing your job.... What emotion comes up with that one, with thoughts about losing your job?" (*Therapist refrains from being hooked by client's worry about losing his job—that is, he doesn't work with the worry itself but stays on track with defusion and self-as-process.*)

Client: "Fear."

Therapist: "Yeah, I would think! Even now, as we're talking about this, does fear show up?" (*Therapist joins in the experience, thus normalizing and validating, and moves to present-moment awareness and self-as-process.*)

Client: "Yes, fear, and anger too. I don't need this."

Therapist: "So that's another thought your mind just handed you: 'I don't need this.'" (*defusion, present moment*)

Client: "Yes."

Therapist: "What do you do at work when these sorts of thoughts and feelings show up? I ask because I've noticed that you have always seemed to work hard at your job." (*The therapist is promoting self-awareness, particularly the distinction between the Experiencer and the experiences, or self-as-process, and is starting to point to values.*)

Client: "Yeah, I just try to do my job and not worry about what he thinks. But he's such a jerk!"

Therapist: "That's pretty amazing. Even though your experience of your boss is that he doesn't notice or care about the work you do, *you* care enough to do it right." (*Therapist again does not bite with the new "jerk" content but remains on target with the self-as-context and values processes.*)

Client: "Yep. I'm just not comfortable putting my name on crappy work."

Therapist: "So let's look at this carefully, because it's a big deal. Sounds like you have a value around work. You clearly value doing good work, and you have put that value ahead of the thoughts and feelings you have about your boss. Even though he does his thing and you have your reactions to it, you make sure you do a good job." (*Here the therapist leans in with "...it's a big deal," and spells out the distinction between the self that chooses and the thoughts/feelings of the moment. "Response-ability" for making valued choices is now resting squarely on the client.*)

Client: "I guess that's right."

Therapist:	"It looks to me like it's you, not your boss, who decides how you are at work." (*The therapist highlights the freedom this gives the client.*)
Client:	"Yeah!"

As you can see, this exchange is conducted at the process level. The therapist is not serving as an arbiter of the client's work situation, but is homing in on the cognitive fusion and experiential avoidance that could keep the client from moving forward in his life according to his values. In terms of style, it is empathic, direct, and yet uncompromising when it comes to the notion that the client is fully able to make choices that move him closer to, not further from, his values.

At the risk of beating this into the ground, it can be informative to play with different iterations of the therapist's first response in this exchange as a way to highlight the functional differences of even slight wording changes:

Client:	"I'm so fed up with my boss. He has never once told me I am doing a good job; in fact, he jumps at the chance to point out any little thing I do wrong. Even when I go above and beyond, it's like it's nothing."
Therapist:	"Like he's taking you for granted." (*This response could function in a couple of ways. The therapist could have recognized the client's cognitive fusion and meant to simply reflect back a version of what the client's mind is giving him. However, because this isn't made clear by his choice of words, and because the client is so fused with his thoughts, the therapist's response would likely be received by the client as agreeing with the client's perception, and would actually serve to extend the relational network by adding the taking for granted idea. It is not uncommon for therapists who are targeting a core ACT process to inadvertently undo what they are hoping to accomplish because of the language they use.*)

Here's another version:

"He's taking you for granted." (*Here we have the same issue, although it seems even more likely the client will perceive this statement as the therapist endorsing his thought process. This response could also strengthen the pull to get caught up in right and wrong, as taking someone for granted is perceived as wrong in our culture.*)

And another:

"You feel like he's taking you for granted." (*This is a bit better as it emphasizes the client's experience rather than suggesting that the therapist agrees. However, with this statement the therapist has still added an interpretation that probably doesn't serve the client so well—the idea of being taken for granted.*)

"So even when you have been working really hard you feel as though it's nothing to your boss." (*This statement is more on track, as it reflects back what the client has said without adding additional problematic content, and it indicates (albeit subtly) that this is an experience the client's having.*)

Notice that the first response I suggested in the remedial dialogue, to simply state something along the lines of "I can see this whole work thing is pretty upsetting," lifts the therapist and client right up out of the content and onto the process level. The therapist immediately points to the client as Experiencer, and in doing so is able to offer support and compassion to the client-as-context, rather than aligning with his thoughts.

There are innumerable such decision points in the course of a single therapy session. Referring to the above example one last time, the response the therapist chooses can also depend on where the client is in the therapy, and I have promised to explore that issue further in chapter 6. This is one of the things I find most exciting about this work. There's simply no one way to go, and no possible way to roll out all the various iterations to compare effectiveness. That means we are in an unending process of discovery, with no cap as to how clinically effective we can become. Woo hoo!

SUMMARY

This chapter has focused on therapist style as per the ACT model. My focus has been on some missteps and misunderstandings that commonly stand in the way of therapeutic progress. I would like to add that therapist style is one of my favorite ACT topics to ponder and work on. It is fascinating how relatively small changes in tone or demeanor can make a significant difference in how a session goes, and how shifting one's basic stance in the relationship can powerfully and positively impact both therapist and client. That is fun. And it is good news. In short, I mean for this discussion to be encouraging, rather than an indictment of some sort. Just as (if your life is anything like mine) there are innumerable ways we can improve how we relate to the people in our lives, so too can we continually build our skill in the therapeutic relationship.

CHAPTER 4

Let's Talk About Timing

In chapter 3 we explored therapist style as viewed in ACT, focusing on specific in-session behaviors that can either enhance or impede the therapy. A closely related issue is that of timing—those moment-to-moment decisions regarding what to do when. Timing also includes pacing—how quickly or how slowly you move through an exercise or discussion. Timing in ACT could also refer to your overall strategy for moving through the core ACT processes. For instance, will you be utilizing a more linear building block approach, such as the one initially presented in the original ACT text (Hayes et al., 1999), or will you be moving more flexibly through the hexaflex? In chapter 5 we will take a closer look at the issue of overall approach. Here, we will explore timing as it pertains to individual therapy sessions and to moments within those sessions.

Let's begin with the obvious: timing is an important consideration in any therapy. It is safe to say that the sharper the timing, the more effective the therapy will be. In ACT, any consideration of timing is done from within the ACT framework. That is, in deciding whether or not to introduce a particular exercise or concept, for example, the therapist identifies the core processes at play in the current context, and considers what will best help the client progress toward psychological flexibility. This decision necessarily involves a consideration of the client's current ability level with each core process (as they are interdependent) and how it will play into the effectiveness of the intervention in question. When a response or intervention is not well timed, it can be misunderstood or misapplied, or simply fall flat. An ill-timed move can also reflect a struggle on the part of the therapist—for example, avoidance of something in session, or not being present. As I mentioned before, every exchange in ACT carries the potential to further or work against the therapy. Timing often determines whether an intervention helps clients progress or actually helps keep them stuck. In the following sections we'll explore clinical decision points as they relate to timing, including common missteps and how these can affect our work with clients.

THE IMPORTANCE OF BEING PRESENT

If I could recommend just one key strategy to assist you with timing during your ACT sessions, it would be simply getting present. It's pretty hard to make a decision about whether or not it's a good time to do or say something when you're not actually in the moment. Of course it's more complicated than that, as part of any decision is considering what has come before and what is likely to come next. But I'm comfortable saying that when a session is not going so well, poor timing is often the issue, and poor timing often stems from the therapist not being present to what is happening in the therapy room. In chapter 3, I provided an example of a dialogue between a therapist and her client who had recently contacted a daughter she had given up for adoption. The point of that example was how powerful it can be when the therapist authentically joins the client by sharing her own experience in the session, rather than simply focusing on the client. But I imagine you also noticed another significant difference in the second exchange, which is that the therapist's first decision was to refrain from doing anything except be in the moment with her client. As it pertains specifically to timing, she made the decision to hold the moment and lean in. This is a good move whenever there is intense affect in the room. However, there is more that went into the therapist's consideration here. What was not conveyed in my depiction was all the other information that contributed to the clinical context in question. That is, based upon her previous work with this particular client, the therapist suspected that the client was trying to hold emotions in check due to verbal rules about emoting in public along with general avoidance of strong affect. She also knew the client's childhood included a fair amount of emotional neglect, and that the client had long been fused with the thought that her emotions did not matter. The therapist accordingly chose to undermine the avoidance and fusion by compassionately making space for the emotion that was not being fully contacted. To refer specifically to timing, she chose to hold the moment, to slow down rather than speed up, to demonstrate nonverbally both her awareness of how huge this development was for her client and her willingness to simply be with her client as a fellow human being. These responses—contacting the present moment, being willing, defusing—were intentional and designed to help the client progress in ACT and learn by experience the vitality that comes when we are willing to have what we have.

The main point I am making is that there is an intended function to the intervention here, which in turn depends on the particular context. We can imagine a similar scenario with a different client who would be better served by a different therapist response. The key is to actively consider timing in terms of context and intended function of the intervention, as this intentional, theory-driven approach to timing is one of the most powerful ways to maximize the clinical opportunities that unfold in ACT.

Active Welcoming

You may have heard the saying "In ACT, everything is welcome." I use this idea a lot to help me effectively respond to what is showing up in session, rather than reflexively jump in to fix or control discomfort or something else I did not expect. A visual image nearly always comes to mind in such instances, one that arose when I first heard the following Chinese proverb: "Sorrow comes unsent for, and, like the unbidden guest, brings his own stool." I picture a big, old wooden table strewn with various items, and then I see my arm sweeping everything aside to clear a nice big space for the "unbidden guest." This image of active welcoming has really helped me choose an accepting rather than avoidant stance toward whatever is happening in therapy.

An approach that I and many others have learned from Robyn Walser is that of leaning in. Having had the good fortune to work with Robyn, I have had the opportunity to observe her as she literally leans in, pressing in on the moment, if you will, as a way to directly counter the avoidance that is occurring. Typically Robyn becomes very still, allowing herself to pause and actively contact the present moment as fully as possible. She then puts what is happening on the table before the client, so that they can look at it together.

Examples of leaning in:

"I'm feeling stuck here, like something's not working. Are you experiencing that?"

"It seems like something funny is going on here—like there's something unsaid."

"I'm concerned that if something doesn't change, you and I will be having this exact same conversation five years from now."

At many times the leaning in is simply remaining silent but expectant, clearly conveying a sense of waiting or of simply sitting in whatever is happening in that moment. Asking yourself the questions I've listed above can help you determine whether it's one of those times to sit in stillness.

One important thing to note is that the sorts of comments listed above are not intended as rote responses. That is, this isn't about the particular words used but about how they ultimately function in the session. Leaning in can be articulated in many ways; as I mentioned, it can be accomplished by nonverbal behavior alone. Simply memorizing a phrase and using it does not mean it will serve its intended function; in fact, care must be taken that it not be reduced to ACT-speak. That is, there are certain ACT phrases that are heard often in the ACT community—such as "Thank your mind for that thought" and "Check your own experience"—that can be not only overused, such that they lose their effectiveness, but misused. For example, Robyn recently observed that the phrase "Thank your mind for that thought," which has the intended function of furthering the processes of defusion, willingness, and self-as-context, was becoming an automatic response for many therapists to any "negative" thoughts their clients shared. Depending on the context, this response was sometimes received as an invalidation or a dismissal, even an avoidance move on the part of the therapist (in other words, a quick and easy way to deal with a problematic thought). However, I've found that when used sparingly and in the right context, this type of suggestion can be a humorous reminder of the capriciousness of the mind and can be quite helpful to clients. It can be really helpful to not take our minds so seriously. To summarize, remaining in the present and focused on the processes in play (being aware of what you are targeting and why) will help guide you to use words in a way that moves the client forward.

THE GIFT OF SILENCE

In the above discussion I made the point that pausing and refraining from getting busy in session (being present and willing) is in fact a powerful ACT move. Another way to say this is it can be powerful to make the choice to be silent. After the many hours I have spent observing providers (or listening to their recorded sessions) as they learn the therapy, it has become clear to me just how very important silence is in ACT. This realization should come as no surprise, given that languaging and its attendant stickiness is one of the reasons we humans struggle so. It should also come as no surprise that laying aside our verbal repertoires for a moment or two can really be a challenge. I have noted that as providers become more facile with the therapy, silence plays an increasing role in sessions. This is about using silence functionally, however. That is, it's not a technique to check off, as in being silent for silence's sake. Rather, we use silence as a way to make room for the present moment, refraining from using words to defend, manipulate, or move away from what is happening. We use silence to hold what is there to be had. When I hear consultees and supervisees allow for such space in their sessions, I know they are building their own ability to simply be in the moment, fully and without defense.

Here is a quick tale about one of my supervisees and her work on this issue: She had been working with an avoidant young man who came to therapy for treatment of depression. My supervisee knew from his history that this man had lost his young son three years prior in an unfortunate car accident, after which he had developed a significant problem with alcohol abuse. Now in recovery, the client described his life as aimless and unrewarding. He was highly verbal and socially skilled, but there was a clear sense that he was using words and stories to keep feelings away. When asked about his son he quickly acknowledged the loss and just as quickly changed the topic. During her work with this individual, her first ACT client, my supervisee had been working on refraining from problem-solving or otherwise "helping" the client with his feelings or negative thought processes. In particular, she was trying to talk less in sessions, as in the past her words had been mainly in the service of fixing. In a session that proved a turning point in the therapy, the client began by telling my supervisee that, for the first time in three years, he had finally gone into his garage, something he'd been avoiding because the car that had been in the accident was being stored there. To my surprise, my supervisee made no response to this sudden announcement. The client, seeming a bit surprised himself, paused for a moment, and then went on to talk about when he first bought the car, the other cars he almost bought, what his then-girlfriend had thought about the car….Still no response from the therapist. The client wandered off on another topic, then eventually wound back to the car:

> Client: "And then, you know, I just sat in it. I sat in that car." (*Pause.*) "I haven't been in that car for three years!"

(*Silence. This time the client stayed silent for a few moments as well, lost in the memory.*)

> Client ….(*eventually resuming*): "And then, you know, I just sat and let myself think about him, about Jason." (*His throat sounds tight.*) I still can't believe he's gone, you know?"

Silence.

And then the client began to cry, softly at first and then finally letting his grief pour out. My supervisee told me later that she also had tears rolling down her face, but silent she remained. The silence lasted for a while. Finally, the client began to breathe more easily, and (as I learned later) looked at last at his therapist—apparently one of the first times he had ever looked her fully in the eye.

> Client: "I've never talked about this before."

(*Silence.*)

> Client: "It hurts so bad."

> Therapist: "Yes."

They sat for a bit longer, and then it was time to end the session. I remember that I sat staring at the tape recorder for a long time, thinking about what I had heard, feeling my own sadness and contacting my own fears around losing a child. I was also very impressed by what my supervisee had managed to accomplish. By simply clearing space, by not taking them both away from the experience of the moment with words, she enabled her client to finally bring his grief to the table. Her willingness to just be with him in the moment helped him do the same, and to discover that he didn't need to continue trying to escape his grief. You are correct if you are guessing that after this breakthrough, progress was swift. The client, no longer pitting himself against his own feelings of loss and grief, found that he had many values and goals for the future, and that he was well able to carry both his sorrow and his love for his son along with him into that future.

WHEN IN DOUBT, LISTEN

Have you ever participated in the listening exercises often done during ACT trainings? In one of these exercises, one person is paired with another and both sit facing one another, knee to knee. Instructions are given for one person to speak while the other person is to simply listen. The speaker relates something he has struggled with (or a personal joy, or whatever has been instructed), and the listener is to give her full attention but no verbal response. I found this to be an eye-opening experience, and when I use it in my own trainings the response I get is almost always along the lines of how difficult it is for the listeners to keep from making verbal responses, to get in there or somehow "help" their partner, and how fulfilling it is for those sharing to simply be listened to so completely. This is an important lesson for us therapists. To share a personal example, I once was assisting with an ACT training, the first after the birth of my daughter, and was asked to pair with an attendee for the listening exercise as they were one person short. I can picture my partner to this day, well dressed and somewhat refined in appearance and manner, quite calm, maybe ten or so years older than I. When it was my turn to speak I found myself, to my surprise, sharing feelings of regret about waiting so long to have a child. I told my partner that I hadn't known how much I would love being a mother, and that because I had been on the fence about being a parent for so long it was realistically too late for me to have a second child. I shared my feelings of guilt for having any regrets at all, given how lucky I was to have my little girl. I spoke of how much I loved my brothers, and of my sadness that my daughter, being an only child, would never know this joy. I cried when sharing how afraid I was that she would be lonely in life. And I remember being very surprised that I had been carrying all this around.

But what I remember most is that, after my time was up, this woman simply sat for what seemed like a very long moment, thinking over all I had said. Then she looked at me, smiled gently, and said, "I'm thinking of the beauty of a mother's love."

I am still moved as I write this. What a gift! You see, there was—is—no fixing here. It is what it is. And I have what I have—gratitude, love, joy, sorrow, and regret. By first giving me the gift of her listening with no attempt to fix, and then by simply pointing to the value at the heart of all I was experiencing, she helped me understand that I could carry all this stuff, and that it is truly beautiful. To tie this all in with clinical decision-making, you could do worse than to have active listening be your default move. Simply listening with all your heart is a powerful and generous clinical intervention and entirely consistent with the ideas we hope to further in ACT. Therapy can be a pretty "mind-y" business. We can easily become fused with thoughts about how to respond to the client, what to do next (or what's for lunch), to the point that we actually "miss" our clients altogether. By engaging in the processes of getting present and defusing, we model these processes for clients and enable ourselves to see and experience what is actually in the room.

EXPLICIT VS. IMPLICIT WORK

When faced with a timing decision, I have found it helpful to make a distinction between whether it is time to work on something explicitly or more indirectly. For example, my client may do or say something that points directly to a core ACT process, but that doesn't mean it's the best time to talk explicitly about that process. In such cases I might choose to work with it indirectly, filing away whatever the client had revealed for use when the timing is more optimal for direct discussion. Consider the following scenario: The therapist is conducting his second ACT session with his client, a thirty-eight-year-old male who is seeking therapy for help with depression and "anger issues." So far, it is apparent that the client is highly fused with his thought content (for example, he has a trove of stories about the people in his life and the ways they "trigger" his anger), and believes that reasons are causes (for example, that others make him angry and that his anger causes his aggressive behavior and temper outbursts). He is also quite experientially avoidant—anger and other uncomfortable emotions are a sign that something is wrong; any emotion that arises in session is quickly talked away. He has poor ability to be in the present, staying in the moment with the therapist only briefly before being reeled back in by his thoughts about the past. Finally, he holds a conceptualized view of himself as "man with very bad temper." He claims to value relationships and feels that getting rid of his anger is a requirement for building and improving his relationships with family and friends. So much to do!

I find it easier to approach this discussion by talking about what I wouldn't suggest doing in this situation. For example, it doesn't seem that it would be very effective to explicitly tackle the client's notion that others need to change (so that he doesn't experience anger) before he can make behavioral choices that take him closer to his values around relationships. This is where we hope he will eventually arrive (not that the notion will change, but that he won't continue to buy it), and the shift will require having all the core processes under his belt. I also wouldn't start explicitly talking about how he has a conceptualized and misleading view of himself—such discussion would entail concepts such as the Self being distinct from private events, and is beyond where the client is at this point. If someone is unable to look *at* his thoughts rather than *from* his thoughts, it is pretty hard to access a self that's distinct from such processes. I have observed providers make such moves, though, and what often happens is that the therapist easily falls into a persuading, teaching mode that actually counters the model. For example, consider if the therapist says to this client: "You have a view of yourself as Angry Man, but that's just a thought, something you learned and associated with yourself." If this statement were made in the context of explicit work on the role of self-as-context and the role of language, it is more likely that the client would understand the statement as intended in ACT. Early in the therapy, however, before concepts such as cognitive defusion have been put in place, this sort of statement can function as an endorsement of the idea that something is wrong with the client's thinking—in other words, "You need to have a different view of yourself because I say so."

That you have decided it is not the time to address something explicitly, however, does not mean you need to ignore it. There are many ways to begin addressing issues of clinical significance that, while indirect, can be quite effective. Taking the first idea as an example (that the client thinks others need to change so that he can feel the way he wants, so that he can then have good relationships), the therapist can begin to work on this idea by simply delineating and highlighting the system currently in place:

Therapist: "You mentioned that you aren't happy with your relationships. Can you tell me more about that?"

Client: "Well, my wife and I hardly talk unless it's something about the kids, and then it's always about some problem. She's constantly complaining about this or that; there's always something that I haven't done right. She just keeps on me till I just finally lose it, then it's *my* fault, you know! I just mostly avoid her these days.... At least we won't get in some stupid argument."

Therapist: "So help me understand this a bit better. Can you say more about your experience when she's 'keeping on you'? What goes on with you when she does that?"

Client: "You mean when she's nagging me to death?"

Therapist: "So that's what it feels like? Is that a thought that comes up at those times: 'She's nagging me to death'?"

Client: "Yeah."

Therapist: "And then what happens?"

Client: "I go off."

Therapist: "What does that look like?"

Client: "I don't hit her or anything. I've never hit her or the kids....I just get mad, throw stuff, cuss her out sometimes."

Therapist: "So she's saying something, you have thoughts about her nagging you to death, and then...anger shows up at some point."

Client: "Yeah. All of a sudden I just feel this rage. I feel like I'm gonna explode."

Therapist: "What are you feeling right now?"

Client: "Huh?"

Therapist: "Looking at you, it seems as though you are feeling some of that right now, that anger."

Client:	"Yeah, just talking about it makes me angry all over again."
Therapist:	"But you aren't exploding. At least you haven't thrown anything yet."
Client:	"Well…you're not her." (*Laughs.*)

In this exchange, the therapist is actively working with several core processes, even if they are not being explicitly put on the table. Let's pull them out:

Therapist:	"You mentioned that you aren't happy with your relationships. Can you tell me more about that?"
Client:	"Well, my wife and I hardly talk unless it's something about the kids, and then it's always about some problem. She's constantly complaining about this or that; there's always something that I haven't done right. She just keeps on me till I just finally lose it, then it's *my* fault, you know! I just mostly avoid her these days.… At least we won't get in some stupid argument."
Therapist:	"So help me understand this a bit better. Can you say more about *your experience* when she's 'keeping on you'? What *goes on with you* when she does that?" (*Here the therapist is pointing to self-as-context and self-as-process while subtly shifting emphasis from what the wife is doing to how the client responds.*)
Client:	"You mean when she's nagging me to death?"
Therapist:	"So that's *what it feels like?* Is that a *thought that comes up* at those times: 'She's nagging me to death'?" (*Again, self-as-context, self-as-process, and laying some groundwork for cognitive defusion.*)
Client:	"Yeah."
Therapist:	"And then what happens?" (*Self-as-process, although the client could potentially take this as a question regarding what his wife does next in these scenarios. If so, the therapist could simply redirect him to his own experience.*)
Client:	"I go off."
Therapist:	"What does that look like?" (*The therapist is subtly pointing to self-as-context, asking the client to relate to his behavior as an observer.*)
Client:	"I don't hit her or anything. I've never hit her or the kids. I just get mad, throw stuff, cuss her out sometimes."

Therapist:	"So she's saying something, you have thoughts about her nagging you to death, and then…anger shows up at some point." (*Self-as-process, self-as-context.*)
Client:	"Yeah. All of a sudden I just feel this rage. I feel like I'm gonna explode."
Therapist:	"What are you feeling right now?" (*The therapist goes to the present moment, both to continue to help the client build awareness of himself as the Experiencer and to begin to undermine experiential avoidance. The therapist is helping the client become aware of, and therefore have—if even for a moment—his emotions.*)
Client:	"Huh?"
Therapist:	"Looking at you, it seems as though you are feeling some of that right now, that anger." (*Still assisting the client to become an observer of his thoughts and feelings, working on building willingness.*)
Client:	"Yeah, just talking about it makes me angry all over again."
Therapist:	"But you aren't exploding. At least you haven't thrown anything yet." (*The therapist is undermining the idea that emotions cause behavior.*)
Client:	"Well…you're not her." (*Laughs.*)

Hopefully it is clear in this exchange how the therapist is advancing core ACT processes while paving the way for more explicit work in the future. It should also demonstrate a point made in the first chapter of this book—the importance of language in ACT. Nearly every exchange can be used to further the work. In fact, I sometimes imagine language in ACT as a sort of chisel that therapists hold throughout the therapy so they can chip, chip, chip away.

This section described just another way to approach the decision-making process in ACT, one that emphasizes considering indirect versus explicit intervention. I have found this approach helpful, as it takes me out of falsely thinking I have to make an "either/or" decision and seems to enhance my clinical flexibility.

COMMON TIMING MISSTEPS

We have been exploring different aspects of timing, an important part of doing any therapy well. I have had the opportunity over time to note where therapists tend to struggle when it comes to timing in ACT, and I'll use this section to present those observations along with ideas about how to think about timing that I have found to be helpful.

Guiding, Not Yanking

Learning to guide rather than yank is something I've really had to work on and it is a challenge for many other providers, as well. My desire for my clients to get it, to understand something that I think will be a game changer for them, combined with my unwillingness to sit with impatience, has led me to attempt to pull my clients along, at times, rather than walk beside them at their own pace. This tendency was particularly strong when I was starting out with ACT. I was so excited about this new therapy that made such sense to me that I wanted to either yank my clients to the finish line or just dump every concept in their lap and say, "See?" This tendency can be especially evident at the start of therapy, when the therapist tries to explain ACT to the client, expecting that she will see the light and immediately make behavioral changes. For example:

> *Therapist (after having the client list all the experiential avoidance strategies she had been using, and doing the man-in-the-hole exercise):* "So you've been digging. And now it's time to drop the shovel. Instead of digging, you can choose to accept it. All this stuff you've been trying to avoid—your anxiety, the depression, the thoughts about not being good enough—if you can just be willing to have that and see it for what it is, you are free to do what works in your life. So despite what you are thinking and feeling, you can move forward and do what you value."

I see this sort of move a lot actually, and understand the impulse. It's as though you as the therapist know you are holding a fistful of really fertile seeds. And because you are aware of the seeds' promise, you excitedly toss them in the nearest patch of dirt and wait for them to blossom. The problem is that no care has gone into the soil. No removal of rocks and weeds, no tilling, no fertilizing. The seeds won't flourish if the soil is not adequately prepared. Now, if you are like some of my clients, you will have immediately found flaws in that metaphor. For example, do we actually know that none of the seeds will bear fruit? Isn't it possible that even if they are sort of dumped in this way, one might actually land and take hold? Sure, such a thing seems quite possible; in fact, I've seen it happen and it has happened to me—something I've done in session unskillfully, downright clumsily, or even accidentally has ultimately proven fruitful. The point of this metaphor is to have timing be a consideration—to consider the condition of the soil and the purpose of the seeds. The core processes in ACT will arise again and again, offering you repeated opportunities to work with them. There are also many pertinent exercises and metaphors to work with, not to mention those in your head that have yet to be created. The idea is to give yourself room to place particular seeds when and where you think they will grow best.

Initially, I worried that throwing the entire gist of ACT at clients in the first session or so would ruin it—sort of like telling the punch line before the joke. But in general, my observation is that it has a more negligible impact. That is, clients are initially so unprepared for the ultimate message of ACT that they can't even hear what the therapist is saying. I *have* seen clients react negatively to the word "accept" when it is pulled out early on; they assume what the therapy is going to be about based on previous associations with the term (such as the idea that they need to just get over it; accepting means feeling differently about it; if they could just accept, it would go away). I have also seen scenarios in which a particularly high-functioning client grasps the full intent and theory of ACT in just two or three sessions. I tend to be wary when this occurs, as it usually turns out that the control agenda has simply gone underground. The client gets the principles of ACT, buys them, and yet is just as easily thrown when life throws a curveball. To repeat myself, the experience of the therapy—not just the conceptual information—is needed to facilitate the significant shifts proposed by this model. Just as we help our clients understand the difference between living as a process and living as an outcome, I believe it is the process of the therapy (followed by active practice), not the punch line, that promotes enduring behavioral changes.

Remember, It's a Process

I mentioned a moment ago that providers sometimes forget ACT is a process. I know this idea sounds elementary. But providers frequently rely on verbal learning as *the* mechanism of change, expecting that if the client understands something intellectually it will lead to behavioral change. For example, although the willingness component of ACT is often introduced fairly early in the therapy, it is interesting how often there is a subtle (and sometimes not so subtle) expectation on the part of the therapist that explaining this concept will cause the client to move from experiential avoidance to willingness. You can actually hear this expectation in the session; at some point there is a subtle switch from the therapist talking with the client about willingness as an alternative to control, to the therapist trying to persuade the client to be willing. The implied message is along the lines of "You can see this, can't you? Great, so you're going to be willing now, right?" Prepare yourself—here comes another metaphor: This time, you and your client are standing together at the near end of a long, dimly lit corridor. You reach over and flip a switch on the wall; a door at the far end of the corridor slowly slides open. Sunlight streams through; there is a glimpse of blue sky...but there's also a lot of hallway between here and there. I think therapy is a lot like that. We can give clients a glimpse of what's possible; we can help them see what's available out there; but they're going to have to walk down that corridor on their own two feet. It is the walk, not the therapist flipping the switch, that gets clients down the hallway and into their life. Willingness is a behavioral process, a moment-to-moment choice. It is not about just understanding the concept and verbally agreeing with it. This is why it is so important to allow both yourself and your client to fully experience the process of ACT.

Going for Gold vs. Going for Broke

One of the things to consider when deciding whether or not to introduce a particular idea, exercise, or metaphor is whether doing so will *optimize* its message. If you'll excuse me for referring to the dirt patch metaphor again, it's about adding an additional level of gardening sophistication. That is, the soil might be adequate for a seed to grow, but is this the *optimal* time for planting that particular seed? If you were to wait for another session or so, might that seed fare even better? For example, I have found the chessboard metaphor to be one of the most clinically powerful in ACT. Along with "passengers on a bus," the chessboard metaphor typically resonates particularly for those clients who are struggling with a very negative conceptualized self or the perception of having no self. (As one such client stated, "If I let go of my anger, there's nothing there; there's no There, there.") While there are many opportunities throughout ACT where the chessboard metaphor and passengers on a bus might reasonably be applied, I like to hold these two back a bit until I feel the client has really been primed for them. I have listened to many sessions during which the therapist brings the chessboard metaphor in early on, and it just doesn't really land. The metaphor is received more as an intellectual idea, rather than resonating at a personal level. Or the client might take it very literally (that there's no winning, for example) and completely miss the main message (the self that is larger than the pieces). This misunderstanding is often due to the client's inability to defuse from the content of her mind, to contact herself as Thinker having thoughts. In these cases, the metaphor functions as just another idea, rather than representing the distinction between self and thoughts (and feelings, and so forth). If the client can see that the control agenda is futile and costly, if she is at least considering willingness as an alternative and understands the distinction between looking *at* thoughts and *from* thoughts and has built some skill there, then she is in a great place for an explicit discussion about the Self being larger than the internal phenomena of the moment.

Similarly, the "passengers on a bus" metaphor works very well in many places, as it so nicely embodies all the core processes. That is exactly why I like to save it, and use it toward the end of therapy as a powerful way to tie the processes together and bring committed action home. That said, there are many times I introduce it earlier because I think it will be the most effective strategy for a particular client at a particular point in time. I will explore clinical decision-making around metaphors and exercises more specifically in chapter 10. For now, my suggestion for ACT therapists who want to enhance their timing in session is to pursue a questioning process along the following lines:

1. Does the idea, exercise, or metaphor pertain to what's actually happening in this session (in other words, getting present and considering the core processes currently in play)?

2. How will introducing it serve to further the therapy? (What is its intended function?)

3. Is there a reason to hold off? (This question could also be phrased as follows: Is there a more optimal time for it, given the current context and where the client is in terms of psychological ability?)

When engaging in detailed analysis of timing with supervisees and consultees, I have often seen that the therapist introduced a concept, metaphor, or exercise simply because the client said something that made the thought or exercise come to mind. Sometimes that's going to be spot on, sometimes not. Many providers have described times when they had some niggling sense that this may not be the best time to tackle or introduce something, but they "just couldn't resist trying." At times like these, it's important to give yourself permission to simply stop and attend to what's happening. Is it really time to go for broke, or is it time to sit with the impulse? Allowing yourself the opportunity to think about timing specifically will raise the odds of having good timing in your sessions. I'll also say again that there will likely be many opportunities to work with a particular process, as these behaviors are persistent and can manifest any number of ways. Keeping that in mind can help you resist the urge to jump on something too soon.

A related misstep I have seen is when the therapist is following a particular agenda, and presents a metaphor or exercise based upon his session plan rather than considering what is actually happening in the room. What often happens in this case is the exercise or metaphor falls flat or increases confusion because it simply doesn't fit. More importantly, as discussed in chapter 1, the therapist is conducting the therapy at the content level rather than process level—the cost being effective work with what is actually happening during the session.

SUMMARY

My intention with this chapter was to offer some ways to think about timing that can assist with clinical decision-making. I included some of the ways ACT therapists can jump the gun with timing as a way to highlight the factors that go into good timing, as well as point out the clinical implications of making missteps in this area. I find this particular terrain—exploring the role of timing and its limitless manifestations—very intriguing and have no expectation of its mastery. It now seems timely (sorry, couldn't resist) to extend this discussion to overall approaches to the therapy and general strategies regarding the introduction of core ACT processes.

CHAPTER 5

Know Your Approach

This chapter will be devoted to a discussion about the overall application of ACT. I am referring to general strategy—how to approach ACT such that over the course of therapy the six processes considered to be central to psychological flexibility are advanced to such a degree that clients are able to lead vital and meaningful lives. This strategy necessarily includes assessing, targeting, and developing those processes where clients demonstrate difficulty, which in turn involves coherently furthering ACT constructs by way of dialogue, metaphor, and experiential work. When I review what has been written on the clinical application of ACT, I am repeatedly impressed by the quality of these materials. There are simply many texts available that do a beautiful job of laying out how to apply the therapy, from case conceptualization to working with specific populations, and I do not feel it necessary to revisit what has already been said so well (see chapter 12 for recommended reading). Rather, since my intention with this book is to help ACT therapists optimize what they are doing and address areas that can be challenging, I will approach this topic from that angle.

It is important to clarify my use of the term "content" in this chapter. I refer to the various topics, constructs, metaphors, and exercises by which practitioners illuminate and further the core ACT processes such that psychological flexibility is enhanced. So, for example, content can refer to the "lemon, lemon" exercise and also to a discussion around reason-giving, both being geared toward advancing the process of cognitive defusion. I will also at times refer to a "content area," meaning the collection of ideas, exercises, metaphors, and so on, that together target a given process. For example, creative hopelessness is an example of a content area that focuses on furthering acceptance by undermining experiential avoidance. The content area of self-as-context is meant to refer to metaphors, exercises, and dialogue that target that core process (which may involve undermining a conceptualized self, and so forth).

TO SEQUENCE OR NOT TO SEQUENCE

I would like to begin by pointing to what can be described as a sort of divide between the various methodologies when it comes to applying ACT. That is, many of the published materials present a certain order for working through key content areas, such as the sequence initially presented in the original ACT text (Hayes et al., 1999), whereas other authors propose a less linear approach, targeting various processes depending on initial and ongoing assessment as the therapy unfolds. Regardless, every ACT expert, author, trainer, or consultant I've ever encountered has made it very clear that there is no one way to conduct the therapy. As it happens, the majority of consultees and supervisees with whom I have worked have approached the therapy using a sequential pattern, providing me ample opportunity to closely observe some of the advantages and disadvantages of conducting ACT in this manner.

What Difference Does It Make?

Let's take a look at what the difference between moving through content areas in a sequential fashion and working with processes more fluidly might actually mean in the therapy room. If you were observing or listening to a typical session within the sequential approach, for example, you would be able to clearly discern the central topic for the session—such as control as the problem, or self-as-context, or committed action. The session might begin with a chronological review of the core ideas covered so far, and then segue to the next component of the therapy, which would then constitute the bulk of the session. The metaphors and experiential exercises incorporated in the session would have been selected based upon their utility in furthering that particular session topic. Although the client could well introduce content that points to other ACT components, the therapist would likely work with it in terms of the central topic for that day or concepts explored in previous sessions. This agenda continues until they have moved through the key content areas (creative hopelessness, control as the problem, willingness, present moment, self-as-context, values, and committed action) over the course of therapy. A more fluid, less linear approach might entail beginning the therapy by targeting a core process that the therapist has assessed as a good starting point for that client, such as defusion or contact with the present moment, and drawing from the various content areas depending upon ongoing assessment as the therapy unfolds.

When done well, the actual clinical differences between these two approaches might not be so great. That is, if the therapist is conducting ACT with fidelity to the model, she is present to each session, looking for the core processes that constitute psychological flexibility and how these apply to the particular client, both in session and in daily life. The therapist who is not following a preplanned sequence might feel freer to pull in a new concept (or several) during a given session, but both therapists would be working with core processes as they arise. The actual difference might be more a matter of what is being addressed directly and what is being more indirectly targeted. That is, a therapist who intends to cover the ACT content areas in a particular sequence might refrain from explicitly introducing a new concept in order to work with something that has shown up in session, because that concept will be covered in detail at a later point; but she could choose to work on the concept in other ways—by the language used, by modeling, or by experiential demonstration, for example. Additionally, the further along they are in therapy, the more likely it is that even therapists following a certain sequence will move freely from one content area to another, because the central ideas from each have been previously explored and are in play. To emphasize, when conducting the therapy with fidelity the therapist is first and foremost in the present moment with her client and working with what is happening in terms of relevant ACT processes. Even if the therapist is clearly following a linear pattern, being present and operating from a principle-based—as opposed to a technique-based—stance naturally leads to more flexible and effective clinical decision-making.

Advantages to a Sequential Approach

To date I do not know of any empirical data comparing the relative efficacy of these two approaches to conducting ACT. I *can* offer that the many opportunities I have had to observe therapists as they conduct the therapy has led me to appreciate the accessibility of the more sequential approach. Chiefly, it offers a sensible framework for working through the many domains of the therapy, ensuring that all six behavioral processes are adequately covered. Although the more fluid approach has the obvious benefit of clinical flexibility, it can seem daunting to therapists who are newer to ACT. As discussed at the beginning of this book, one of the most important competency milestones for many therapists is making the shift from basing what they do in session primarily on verbal content to considering the function of what is being said or done (or not said or done), and how that is reflected in the core ACT processes—in other words, looking through that ACT lens and discerning what core processes are currently in play, and then determining how to work with them in an ACT-consistent fashion. Doing so in a way that manages to meet clients where they are while also introducing new concepts and tying it all coherently together can be quite challenging. Because the core ACT processes are not actually distinct entities but rather interdependent, almost any interaction can be meaningfully approached from a number of content areas, further increasing the clinical options and decision-making complexity. When used correctly, a sequential approach to moving through the respective content areas of ACT serves less as a clinical blueprint and more as a framework from within which the therapist can work effectively.

Another advantage to the sequential approach is that the various ACT content areas can be used almost as building blocks, with work in one paving the way for work in another. For example, creative hopelessness is often brought in at the beginning of therapy to loosen the grip of the control agenda, creating an opening for the rest of the work. Control as the problem then orients the client away from the fix-it ideal and toward what might actually be keeping him stuck, paving the way for willingness to be considered as a more workable alternative. Mindfulness is presented as a way to increase contact with the present moment (which requires at least some willingness), and from this stance the client can begin to build both willingness and self-awareness. This increased ability to observe thoughts paves the way for cognitive defusion, which helps clients deliteralize thoughts and distinguish between Thinker and thought—an ability that is extended when moving into self-as-context. Once it has been established that there is a Self that is larger than the cognitive, emotional, and physiological phenomena of the moment, and free to make behavioral choices regardless of those phenomena, values are introduced as a way to clarify and guide the manner in which clients actually want to be living. Finally, committed action, as the behavioral manifestation of all these processes, is brought in to help the client put all this into action. In this way the content areas build on one another, and the client's developing skill with one core process enhances skill with another.

The Trickiness of a Sequential Approach

When the therapy is approached in a sequential fashion, therapists can be even more apt to base clinical decision-making on where they are in the progression, at the cost of discerning and effectively working with the ACT processes that arise in the moment. As discussed throughout this book, there are multiple and significant problems with approaching ACT as a collection of techniques or topics rather than working at the level of core behavioral processes. For this reason, there is valid concern that the various texts, manuals, and protocols presenting a sequential order for applying ACT can be misunderstood to suggest both separation and linearity in the core processes—even though the authors of these approaches are clear that this is not the case. Nonetheless, because the various content areas are designed to target specific core processes, and because these content areas are sequentially presented, many therapists are still prone to perceive the processes themselves to be separate entities when in fact they are highly interdependent. Similarly, the sequential content presentation can suggest that therapeutic progress follows such a sequence, rather than ability being on a continuum, not only within each core process but in terms of psychological flexibility overall. Because the core processes are interdependent, many of the metaphors and exercises presented in one content area can also be used to demonstrate a different core process. This versatility is a strength of the model, as it enhances clinical flexibility—the therapist can use the metaphors and exercises where they will be most effective for a particular client. But it can also be overlooked when working through the therapy in a typical pattern.

In short, while there may be some advantages to approaching ACT by moving through the content areas in sequence, it is crucial that such an approach not be at the cost of being present and working effectively with what is actually occurring in session. Here's an example of how a therapist following a building block sequence might further the topic of the day while also working with what occurs in session. In this scenario, the therapist and her client, a female in her late twenties, are in their second session, having explored creative hopelessness the previous week:

Therapist: "So last week we talked quite a bit about what brought you into therapy, what you are hoping for here."

Client: "Yeah. When you basically told me it was hopeless."

Therapist (laughing a little but responding compassionately): "Is that really what you heard?"

Client: "Well yeah! You told me about that man in the hole and how everything I've done hasn't worked. That I've just been digging."

Therapist: "Yes, I remember. But it's important that I don't send the message that you're supposed to believe the stuff you've tried hasn't worked simply because I say so. What I mean is, it's truly for you to determine whether the various things you've tried to control or to not have unwanted thoughts and feelings has worked. You are the best judge of that—you'll know by checking your own experience." (Here the therapist is making the point that this isn't about following a new rule provided by the therapist. Rather, the client is encouraged to contact the direct contingencies around her behavior.)

Client: "Well, it hasn't worked, obviously. Here I am."

Therapist: "Yes, here you are." (Pauses, unhurried.) "I also want to stress that there's an important difference between that control agenda being helpless and you being helpless. You are far from helpless. The main thing at this point is to get clear on the bind you've been in."

Client: "Oh, I'm clear, believe me."

Therapist: "What are you experiencing right now? In this moment with me?

Client: (Starts to say something; falls silent.)

Therapist: "When you said that, it seemed like maybe you were feeling angry, or frustrated." (Even though the therapist was prepared to move into the topic of control as problematic during this session, she is tuned in to what is happening in the room and perceives that the client is upset.

*To ignore the client's feelings and move on at this point would actually
be an avoidance or control move on the part of the therapist.)*

Client: "I guess I am frustrated. I was actually really bummed out last
             week. Well, at the time, I was confused, then bummed out, and
             now I'm just mad or something. This pisses me off. Like, what am
             I supposed to do?"

Therapist: "Yeah." (*Rests with it a moment.*) "I'm wondering if fear is there
             as well? I thought I sensed a little bit of that there too, just now,
             along with the anger." (*Here the therapist remains focused on the
             client's affective experience, rather than answering her question.
             Doing so would be to move away from the affective experience and
             into content introduced by the client as a likely avoidance move.)*

Client: "Definitely. What if I never get out of this?"

Therapist: "Yeah! So scary thoughts are going on about being stuck, what it
             would mean if you never got out of this….You've got frustration,
             confusion, fear. There's a lot going on right now."

Client: "Definitely."

*(The therapist is silent but in a patient, attentive, and compassionate way. If her
nonverbal behavior could speak, it would be saying, "I hear you. I'm here with you.
While this is uncomfortable to experience, we don't actually have to do a thing with
it." With this move the therapist is working on contact with the present moment and
willingness in an implicit, rather than explicit, manner.)*

Client   (*after waiting a bit for the therapist to say something*): "So what do
             we do now?"

Therapist   (*pauses before answering*): "Hmmm. You know, on one hand I feel
             pulled to answer that, and on the other I am wondering if that
             isn't something we should add to our list here (*gesturing to a list of
             control strategies generated in the previous session*). Is it safe to say
             that asking questions or asking for the solution is something you
             do to get out of feeling uncomfortable? Like, you're experiencing
             some really tough stuff right now, and you're asking me what
             we need to do to get out of that experience?" (*Even though they
             won't be worked on directly until later in the therapy, the therapist is
             introducing cognitive defusion and self-as-context indirectly by using
             words such as "I feel pulled here," and by helping the client build
             awareness of self-as-process. She is drawing upon what was covered in
             the previous session and continuing to work explicitly with experiential*

avoidance—using different words for it, though—by pointing out the function of what the client is doing.)

Client: "I guess so."

Therapist: "So let's just notice that." (*Long pause as the therapist and client just sit. Although the therapist hasn't introduced willingness as a topic, this move is very much about that process, as well as continuing with the implicit self-as-process work—in other words, who's doing the noticing?)*

Therapist   (*eventually continuing*): "Asking questions or asking for solutions are ways we attempt to get out of discomfort. We humans are pretty amazing creatures, aren't we? Very inventive, very determined. We can come up with endless strategies to try to get away from discomfort or pain, just as we saw last week. When we are in that hole, we just dig away." (*The therapist is normalizing the struggle and pointing to the ultimate futility of the control agenda.)*

Client: (*Nods.*)

Therapist: "Yes." (*Long pause.*) "Here's the thing: what if it's the digging itself that causes us the most difficulty?" (*With this the therapist begins to bring in the new content—control as the problem.)*

Client: "What do you mean?"

Therapist: "What if the effort to not have unwanted thoughts, painful feelings, and so on, is the real culprit here? What if that very control agenda is what keeps us stuck?"

(Now the therapist can move fully into the content area of control as the problem, hopefully using a combination of experiential exercises—tug-of-war, for example— and metaphors, such as the polygraph, to bring the point home. However, in-the-moment dynamics will continue to be addressed from within the ACT framework as the session unfolds. Note that she is still using "us" rather than "you," continuing to highlight that this is a human dilemma as opposed to being specific to the client. This is especially important to do in the beginning of therapy, as clients are prone to hear what the therapist is saying as further evidence that there is something wrong with them, or that they are not doing it right. Such language also helps establish the horizontal therapist/client relationship that is so important in ACT.)

Here's another example to demonstrate that sequentially working through the core content areas of ACT does not mean the therapy itself is a linear process. In this scenario the therapist and male client have worked through the content areas of creative hopelessness, control as the problem, willingness, present moment, cognitive defusion, and self-as-context, and have started to explore values:

Therapist	*(reviewing a values worksheet assigned as homework during the previous session):* "I see that you have put down 'make a contribution' in the 'Citizenship' domain."
Client:	"Yeah. I like to feel like I'm making a difference."
Therapist:	"I can see that. So, in terms of citizenship, what are some specific goals that would be in the service of making a difference?"
Client:	"Well, I thought I was making a contribution by serving in Vietnam." *(Pauses.)* "You'd think that would count, but apparently not according to folks here."
Therapist:	*(Silent, considering.)*
Client:	"Believe it or not, that was the hardest thing about it—coming back and being treated like a piece of crap."
Therapist:	"I've no doubt! I can't imagine what that was like after having made that sort of sacrifice." *(Although they have talked quite a bit about the client's tour in Vietnam, he has never really expressed this before, and the therapist feels it is important to validate his experience.)*
Client	*(suddenly worked up):* "It really hurt, you know? I was like, 'SCREW YOU!'"
Therapist	*(silent for a bit, just sitting in the emotion that has shown up, then):* "Do you notice what is happening right now? Here, in this moment?" *(This move pulls in contact with the present, and also reflects self-as-process and willingness processes.)*
Client:	"Yeah, I'm pissed off just thinking about it."
Therapist:	"Yeah, I can feel the anger, and the hurt, from over here. Let's just honor that a moment." *(Long pause as they simply sit together. Therapist eventually resumes.)* "Well, let's play it through. We were working on the idea of values, of valued living—what you want to be about in your life going forward. You identified 'making a contribution' as an important value, and then what happened?" *(Willingness and self-as-process are furthered by the therapist's word choice—"I can feel," for example—and by her choosing to simply sit in the moment, holding the experience. Next, the therapist assists the client's ability with self-as-process by asking him to "play it through.")*

Client:	"I dunno. All of a sudden I was thinking about Vietnam and what went down. I can't believe I'm still this pissed off after all this time."
Therapist:	"Let's stick with this—this is important. It's a perfect example of how our minds work, of what happens for us that can make it hard to actually get out there and start living life in the way we want. Even just now, your mind is scrambling around handing you stuff about being pissed off after all this time—it never stops!" (*The therapist is normalizing the client's reactions and also working against the ongoing control agenda—for example, the idea that he should be fixed by now and no longer pissed off. Cognitive defusion is furthered by pointing out what the client's mind has been doing and continues to do.*)
Client:	"No, it doesn't. Happens so quickly, too!"
Therapist:	"Yup. And am I correct in saying that tucked into 'I can't believe I'm still this pissed' is the idea that you shouldn't feel this way? That somehow you should not have these feelings about it?" (*The therapist is homing in on the ongoing control agenda.*)
Client:	"Yeah! I'm still trying to control."
Therapist:	"How great that you see that. And now you might be evaluating the fact that you're trying to control." (*The therapist continues to home in on the control agenda, working on the core processes of cognitive defusion, self-as-context, and ultimately, willingness.*)
Client:	"Oh, man."
Therapist:	"Yeah, our minds are busy, busy, busy, aren't they? (*Here we have cognitive defusion, self-as-context, and promoting willingness by normalizing.*)

(*Again, the pace is unhurried, with plenty of pauses to simply experience the moment.*)

Therapist:	"So let's keep looking at what you experienced in here. The 'making a contribution' idea brought up the memory of Vietnam and a bunch of experiences, thoughts, and feelings that you have associated with that. It's as though, instead of being in the room with me, talking about your life now and how you want to be living your life, you fell into a story about your past." (*The therapist works on contact with the present moment by pointing out the domination of the conceptualized past.*)

Client:	"I sure did."
Therapist:	"Well, as we've talked about many times, our minds are very ready to go there. But you have also come a very long way in being able to catch and work with that process so that it doesn't stand in the way. So what's at stake here? What I mean is, you are clear that you value making a contribution, and you have had a super-painful experience around the contribution you made by serving your country in Vietnam. What does your mind hand you around this?" (*The therapist seeks to enhance the client's learning by engaging him in the inquiry, rather than spelling everything out.*)
Client	(*thinks*): "Hmmm. Something along the lines of since my contribution wasn't appreciated then, why bother now?" (*Laughs.*) "Real mature, huh?"
Therapist:	"Real human." (*The therapist normalizes and promotes acceptance with these two small words. She could also continue with defusion and self-as-context by pointing out the client's quick evaluation.*) "But do you hear the trap in it?" (*Leaning in.*) "Making a contribution is *yours*. It is *your* value—you get to decide what you care about, what you want your life to be in the service of. You are not dependent upon other people, their reactions, their values, for determining what you want *your* life to be about." (*Now they are back into full-on values work, having incorporated what occurred in the sessions and worked on the core processes that seemed most pertinent.*)

I have included the above examples to demonstrate how approaching ACT by moving sequentially through the key content areas does not preclude working with whatever core processes should arise. Hopefully this discussion has continued to help make the distinction between working at the level of the processes and having sessions be about covering certain content.

OTHER CONSIDERATIONS

I have been focusing on some things to consider when determining your overall approach to ACT. It is important to note that these considerations aren't always simply a matter of preference. For example, some treatment settings (such as an inpatient setting, where the patient's stay may be quite brief) preclude moving through the content in sequential order. Sometimes the therapy is delivered in daylong workshops, or just a few sessions according to a research protocol. Another example is group work. I have conducted many ACT groups, and when the group is closed and treatment length is not an issue I prefer to move through the content areas sequentially. When it's an open group, with participants coming and going, a more fluid approach wherein the core processes are touched upon in each session has made more sense. Fortunately, there is good information out there on how ACT can be effectively conducted in these sorts of settings. Some of these materials are listed in chapter 12; others can easily be found by perusing the Association for Contextual Behavioral Science (ACBS) website: http://www.contextualscience.org.

My emphasis in this chapter has been on the sequential approach, as that has comprised the bulk of my consulting and supervising experience, and has also been shown to hold some real challenges to conducting ACT with fidelity. However, a very common progression for therapists as they advance in ACT is to move to a more fluid approach. Most, if not all, the therapists I have worked with have become more and more fluid as they gain experience. For many, this progression has become apparent after only having done one full course of ACT. The therapist might, for example, report that it made better sense to start a particular client off with values rather than creative hopelessness, or that she had found a client to be so experientially avoidant that she felt the client needed to spend some time building contact with the present moment before moving into any other content area. Such flexibility is the hallmark of approaching the therapy from the basis of principle versus technique, and leads to the experience of clinical freedom I mentioned at the beginning of this book.

WRAPPING UP WELL

So far, I have concentrated on some clinical implications of the general strategies therapists use to approach the application of ACT. Regardless of the strategy used, at some point therapy comes to an end. I will spend a bit of time here on terminating ACT, as the manner in which the therapy ends is as important as how it begins.

The main reason I would like to explore this issue is because I have observed that therapists don't always optimize their final ACT sessions. It has sometimes seemed as though the minds of both client and therapist have managed to lead them out of the therapy room and into the future, when what is needed most is continued work on what is happening in the present. This section explores ways in which this shift from the present can manifest in final sessions, potential consequences, and ways to milk every last drop of clinical opportunity when terminating with clients.

The End Is Just the Beginning

An interesting phenomenon I've noticed during final sessions is that the therapist can subtly promote the idea that the client has been fixed by neglecting to address ongoing issues (which suggests that they no longer need to be recognized and worked on). This tends to occur when the therapy has gone well and the client is no longer stuck. That is, the therapist, well aware that the client has begun to move in valued directions, overlooks ongoing ways of thinking or behaving that can lead to future problems. For clients, too, the notion of being fixed can suddenly reveal itself, as though it has been in hibernation and woken up just as they are headed out the door. I have noticed that even therapists who have consistently homed in on ongoing control efforts often miss them at the end. They can even inadvertently strengthen the control agenda by stepping out of the ACT framework a bit during final sessions. Here's an example:

Client   (starting out the session with a reference to homework): "So I completed my goal this week, and redid my résumé."

Therapist: "That's great! How did it go?"

Client: "It was a total pain, but I think it turned out pretty good."

Therapist: "Well, well done for completing that. I know that was an important one for you. I think you were also going to send it out to a couple places?"

Client: "I didn't get to that yet. But I found out yesterday that the company where a friend of mine works is opening a branch office here, so I'm thinking about applying there….This is the friend who was visiting over the weekend."

Therapist: "The college buddy?"

Client: "Yeah, Dan. We haven't seen each other in years—just talked a few times on the phone….It's been really great to see him. He says he can definitely tell that I've changed."

Therapist: "Really? In what way?"

Client: "He said I'm way more positive now, not this depressed person all the time. He said I'd been a real drag to talk to for a while there. We have really been able to connect on this trip."

Therapist: "That's great! I know reaching out to friends was something you identified as a goal when we were talking about values."

Client: "Yeah, it was so much easier to be around him than I was expecting—it just seemed natural, you know?"

Therapist: "That's great."

Before going over this example with an ACT-toothed comb, let me say again that this sort of exchange is not uncommon as therapy is wrapping up. At one level, things seem great, as the client clearly feels as though his life is going well right now. Especially when this has not always been the case, and the therapist and client have experienced some tough times together, there is an understandable pull to sit back and celebrate. There is no harm in celebrating the good moments with a client—in fact, I would add that is important to do—but it should not be at the cost of addressing other things going on that could put the client at risk for future problems. When the therapist does not address these issues as well, it sends a sort of "we're done with ACT" message, right when it's most important to knit ACT processes and the client's daily life more firmly together.

If you read over the above dialogue again, focusing on identifying any additional sticking points the client might have in terms of ACT processes, what do you see? Here's what occurs to me:

Client	(starting out the session with a reference to homework): "So I completed my goal this week, and redid my résumé."
Therapist:	"That's great! How did it go?"
Client:	"It was a total pain, but I think it turned out pretty good." (You could leave this alone, as the identified goal—to complete his résumé—was accomplished. However, there is an opportunity here to spell out for the client what he was doing that was effective. I tend to grab such moments, even if it's not likely to be news: "When did that thought—that it's a total pain—show up?" or "So even though you were having that thought about it being a pain, you made a choice that took you closer to your values around working.")
Therapist:	"Well, well done for completing that. I know that was an important one for you. I think you were also going to send it out to a couple places?"
Client:	"I didn't get to that yet. But I found out yesterday that the company where a friend of mine works is opening a branch office here, so I'm thinking about applying there….This is the friend who was visiting over the weekend."
Therapist:	"The college buddy?" (Although it may seem a light wind, the therapist has nonetheless been blown off course here. That is, he was hooked by the content of what the client said about his friend, and with this question has moved off of committed action. In fact, his client's response—"I didn't get to that yet"—potentially points to a barrier to committed action.)
Client:	"Yeah, Dan. We haven't seen each other in years, just talked a few times on the phone….It's been really great to see him. He says he

can definitely tell that I've changed." (*My antennae always quiver when I hear something like this. Does he mean that he is behaving differently and others are noticing that, or does he mean that he's a different—as in fixed—person?*)

Therapist: "Really? In what way?" (*To a fused client, one who is thinking that he's different and fixed now, this question would likely be heard as an endorsement of that idea. The therapist has also now completely moved away from working with the client on committed action before it was adequately addressed.*)

Client: "He said I'm way more positive now, not this depressed person all the time. He said I'd been a real drag to talk to for a while there. We've really been able to connect on this trip." (*Although the client is talking about his friend's perception here, it is likely he is viewing things similarly since he is not commenting otherwise. The concerning elements include [1] attachment to a control agenda—that a person can, and should, be positive; [2] attachment to a conceptualized self—as either positive or depressed—rather than seeing the distinction between the self and depressive or positive thoughts, feelings, and behaviors; and [3] an "in with the good, out with the bad" orientation that is leading the client to think he's fixed, which sets him up to think he's broken when—not if—the positive experience changes.*)

Therapist: "That's great! I know reaching out to friends was something you identified as a goal when we were talking about values."

Client: "Yeah, it was so much easier to be around him than I was expecting—it just seemed natural, you know?"

Therapist: "That's great." (*We get to be happy for our clients when something goes easily for them. But we've done them a disservice if they leave therapy thinking that the reason something was successful was because it was easy. The point is to make a valued choice—whether easy or not.*)

I admit to hypervigilance about this sort of thing, stemming from what I have noted over time observing clients who have completed a full course of ACT. For example, I facilitated a weekly ACT aftercare group for several years that was comprised of female veterans who had completed a full course of ACT while in our PTSD treatment program. In the course of the seven or so years I ran this drop-in group, I gained invaluable insight regarding the challenges of applying ACT concepts to daily life. One lesson I learned was that the idea that one's life can be fixed is an idea that clients often aren't ready to entirely give up. That is, even when clients have fully grasped the idea that there is no ultimate destination in living a good life, no ultimate point of arrival where we say, "At last, I've done it," the notion that they can somehow finish working at it lives on.

An example just came to mind, one that involved a young woman who had experienced sexual trauma in the military. She was experiencing severe symptoms of PTSD, depressed mood, and suicidal ideation, and she was abusing alcohol as well. This young woman really took to ACT and after her discharge began to turn her life around. She remained sober, got her own apartment, and enrolled in college, where she was earning A's, and she managed to finally end a destructive relationship. Then one day she arrived late to the group, noticeably disheveled and unkempt. She was uncharacteristically quiet, and the few comments she made were very passive and hopeless sounding. In fact, her presentation was reminiscent of where she had been when she first presented for treatment. This pattern continued for about three weeks, with the most striking feature being the degree to which this woman had moved from actively and intentionally moving through life to identifying with a victim role. Finally, during one group she was able to access and give voice to her anger. In essence, it turned out it was August, the anniversary of her trauma, and she was experiencing all-too-familiar feelings of anxiety, dread, sadness, and shame, and the same old thoughts involving self-blame and low self-worth. And here came the anger:

Client:	"And there's just no point, you know?"
Me:	"No, I don't know what you mean by that."
Client:	"Why bother? This is all so unfair. The rape just ruined my life. I just don't care anymore."
Me:	"Sounds like you care a great deal."
Client:	"But there's no point. I'm tired."
Me:	"Tired…"
Client:	"Tired of everything! I'm tired of feeling this way, of trying. I've been trying so hard." (*Starts to cry.*)
Me	(*pausing and letting the emotion be there, not rushing*): "What have you been trying to do?"
Client:	"To get my life together! To be a normal person with a life, a degree, a good job…"
Me:	"Looks to me like you haven't been trying."
Client:	"What?"
Me:	"Looks to me like you've been doing. You've been out there living, enrolling in school, going to classes, moving toward that

degree and good job. You are also experiencing the stuff that life continues to hand you, including feelings of sadness, shame, thoughts of self-blame, all the stuff that comes along with the memory of what happened to you in August, three years ago. Sounds normal to me."

Client   (really angry): "But I don't want that anymore! I've been doing everything right, working so hard. There's no point!"

Me: "No, there isn't." (Pause.) "No point at all if it's all in the service of not having what you have."

(Silence.)

Me   (more gently): "I am truly sorry that this is something you have to carry, that you were raped and that you experience the incredibly painful thoughts and feelings that go along with that. And this is when it's so very important to remember that you are larger than even these feelings, these memories." (Pause.) "You've been thinking that they were gone, that if you did everything 'right' you would get out of having to experience them again."

Client   (after a long silence): "Yes."

Me: "And yet, how could that be? What happened happened. There's no erasing that. And the thoughts and feelings you have around that are what belong to that sort of experience. If something brings the experience to mind, those thoughts and feelings are there as well. And who would you be, what sort of person would you have to be to not feel that way about being raped?" (Long silence.) "But the most important thing to see here is that you are fully capable of carrying the memory of this experience and everything that goes with it. You are carrying them. The question is whether you will stop now and sit on the side of the road with a sign that says, 'I don't want this,' or whether you will choose to continue to build that life that you envision."

This exchange led to a good group discussion on process versus outcome, on what it means to "live a good life," and so on. It is just one of many, many similar scenarios I have seen in which the desire for an ultimate fix, an ultimate destination or arrival point, has been revealed. I have accordingly come to believe that the fix-it agenda never goes away but, like any passenger, will continue to ride the bus and give a shout-out every now and then. This is why I actively look for this agenda in my sessions, particularly as therapy comes to an end, and use every opportunity to undermine that agenda, even if it is in the last minute of therapy.

Another way in which therapists can shortchange a final session is to rely on verbal exchange rather than implementing an experiential exercise. Sometimes this choice is simply a continuation of a larger pattern, which I will explore further in chapter 10. But especially at the end of therapy, there can be a tendency to think that now that the client "gets it" and is actively applying ACT principles to her life, there is simply no need for any fancy stuff. Here we revisit the idea of adequacy versus maximization. That is, while an experiential exercise might not technically be needed, pulling one in adds emphasis and takes advantage of experiential learning processes that are just as relevant at the end of therapy as they were in earlier sessions. I also think it's important to be perennially wary of our reliance on language and the very real potential for using words to stay off of emotions, even if it makes us only a smidgeon more comfortable. I believe that as ACT therapists it is important to remind ourselves that while useful, words aren't the only game in town. Finally, a well-executed experiential exercise brings in that clinical oomph we've talked about, and does justice to the remarkable, life-changing journey you and your client have made together.

Hallmarks of a Good Wrap-Up Session

Just as there's no one way to conduct ACT, there is certainly no "right way" to finish. That said, I personally really like to see the therapy end in such a way that it does justice to the work—to the client, to the therapist, to this life-changing form of therapy. I have also found, in the course of exploring final sessions with therapists after the fact, that experiential avoidance sometimes shows up in these sessions in sneaky ways. For example, it is not that unusual to discover that the therapist stayed away from fully contacting the emotion that was in the room without even realizing it. Being thoughtful about the final session can help therapists remain aware of their own experience and take full advantage of the clinical opportunities that arise. The following list contains the central elements that can be incorporated to create a powerful final session:

1. Acknowledgment of the therapeutic relationship

2. Review of the journey (key concepts, clinical progressions, and turning points)

3. Next steps

4. Experiential finish

ACKNOWLEDGMENT OF THE THERAPEUTIC RELATIONSHIP

I once worked with a consultee who had struggled quite a bit with stepping out of the therapist role while doing ACT with her clients. Her training had emphasized the importance of "maintaining appropriate boundaries"—which meant, among other things, keeping personal information out of the session. As our work together progressed, it became clear that there was a larger struggle going on for this therapist, for despite having strong clinical skills and a solid understanding of ACT and why a more horizontal therapist/client relationship made theoretical sense, she continued to operate firmly from the therapist chair during her ACT sessions. During our consultation she confessed that the idea of sharing herself in session felt vulnerable and unsafe, particularly with certain clients. Nonetheless, she was willing, and toward the end of conducting her first course of ACT therapy she was starting to make small steps in that direction. Her small steps did not prepare me, however, for the bold move she made in her final session with one of her clients, a young woman who had entered therapy with an extremely painful history and had made huge changes in her life over the course of the therapy.

The session began with a short greeting as both women settled themselves and prepared to do a mindfulness exercise per the usual procedure:

Therapist: "So let's get settled and in a comfortable yet upright position—" (*Cuts herself off suddenly, hesitates, then:*) "Before we begin, though, I'd like to say how nice it is for me to be here with you today. To see your smile and the brightness on your face."

Client (*surprised and greatly pleased*): "Thanks! I feel good to be here, too!"

Therapist: "I just want you to know what a pleasure this has been. I've had thoughts come up repeatedly as we've worked together about what a remarkable person you are. You really are. It is wonderful to see you out there living the life that you deserve. And I'm so grateful to you for your perseverance and your patience as I've been learning this new therapy. I really appreciate it."

Client (*a little choked up*): "I am grateful to *you* for being there for me! Seriously, I…I don't know what I would have done; you've really been there for me." (*Pauses, then confesses:*) The next step for me was suicide."

Therapist: "Well, you're welcome." (Smiles and just holds the moment for a bit). "And of course I can't let that one slide by, right?"

Client: "What?"

Therapist: "How might you rephrase that, that the next step for you was suicide?"

Client (*thinks*): "Um…My *mind* was telling me that was the next step."

Therapist: "Excellent! Nice work! Yeah, painful stuff. I'm so glad you and I have had this chance to see that type of thought for what it is."

Client: "Me too!"

While this example demonstrates taking every last opportunity to further ACT principles, not letting even a simple comment about past suicidal ideation slide, the larger point was to illustrate the depth that comes with authentic self-disclosure. I doubt the printed page can do it justice, but as soon as the therapist abruptly shifted and authentically connected with the client in the present moment, the session became riveting. It became something to be remembered.

REVIEW OF THE JOURNEY

I like to use time in the final session to revisit the core content areas of ACT as they have pertained to the particular client. Even though these ideas will have been well covered, the final session presents an opportunity to highlight those areas that seem most central to the client, to underscore ongoing areas of concern, and to inoculate against further difficulties. For example, if the client had been particularly fused with the idea that the problem was that he "lacked motivation," you could remind him of this idea and how he had learned that making a value-driven choice is not dependent on the feeling of motivation. I would also use this opportunity to undermine the "I'm fixed" idea by making the point that the experience of not being motivated will continue to show up. In this sense you are very clearly connecting the dots for this client in terms of how ACT pertains to him in particular, and how it will continue to apply to his life going forward. I also make a point to remind myself that the ideas promoted in ACT are a far cry from the messages encountered in our culture. Once my clients leave the room they will essentially be paddling a little ACT boat upstream, so I am hoping to leave them with some good oars and an idea of where the strongest currents will be.

NEXT STEPS

The sort of review just described paves the way nicely to a discussion about the client's next steps. This is a good opportunity for the client to articulate the "larger pattern of committed action" we look for as the therapy comes to an end, and also provides the therapist an opportunity to check for any remaining sticking points.

Client: "So now that I'm reconnected with my son, I'm going to just keep strengthening my relationship with him. I want to get to know him again, to be a true granddad to his boys. Just be there for him, you know?"

Therapist: "Well, I know how huge it was for you to make that step, and how important it is to you to be the sort of dad and granddad you want to be."

Client: "Yeah. I just want him to know that he can trust me. That he doesn't have to worry about me disappearing again."

Therapist:	"I hear that. In fact, I'm remembering that being trustworthy was one of the very first values you mentioned."
Client:	"Yeah. I want to be trustworthy, not just to my son but in my life."
Therapist:	"We talked quite a bit about what that meant to you, *being* trustworthy. Like what sorts of things would you be *doing* if you were being trustworthy? Just now, when you said you want to 'be there' for your son and grandkids—what sorts of actions can you take that together represent 'being there' for them?"
Client:	"Remembering birthdays, reaching out, offering to help with stuff, going to the boys' games, things like that."
Therapist:	"Exactly. And something really important to see here is that what we're really talking about isn't how your son is feeling. You said you want him to trust you, as though you want him to have the feeling of trust. And you also said you didn't want him to have worries about you disappearing...."
Client	*(laughs):* "Oh, so that's me trying to control him."
Therapist:	"Not just that, but that even your son, try as he might, can't *make* himself have the feeling of trust. He may have it, he may not; it may come and go like crazy for a while. He also can't make himself not have worries about you."
Client:	"That's right."
Therapist:	"But what we've learned here is that you don't need him to be feeling a certain way to honor your values around this. In each moment, regardless of what either of you is thinking or feeling, you will have the opportunity to make a choice that will take you further from, or closer to, your values around *being* trustworthy."
Client:	"Got it."

EXPERIENTIAL FINISH

Ending the work with an experiential exercise is a powerful move. When Robyn Walser and I were cofacilitating ACT groups, we almost always ended on an experiential exercise such as Stand and Commit (in which therapist and client physically stand and verbally state "what [they] stand for") or the Child Exercise (in which clients are guided via imagery to contact a compassionate self). We made it a point to not process too much, if at all. Stand and Commit, in particular, seems to benefit from letting the exercise speak for itself. When the therapist refrains from filling space afterward with talking, the importance of present-moment experience over the incessant chatter of the mind gets one last exclamation point. Be sure, though, to rest fully in the moment. That is, when the exercise is done, allow yourself to be fully engaged with the client, fully in contact with what has just been experienced and the emotions that have been evoked. It is important to focus in, rather than move quickly ahead to whatever's next. Take this moment to truly honor yourself and your client for being willing to have the scary, exciting, painful, and powerful intimate experience we call therapy.

SUMMARY

My intention with this chapter is to point to some things to consider when determining the overall strategy you are going to use to conduct ACT. Many of those with whom I have worked have struggled with the idea that there is so much clinical flexibility in ACT, even as that is one of the therapy's greatest strengths. I have attempted to shed some light on one of the areas of confusion regarding two main approaches to ACT: sequentially moving through content areas and targeting processes more fluidly. I have discussed some of the perceived and actual differences, their respective advantages and disadvantages, and how to avoid some of the more common pitfalls. I concluded with a section on how to optimize a final session, as this important piece of the therapy is often not maximized. My central goal is to encourage therapists to be thoughtful about the approach they are using all the way to the end of therapy, so that the full power of ACT can be harnessed regardless of overall approach.

PART 2

Tricky Little Pieces and Common Missteps

CHAPTER 6

That Little Problem Called Language

L anguage plays a starring role in ACT. In fact, much of the therapy is about unveiling language. We help clients see language for what it is and isn't. We work to lessen the influence of certain forms of language processes (such as fusion with unworkable rules and rigid self-concepts) while increasing the influence of language processes in other areas (such as making value-driven choices). In short, the way words are used is important in ACT. Every verbal exchange has the potential to either further or work against the therapy.

It might be fruitful to focus on two main ways in which therapists miss the mark with the words they use in session. One is by using language that works against the principles in ACT; the other is more about missed opportunities. Starting with the first, missing the mark might include making statements that directly oppose the model, such as suggesting to a client that acceptance will decrease discomfort, or that the point of defusing from thoughts is to make those thoughts less painful. It also could include less obvious examples that nonetheless contradict the therapy. For example, I have often advised consultees to stay away from using the term "depression" with their clients, because they tend to use that term in the same way as their clients do (for example, "How long have you been struggling with your depression?" or "What happens on the days when you're depressed?"). This word usage runs the risk of supporting the idea that depression is a thing that is in the client, or that something called depression somehow lands at certain times and as such has a lot of power. Even if this choice of words occurs as part of an explicit conversation about self-as-context, the therapist could potentially reinforce cognitive fusion and a conceptualized self by making such statements. Similarly, something as simple as reflecting back a client's statement that she was "overwhelmed" by something (as in "So you were overwhelmed;

what else was going on?") can support the notion that such a thing is possible. There are many, many such examples that I hear as therapists conduct the therapy.

Such statements not only can work against the model but are missed opportunities to actually move things forward. Even if you are just beginning with a client, with thoughtful wording you can begin to undermine cognitive fusion and develop an awareness of self-as-context. For example, you can rephrase these sorts of statements to reflect that the client is the Experiencer who *had*, or *is having*, an experience. If the client tells you that depression has been the main problem for him, you might respond with "Tell me what you mean by the *experience of* depression. What happens for you when you *are having that experience*, those thoughts and feelings about being depressed?" or "So it was one of those times when you were *feeling* down, *having* painful thoughts...." Reframing in this way also helps the client begin to see that, rather than some concrete thing, depression (or overwhelm, or whatnot) is a series of thoughts, feelings, and sensations that are actually fluid and ever-changing. If you can continually turn toward the idea that you and your clients are Experiencers who are constantly experiencing the internal phenomena of the moment, you will be guided to choose words that are more consistent with where you are headed with the therapy.

An oft-mentioned example of the importance of words in ACT is the distinction between "but" and "and." Using the word "but" supports the verbal rule of the moment (as in "I wanted to ask her out *but* I was too nervous"), whereas "and" (as in "I wanted to ask her out *and* I was nervous") helps clients get more in touch with their actual experience. When therapists are careful about the use of such words, clients can better see that they can make such choices regardless of what their minds are telling them. I include this particular distinction as an example of how even seemingly insignificant words have important clinical implications when it comes to ACT.

Another potential mistake, and one I'm certainly guilty of, is saying "right" at the end of a statement—such as "We've already talked about how thoughts and feelings aren't in control, right?" If you are listening for this one, you may be amazed by how often it shows up in your sessions. The problem is that it can function as persuasion. It could pull clients toward therapist pleasing that may not be in their best interests.

Here's another example of a tricky word choice I've heard more than once. Pointing it out may seem to be splitting hairs, but actually the choice can involve important clinical considerations: this is telling a client that a particular thought, or self-concept, is "only one *part* of him," rather than pointing to such experiences as *distinct* from the self that is experiencing them. It's not about one part more than another, or even about balance among the parts. It's about contacting what's *beyond* the parts. We will take a closer look at this idea in chapter 9.

It can seem like a lot, though, can't it? Not only are you trying to coherently introduce particular topics, relate metaphors, and conduct strange experiential exercises in the service of furthering core ACT processes, you are prioritizing being present and adding your reactions to the mix as well. And now you must also think about the particular words you are using? Yup. Here's some really good news: doing this perfectly is not remotely necessary. Doing it smoothly is not necessary. We really, truly, don't have to do this all just right. In fact, it is a red flag for me when I am listening to a session that is very smooth, when there's a slick exchange going on, when the session seems very intellectual and "heady." At such times I picture two brains at a party, kicking back with a cocktail or two and holding forth. The important thing here is to be alert to the role of language and to how it is functioning in the room, so that we can point to it in a way that is useful. As ACT therapists we get to say things like "Did you hear that? I just suggested you should have different thoughts! I can thank my mind for that one!" or "I just realized I was trying to control how you were reacting to all this so that I would feel less anxious. I'm going to just hold my anxieties gently here." One of my consultees was so prone to say "…Right?" after everything she said that she asked her client to join her in catching it during their sessions together. You can see how clinically effective such modeling can be—far more so than doing or saying things perfectly.

Lately I have been likening language to a carving knife. While we use a carving knife because of its utility, we don't forget its edge. We use such tools with intention and care. Handling language in this way can help us maximize its utility while remembering its edge. Here is a short list of things to think about when using this particular implement:

1. Be aware of the words you and your client are using. To repeat, every exchange is an opportunity to further the therapy. Every exchange can also work against psychological flexibility.

2. Be thoughtful as to how words are functioning in the moment. What purpose is being served or intended here? How is this conversation functioning in the session?

3. When given the opportunity to create space between the Thinker and the thought, or the Feeler and the feeling, take it. Even slight changes, such as "You are having the thought about being depressed" can alter how that experience functions for the client.

4. SLOW DOWN. Take time to think things through, even if it means there's a long pause (in which case you can say, "I'm pausing for a moment because I want to make sure I say this in the way I mean….") or you need to take another run at something altogether ("Wait, that didn't come out the way I wanted; let me try that again."). Defuse from what your mind is telling you about needing to have an immediate, perfect response.

LETTING LANGUAGE OFF THE HOOK

Over the course of my supervision and consultation work I noticed a trend that was apparent only after having observed many full courses of ACT. At some point I realized that many therapists had stayed entirely away from working explicitly with the language piece. That is not to say, of course, that this component was absent from the therapy altogether. As discussed throughout this book, the words we use in ACT, the ways things are said (and not said), and the use of metaphors and experiential exercises are very deliberate attempts to move clients toward psychological flexibility. This objective arises from what we have come to understand about the fundamental role of language in psychopathology, which in turn arose from the study of human cognition and language acquisition. Given the importance of language in ACT, it has been surprising to me that the actual topic of language is often not directly explored with clients.

Two questions come to mind: (1) why is this occurring, and (2) so what? For me, the answer to question 2 rests in part upon the answer to question 1. That is, it is significant whether the decision to stay away from an explicit discussion about language is clinically based or due to something else. It could well be the case that the therapist has determined that for a particular client, explicitly discussing the stickiness of language would not be as effective as experientially demonstrating it in other ways. For example, clients who are very concrete thinkers or clients who tend to overintellectualize might become more entangled with language in the course of such a discussion, not less, at least early on. What I find concerning is how often I have been told, after inquiring, that the reason language (or "languaging," to refer to the behavior of acquiring and using language) is not being explicitly explored with clients is because of discomfort with the topic. Many therapists have told me that they only "sort of get" how languaging is viewed within the ACT model, that their comprehension of this subject "glimmers in and out," and so on, and that they don't feel confident they can talk about it with clients in a way that makes sense. I can certainly understand, as these comments reflect my own experience with the language piece of ACT early on. To go beyond the idea that language is problematic to understanding *why* this is so requires understanding of how language develops in the first place and then subsequently functions for us humans—how it is that our relationship with language can become so problematic.

WHY GO THERE?

A question all this raises is: do clients need to understand how language functions in order to fully benefit from ACT? If these processes are not explicitly explained, is the client shorted in some way? While this is an empirical question, I'll not let myself off the hook by simply deferring to researchers. If we remember that there is no one way to do ACT, if we remember that the point of the therapy is to help clients get unstuck (in other words, to have psychological flexibility), then it follows that a client who learns she can make value-based behavioral choices despite the presence or potential appearance of aversive private events—who, in short, can choose to live life in the way she wants to be living—has received what ACT has to offer. Such a person may not fully grasp *why* she is not her thoughts so much as that her thoughts (and feelings and bodily sensations) are not in charge. She may have come to learn that she can hold uncomfortable thoughts, feelings, and bodily sensations without needing to avoid or control them. These discoveries in turn free her up to make choices based on something besides the thoughts or feelings of the moment (or the past or perceived future). All good.

That said, I personally believe that helping clients really understand how language functions, its trickiness and *why* it is tricky, serves to increase psychological flexibility. It seems logical to me that understanding that a thought is a process—a product, if you will—rather than "Truth" would facilitate cognitive defusion, especially from those thoughts that are particularly sticky. So one reason to spend time in therapy helping clients understand how language functions is to help them see language for what it is and for what it isn't—to put language, and hence thoughts, in their proper place. So it's not just that we don't have to be run by our thoughts, but also that thinking is a language-based, learned behavior, and that our tendency to reify our thoughts is not only flawed but can be quite costly. Contained in this message is the recognition that even our most painful thoughts about ourselves are examples of this learned behavior, rather than being literally true. This recognition is a big deal if you've spent much of your life thinking you were fundamentally not okay.

To summarize a bit, here are some key points that working with language explicitly brings to the table:

✓ Thinking is a learned behavior, as opposed to a representation of truth in a literal sense; the content and meaning of thoughts are derived through language.

✓ The nature of language is such that a virtual world is manufactured and then dwelt in, at the cost of living in the present moment.

✓ Certain aspects of language, such as evaluating and reason-giving are not only particularly compelling but also suspect.

Helping clients to understand the role of language and how we come to literalize our thoughts leads to the realization that we don't need to continue to do so—which in turn furthers two of what I think are the most powerful ideas in ACT: (1) that we are behaviorally free from the content of our thoughts, and (2) that we are fundamentally whole and acceptable despite thoughts to the contrary.

Not only are there real benefits to working explicitly with clients on the role of language, but leaving out this piece can undermine the very ideas you are hoping to further in ACT. For example, a very common misstep is when the therapist targets cognitive fusion by informing the client, "You are not your thoughts," without providing any sort of rationale as to why this is so. I have often heard this sort of exchange during a conversation in which the client is sharing "negative" (as perceived by the client) thoughts and self-conceptualizations. The therapist responds with a statement of this sort without having laid the groundwork that makes such comments meaningful. According to the ACT model, the point of making such statements about thoughts is to alter the function of those thoughts. Without having created the proper context these sorts of remarks tend to instead become a "believe this because I say so" instruction, and an example of the unworkable rule following we are hoping to undermine in ACT. In talking with therapists who have made this move, I've discovered that most often, the reason is a lack of clarity about the role of language in the ACT model. It should be mentioned that the therapist's own control agenda can be tucked in there as well. That is, it is not uncommon for a therapist to come in with "you are not your thoughts" as an attempt to ameliorate the client's pain (and hence the therapist's own discomfort). Here's an example:

Client:	"I don't like to go out because I always feel self-conscious."
Therapist:	"What do you mean? What is going on for you when you feel self-conscious?"
Client:	"I always feel like people are looking at me, thinking about how ugly I am."
Therapist:	"You have the thought that people think you're ugly?"
Client:	"Yeah. *I* think I'm ugly. Even after I've done all this stuff I still know I'm ugly."
Therapist:	"Stuff?"
Client:	"I had a nose job a while back. But I still am really self-conscious, especially if I go out to some club or something where there are beautiful people everywhere."
Therapist:	"That sounds really painful! So 'I'm ugly,' or 'They think I'm ugly,' is a thought that shows up a lot for you."
Client:	"All the time, all the time."
Therapist:	"The thing is, even though it's certainly painful, that's just a thought. 'I'm ugly' is just a thought. You are not your thoughts."
Client	*(even more earnestly):* "It is so painful! I'm miserable! I don't even want to go anywhere or see anyone a lot of the time."
Therapist:	"Right, but these thoughts aren't you. You are not your thoughts."
Client	*(unconvinced):* "Yeah…but I *am* ugly.…I'm just so sick of feeling this way."

If the context for these sorts of statements (how language functions, how "I'm ugly" is a subjective evaluation and not *in* a person, and so on) has been previously laid, this exchange might serve as a reminder and segue to a useful discussion around defusing from such thoughts. However, I have heard and observed this sort of dialogue many times when no such framework has been established. The statement then becomes the directive: "You are not your thoughts because I say so," rather than "Ugly is not in you because we have established that such thoughts are a by-product of language and that there's a you that is distinct from such thoughts." Not only is the client understandably unconvinced; she might also hear such comments as an invalidation of her experience—in other words, "It's *just* a thought (and therefore not real and therefore you should get over it)." In fact, the client in the above dialogue seems to have this sort of perception. When the therapist remarks, "It's just a thought," the client stresses even more strongly the degree of her pain. There is an important distinction to make between implying that thoughts themselves (and attendant feelings) aren't real, and getting at the idea that thoughts don't represent reality in a literal sense.

WHAT IS NEEDED?

So what elements are needed to begin to work with clients so that they have a more useful relationship with language? The following concepts are interrelated but have slightly different emphases. All of them provide a useful context for explicit work on language, just as directly working on language serves to extend each of these ideas:

- ✓ The idea that thinking is a process

- ✓ The difference between looking from within our thoughts and looking at our thoughts

- ✓ The distinction between Thinker and thought

These points are contained within cognitive defusion and self-as-context (which also require contacting the present), which is why I tend to wait to tackle language explicitly until after I have introduced and done some work with the client on these processes. A difficulty I have observed is when therapists try to tackle the topic of language too early in the therapy. This tendency has often gone hand in hand with a misstep mentioned in chapter 3—when therapists attempt to "tell" the client the entire therapy in the first session or so. I have seen many examples of this difficulty concerning the topic of language, although I find them hard to convey here, so out of context (as context determines how such exchanges actually function). Following are a few examples of the sorts of statements I'm referring to—the important point being that they are occurring at the outset of therapy, before the laying of the groundwork that would make them more meaningful to the client.

Example scenario: A first session with a young man who has come to treatment for depression.

Client:	"…and I have days where I just don't get out of bed—where I keep telling myself I should do something but I just don't have the energy. And then I beat myself up for it. I feel like such a loser: It seems like I've been dealing with depression my whole life…."
Therapist:	"You called yourself a loser…"
Client:	"I definitely feel like a loser."
Therapist:	"Wow, loser is a powerful word. That's what language does; it can be really sticky."
or	"Because of language we learn to buy thoughts like that. But we're not really our stories."
or	"Loser is an evaluation. That's what happens when we acquire language; we learn to evaluate."
or	"When we learn to have language we learn to give reasons, like why we do or don't do things. But reasons are not causes."

I suppose it could be argued that even if such comments are made early on and essentially in a vacuum, they could still move clients forward in some way. How can we know what actually lands and takes root? However, my sense is that at this stage it is going to be more effective to undermine the literalization of language in other ways, such as with the words you use to reflect the client's experience ("You have the thought that you are a loser") or by altering its function using an experiential exercise (such as having the client sing "I'm a loser," or physicalizing the experience of "loser"), rather than introducing a concept as abstract and complex as the role of language so soon in the therapy.

DESCRIPTION VS. EVALUATION

One of the ways therapists often inadvertently work against the principles we are hoping to further in ACT occurs when discussing the mind's tendency to engage in evaluations. I have observed that many therapists draw a distinction between describing and evaluating, but then neglect to bring home the point of this distinction. That is, they educate the client on how an evaluation differs from a physical description, but leave out how we humans tend to literalize evaluations, how we relate to evaluations as though they are descriptions. When these important pieces are left out, the client is left with a sort of "so what?" experience, or is apt to conclude that evaluating is wrong. I have also observed that many therapists readily go with the idea that evaluation is problematic but then proceed to work with this idea in a fashion that is more reminiscent of traditional CBT than it is ACT-consistent. In other words, rather than help shift the function of evaluative thoughts, they work with them in such a way that the main message to the client is that he needs to stop incorrectly evaluating. For example:

Therapist	*(conducting an individual ACT session with a male Vietnam veteran who is also a participant in a weekly support group run by the therapist):* "I noticed you were pretty quiet in group this week."
Client:	"Yeah, didn't feel like talking."
Therapist:	"Was that a feeling you were having then? Not wanting to talk? Or were there thoughts going on as well?"
Client:	"There's always thoughts going on."
Therapist:	"Yeah, right. I ask because you told me before that you often have thoughts about not having anything useful to say, like you don't have anything to contribute."
Client:	"Yeah, there was some of that."
Therapist:	"Can you tell me more about that? It would help me understand what you experience in those situations. So you have the thought 'I don't have anything to say....'"
Client:	"Yeah, like 'Why say anything if it's just gonna bring everybody down? If I don't have anything good to say, why say it?'"
Therapist:	"Oh, so your mind told you that you would bring people down."
Client:	"I do! That's why it's better to just keep to myself. Why ruin things for everybody else? I'll just be a downer."
Therapist:	"It's like what you were saying last week about being toxic."
Client:	"That's right! Toxic. Better to just keep to myself."
Therapist:	"And yet, you told me last week that your grandson told you he loved you. And your wife seems to want you around more, not less."
Client:	"Hmm. They don't know what's really inside me."
Therapist:	"So even though some people do like to be around you, you still have the thought, the evaluation, that you are toxic, a downer— that if others knew what was inside they would not want to be around you. Like that?"
Client:	"And that they would never think of me the same. If they knew what I really am, how I really feel...some of the things I've seen... they wouldn't want to know, believe me!"

Therapist:	"So because of all the stuff you've just mentioned—the experiences you've had, things you've seen and done, thoughts you have—you have the thought, the evaluation, that you're toxic."
Client:	"That's right."
Therapist:	"And when you have that evaluation, what happens next?"
Client:	"I just keep to myself. That way I won't bother anybody."
Therapist:	"And how does that make you feel?"
Client:	"Lonely. Depressed."
Therapist:	"Hmmm. So evaluating isn't working. You just end up feeling worse. But if you were to check your actual experience, you might see that your grandson, for example, doesn't experience you as being toxic."
Client:	"He doesn't know what's really going on with me, though."

This exchange is actually a pretty typical example of the potential (depending on how it actually functions) misstep I've just described. Taking a closer look at this exchange, we can see that the therapist may have stepped off course a bit at the point he first responds to the veteran's evaluation about being toxic:

Client:	"That's right! Toxic. Better to just keep to myself."
Therapist:	"And yet, you told me last week that your grandson told you he loved you. And your wife seems to want you around more, not less." (*The potential risk here is that the client may interpret this to mean that he needs to have different thoughts. While we might want to bring the client's attention to aspects of his experience, it is important not to convey the message that he should not be having evaluative thoughts. We hope to alter the function of such thoughts by helping the client recognize the distinction between what his mind tells him and his actual experience. One way to approach this would be to help the client track his own experience, observing not only his thoughts around this but also what happens in his interactions with others.*)
Client:	"Hmm. They don't really know what's inside me."
Therapist:	"So you have the thought, the evaluation, that you are toxic, a downer—that if others knew what was inside they would not want to be around you?"

Client:	"And that they would never think of me the same. If they knew what I really am, how I really feel…some the things I've seen…. they would not want to know, believe me."
Therapist:	"So because of all the stuff you've just mentioned—the experiences you've had, things you've seen and done, thoughts you have—you have the evaluation that you're toxic."
Client:	"That's right."
Therapist:	"And when you have that evaluation, what happens next?"
Client:	"I just keep to myself. That way I won't bother anybody."
Therapist:	"And how does that make you feel?" (*I prefer to say something along the lines of "And what sorts of feelings show up at times like this?" to better work against the idea that feelings—having pleasant ones and getting rid of uncomfortable ones—are the objective.*)
Client:	"Lonely. Depressed."
Therapist:	"Hmm. So evaluating isn't working." (*This may be true in this case, but knowing it doesn't stop the mind from evaluating. Rather than the mind doing something wrong, it is doing what it is geared to do.*) "You just end up feeling worse." (*This statement supports the problematic idea that avoiding feeling bad is the goal, and that if we are feeling bad it's because we are having the wrong sorts of thoughts, or evaluations. This idea is what gets clients—and us—stuck in the first place.*) "If you check your actual experience, for example, you might see that your grandson doesn't experience you as being toxic." (*There is a fine line between pointing out that our evaluations might not necessarily be true and implying that evaluation itself is bad. That is the overarching message implied in this exchange—that evaluation is bad, and therefore the client needs to stop it.*)
Client:	"He doesn't know what's really going on with me, though."

As I mentioned earlier, there are many rich metaphors and powerful exercises that help therapists work with language in a way that clients can understand. Here is an example applied to the scenario described above:

Client:	"That's right! Toxic. Better to just keep to myself."
Therapist:	"So one of the thoughts your mind hands you is that you better stay away from people, keep to yourself."
Client:	"Yeah."

Therapist:	"What else is there? What I mean is, what else does your mind hand you around the notion of being toxic in situations like this?" (*Here the therapist is working on cognitive defusion via word usage—"what does your mind hand you"—and building self-as-process by helping the client observe the flow of his thoughts. He is also flushing out at least part of the relational network the client has developed around the word "toxic," and showing that there is a collection of thoughts that tend to show up when the client has this particular experience.*)
Client:	"I don't know what you mean."
Therapist:	"It sounds like there's a problem with being toxic. You need to keep to yourself and hide that you're toxic because…"
Client:	"…because other people will be brought down."
Therapist:	"And that's bad because…" (*The therapist continues to point to the flow of thoughts around the relational network associated with being toxic and is attempting to unearth the experiential avoidance at the heart of the issue—in other words, that the client doesn't want to feel the way he feels when he perceives others to be evaluating him as a downer.*)
Client	(*after pausing to think*): "…they wouldn't want to be around me anymore."
Therapist:	"And that would…"
Client:	"That would really…that would make me feel even worse about myself."
Therapist:	"Huh, that's really tricky, isn't it? Your mind tells you that you need to not be around people so that they won't want to not be around you…." (*The therapist continues to chip away at cognitive defusion, getting at the idea that some of what the client's mind is handing him is suspect. This change may seem slight, but it's quite a difference from how the client has been holding his thoughts. Notice, though, that the point is more that the mind needs to be taken with a grain of salt than that something wrong is happening here—that something is wrong with the client because he is evaluating.*)
Client:	(*laughs ruefully*): "Yeah, that doesn't make any sense."
Therapist:	"It sure puts you in a bind—especially since this is what minds do. Our minds' job is to assess, problem-solve, evaluate…and

it gets really tricky because the way we relate to our minds, to our thoughts and evaluations, can really get us stuck. That is, once language comes along and we learn to label things and start attaching meanings to things, it can get really sticky." (*The therapist makes a point of normalizing what the client's mind is doing and introduces the topic of language itself.*)

Client: (*Listening.*)

Therapist: "Language is useful, obviously, but it also does a number on us in a way, particularly when it comes to evaluations." (*The therapist rises and moves an empty office chair closer to where they are sitting.*) "Take this chair, for example. We English-speaking people have agreed to call this object a chair. In France it would be 'chaise.' We could just as easily agree to call it a 'barg.' In fact, if I said, 'Can you please move that barg?' you would know what I mean, right?"

Client: (*Laughs, nods.*)

Therapist: "And we've also agreed to call this 'metal' (*touching the legs*), and this particular material 'plastic' (*touching the seat back*), and this part the 'seat,' and this (*touching the fabric seat*) 'fabric.' We could just as easily have named them something else, but the point is that we've assigned words to refer to these physical properties of the chair."

Client: "Okay…"

Therapist: "Now, if I were to say, 'That chair is the *best* chair,' or 'That is a *snazzy* chair,' that's a bit different. When we talk about the metal legs, or the cloth seat, we are describing the various physical aspects of this object we are calling a chair. But we aren't going to find 'best' in this chair, like we can find metal or plastic. We're not going to actually find 'snazzy' in there, either."

Client: "Okay, I see that."

Therapist: "'Best' and 'snazzy' aren't in the chair—they are evaluations. Evaluations require an Evaluator. That is, 'best' and 'snazzy' are created by the interaction between the observer and the chair, rather than being a property of the chair itself. Is that making sense?"

Client   (*thoughtfully*): "Yeah, okay."

Therapist:	"What gets so tricky about that is that we tend to relate to our evaluations of things as though they are literally true, as though we could take the chair apart and find snazzy in there. For example, you have the evaluation of being toxic, and you relate to that as though we could open you up and actually find toxic inside of you somewhere."
Client:	"I think I see what you're getting at...."
Therapist:	"And can you see that part of the trickiness here is that knowing this doesn't make it go away? Knowing that our evaluations are subjective doesn't mean we stop evaluating. But we can recognize what our mind is handing us, and that even though the thought 'I'm toxic' is sure to show up here and there, that doesn't represent literal truth. You *are having the thought that* you are toxic, rather than you *are toxic*."

The use of a physical object such as a chair or cup to illustrate how descriptive and evaluative processes function for humans was introduced in the first ACT book (Hayes et al., 1999). I have seen it done effectively with any manner of objects as a useful way to help clients understand the distinction between describing and evaluating and how fusion with evaluations can result in being stuck.

Evaluation: Not "Bad," Just Costly

Though evaluation itself is not inherently problematic, there is no doubt that evaluations can create great difficulty, particularly when we apply them to ourselves and take them literally. I like to use the following short but sweet example to highlight the life-altering difference between buying our evaluations and recognizing them for what they are. Again, using third-person examples can be quite effective, especially for individuals who are more concrete thinkers, or highly fused with their thoughts.

Therapist:	"Let's say that we know of two fathers. Let's say one is a really bad dad. He's just never been there in any way for his kids, okay? And let's say the other is an awesome dad. Just fantastic. Got it?"
Client:	"Okay, got it."
Therapist:	"So we've got these two dads, good and bad. Which one has the greatest opportunity to be a good dad in the future?"
Client:	"The good dad!"
Therapist:	"Actually, I would say both. Both have an equal opportunity, because 'good dad' or 'bad dad' isn't actually in either of them.

Those are evaluations based on past behaviors. Both can do something that we would evaluate as a 'good dad' behavior in the next moment."

Client: "Okay, I see that. Huh."

Therapist: "I used that example to point out how powerful language is, to show how we tend to relate to evaluations as though they are literally real, and the impact that can have. For instance, if the one dad really bought the idea that he was "Bad Dad," that would likely affect not only how he views himself but his behavior as well. It's like how buying the evaluation that you are toxic has influenced your behavior." (*When using a third-person example it's important to bring it back to how it specifically relates to the client.*)

Client: "Yep. That makes sense. I can see that."

A good move at this point in therapy would be to do an experiential defusion exercise such as "lemon, lemon." To review, in this exercise the client is instructed to imagine a lemon. He is then guided to contact the various stimulus functions that have been relationally framed with the word "lemon," such as envisioning its bumpy peel, imagining bringing it to his nose and taking a deep whiff, imagining taking a bite, and so on. The therapist points out that the client is reacting as though "lemon" is actually in the room. Next, the client and therapist repeat the word "lemon" over and over again until it loses its meaning. That is, they eventually experience themselves as making strange bleating noises rather than referencing the object, "lemon." Exercises such as these highlight both the power of language and its arbitrary potential. That is, we can call the lemon anything, the peel anything, and the smell anything but due to relational framing, the words can still make us pucker.

As a general strategy, it is helpful to relate these sorts of exercises directly to the client either before or after the exercise. For example:

Therapist   (*concluding the "lemon, lemon" exercise*): "So we can see that language is pretty darn powerful. Just by using words, it took less than a minute to get lemon in the room to the point where both our mouths were watering! Not only were we able to bring in the object we've all agreed to call 'lemon,' but we also brought in many of the qualities we've learned to associate with that object, like its yellow bumpy peel, or what it's like to bite into something really sour. By using words that have been assigned to the object and to those other qualities, we generated a virtual experience when there wasn't even a lemon in the room! That's pretty amazing, isn't it? But as we've been exploring, there's a dark side to this. Listen to the words (*heavily emphasizing*) 'I'm toxic.' Rather than realizing that you've learned to produce and assign meaning to those words, you relate to them as though they are literally in you, as though we could open you up and find 'toxic' in there. You have your own virtual experience with the words 'I'm toxic' going on."

If the therapist wished, he could then repeat the exercise, replacing "lemon" with "toxic." Hopefully it is not hard to see how these sorts of exercises can effectively alter how language functions for our clients. Even if "I'm toxic" continues to show up for this client (and it will) we can imagine that this exercise will show up as well. It is now a part of the relational network this client has around his "toxic" self-concept. The simple recognition that he is having that thought again about being toxic represents a different way to hold that experience.

THE MIND IS NOT ALL THAT

Some clients are reluctant to defuse from their thoughts because their self-concept is about their thinking (for example, "I am very intelligent"). They can be so wedded with their thoughts that they simply can't or won't conceive of a distinction between themselves and their thoughts. One way to approach it is to ask clients to consider what life was like before they developed language. The idea that there is more going on with them than the language-based ticker tape of cognitions running constantly in their heads can be a really foreign idea and can pave the way for cognitive defusion. Again, I've found that using a third-person example can help these clients see what is hard to see when they are fused with their own thought processes.

Me   (*continuing a discussion about the role of language*): "I remember having mixed feelings about my daughter, Chloe, learning language. I mean, obviously I wanted her to learn to communicate, but because of this work I've become very aware of what gets lost as well. For example, I remember holding her up before a mirror when she was, oh, six months old or so, and she would gaze at herself with pure delight. She was simply fascinated by what she was seeing. She wasn't looking at herself and thinking, 'Geez, shouldn't I have more hair by now?' She had no word for 'hair'—for 'I,' even. She certainly hadn't learned what 'should' or 'shouldn't' meant, what 'more' or 'less' meant. She had no concept of 'not as much as' or 'not enough,' or 'something's wrong with my head.' And yet she existed. She was living, breathing, experiencing, observing. Just as there was an activity of observing going on before the cognition ticker tape in your head got going with all its language-given thoughts. In this moment you are living, breathing, experiencing right along with all those thoughts going on. In fact, we can't begin to capture all the various processes going on with you right now. Your brain is picking up and sending out signals right and left, your heart is pumping, hormones are being released, blood and oxygen cells are running around, the hair follicles in your ear are waving around picking up sound waves…but it's the thought process that has your attention. The thoughts on that ticker tape are so compelling, so seductive, it's as though we fall into them. We don't see that we both produce and experience that ticker tape; we think we *are* that ticker tape."

In this example, the role of language development in our experience and concept of ourselves is highlighted. An exercise such as the Continuous You exercise would be a nice way to extend self-as-context at this point.

Given that we must use language to tackle language processes, it can be particularly useful to draw upon experiential exercises. Note, though, that the "experiential exercises" used in ACT are not purely experiential. That is, we must use language as a means to change the client's awareness. We use language as a tool for the experiential work. I also like the "tell me how to walk" exercise, as it not only demonstrates the limitations of language but does so in an experiential fashion. That is, using verbal instruction alone, the client is asked to tell the therapist how to walk, as though the therapist has never done so. The client is quickly confronted by the limitations of his mind as this task is shown to be fundamentally impossible (as we didn't learn how to send a signal to our leg to move forward because someone told us how), and this realization pokes a hole in the idea that languaging is the only game in town. A common example that is also used to make this point is that of driving: When we are driving a car we are managing to do so without ongoing input from the cognitive mind. We are not giving ourselves internal instructions such as "Now I need to turn my head and look left while pressing on the brake pedal." Both of these examples, and similar exercises and metaphors, highlight how even very complex and important behaviors are not verbally dependent—again undermining the idea that the only reality going on is the one offered by our minds.

SUMMARY

I began this chapter by commenting on the importance in ACT of which words we use in therapy. This is logical, given that the model is based upon what we've learned about language acquisition. I also shared my observation that many of the ACT therapists I have worked with essentially avoid working explicitly on the role of language with their clients. I have argued that including this piece can significantly enhance the therapy, particularly work on cognitive defusion and self-as-context. I have also suggested that excluding it due to therapist discomfort or lack of clarity shorts the client, and that skimming the surface or otherwise mishandling the topic can contradict some of the points we are hoping to bring home in ACT.

Although I have been pretty direct about making these points, I do so with compassion and understanding. I personally found this aspect of the therapy surprisingly difficult to translate into clinical practice, and it was only after many clumsy attempts and simply wrestling with it for a while that I learned ways to make it work for me and my clients. I also revisited the ACT literature and found both old and new gems that deepened my understanding and directly translated into increased skill in the therapy room. In chapter 12 I will share these and other ways to continue to advance in ACT. My hope is that by pointing out some of the trickiness in this area, I will enable others to circumvent common missteps, or at least move through them quickly. By offering examples of how language might be brought into the work effectively, I am hoping that therapists who have not been capitalizing on this aspect of ACT will be encouraged to start pulling it in, and that in doing so they will discover it was well worth the effort.

CHAPTER 7

Help with Creative Hopelessness

I've devoted this chapter to the topic of creative hopelessness. First presented by Hayes, Strosahl, and Wilson (1999), and subsequently included in many ACT materials, creative hopelessness (CH) is typically seen as an important first step in conducting ACT. In my opinion it is also the hardest component of ACT to do with fidelity. In this section we'll explore how and why CH is so challenging, and given its difficulty, whether its contribution merits its inclusion in the therapy. We will explore some points to consider when thinking about whether to bring in CH and, if so, how to approach it effectively. I believe the points of discussion raised in this chapter are quite relevant even if you do not specifically include the CH component in your treatment. That is, while working through CH puts certain issues in stark relief, they are issues that will repeatedly arise throughout the course of therapy.

Let's start with a quick review. The content area termed "creative hopelessness" is used to create an opening for the work to come. It is geared toward flushing out the client's experiential avoidance, putting it squarely on the table as problematic so that therapist and client can get to work. Rather than simply informing clients that experiential avoidance is what has been keeping them stuck, the therapist conducts CH sessions in such a way that clients come into experiential contact with the bind they have been in. While there are many ways to go about this, a common method is as follows: First, the therapist gathers information on what the client is viewing as "the problem," and why she is seeking treatment at this particular point in time. As they talk about what is not working in the client's life, the role of experiential avoidance is revealed. That is, the therapist gradually uncovers the client's stance toward uncomfortable or painful thoughts, feelings, and bodily sensations, and the degree to which the client has been working to avoid or control these unwanted internal experiences. The therapist and client generate a list of the multitude of strategies the client has employed in this effort, and arrive at the simple fact that despite the considerable energy given to this "control agenda," it apparently hasn't worked, as the client has not been fixed. The therapist further challenges the revealed control agenda by extending the client's dilemma to one faced by humans in general—thus normalizing both human suffering and the bind created when humans pit themselves against their own internal experiences. By use of metaphor and discussion the therapist highlights the futility of "trying not to have what you have" and introduces the idea that such strategies—including coming to therapy—"haven't worked because they don't work." In other words, the therapist clearly states that the client is not going to receive what she is looking for in therapy—meaning to be fixed such that unwanted thoughts, feelings, and sensations are vanquished—because this goal is simply not attainable. Further, CH highlights the suffering and cost in pursuing this sort of control agenda. Rather than living a vital, meaningful life, the client has become stuck fighting a battle that cannot be won.

Before moving into particulars regarding conducting CH, it seems timely to consider whether this piece is critical to the therapy. I cannot assert that including this piece makes the treatment more efficacious, as that conclusion would require empirical testing that has yet to occur. It also doesn't follow that excluding it would automatically cost the client something. Just as there is no one way to do ACT because it is a principle-based therapy, there are many ways to get at the processes targeted in a CH session. It is not hard to imagine situations in which CH wouldn't be the best first move, or times when it would make sense to do it very lightly—in fact, we'll be exploring a couple of these scenarios later in this chapter. It could also be argued that excluding this piece might be preferable to attempting it and making missteps that ultimately work against what you are hoping to accomplish. However, it has been my experience that when appropriate, CH is quite an effective start to the therapy. It is a powerful way to shake up clients' preconceived notions about what is needed to have a better life—notions that have stood and will continue to stand in the way of that better life. When done well, a CH session brings a sense of workability to a client's way of thinking. It helps her contact the direct contingencies of her life while reconnecting with a higher purpose. The discomfort that often results, while challenging for client and therapist alike, is a reflection of the struggle the client has been in. Confusion could arguably be preferable to fusion with unworkable rules about what should be happening in therapy (for example, pursuing a fix-it agenda). Helping clients contact this struggle is a move toward accepting the sometimes-difficult experience of being human, rather than aligning with the idea that clients need to be fixed.

In short, an effective CH session functions to loosen the client's hold on the control agenda, making a little room for something new. But that is not all. It seems to me that CH is a fitting way to begin this particular therapeutic journey, as it addresses, right from the start, the initial dilemma faced by the ACT therapist. That is, ACT strives to free clients from a flawed and costly feel-good agenda, moving from unworkable, rigid behaviors toward psychological flexibility. With rare exception, that is not what clients are seeking when they come to therapy. That is, they certainly want a better life, and feeling happier (as a destination) is usually a part of that picture. How do we as therapists reconcile our knowledge of what ACT ultimately offers with the concurrent awareness that clients get to decide what they want out of therapy and life itself? Additionally, the notion of being fixed, and all that comes with it, is seductive indeed. Given the attractiveness of the idea that if the client can just figure this out—if she can just get it together, be fixed, heal, get over it—then she will have arrived, ACT therapists face a daunting task. How do we help clients see that this is a trap when they are so invested in the bait? Why would they want to let go of such an attractive ideal? How can we help clients see that this objective is ultimately constraining, that they already have all they need to begin living well? How can we help them see that they are so much more than the collection of thoughts, feelings, or experiences that drove them into therapy when they think the answer is fixing all that? Tricky stuff.

When done well, creative hopelessness spells out this initial divide between what the client thinks is holding her back and what the ACT therapist perceives as the problem. The therapist isn't waiting until some later point in the therapy to reveal an agenda that differs from what the client is expecting. This different perspective is presented not as the "right" perspective, but as *one* alternative to a strategy that the client's own history suggests isn't working. The client then has the opportunity to choose whether or not to further explore this alternative.

WHY SO HARD?

So why the difficulty with CH? I would say it is a combination of there being no middle ground when it comes to ACT, the timing (CH typically occurs right off the bat), and the fact that the work with CH tends to reveal the degree to which therapists have bought into the model. I have mentioned throughout this book that a common misstep is a therapist's attempt to pull in some ACT principles while fudging on others, and I have frequently observed this misstep in CH sessions. As discussed, such a strategy contradicts the ACT-consistent pieces altogether and impedes progress toward the psychological flexibility that is the overarching goal in ACT. One of the greatest challenges for ACT therapists is to work consistently from within an ACT framework while including their own in-session experiences. In a typical CH session, the therapist not only confronts the client's experiential avoidance head-on, but will likely confront his own as well. An effective CH session requires that the therapist be fully willing to simply experience, rather than fix, the discomfort that arises as the session unfolds. Since this willingness flies in the face of much of what we have learned not only as therapists but as human beings, many of the missteps I've observed have been attempts to reconcile this inherent contradiction.

BAILING OUT

Along these lines, I'd like to talk about a misstep that frequently occurs in the latter part of CH sessions. A common scenario was that the therapist would make an ACT-inconsistent move right at the end of what was otherwise a strong CH session. In fact, this phenomenon occurred so frequently that I came to think of it as the "CH Bailout," in which the therapist, after doing a good job of revealing the futility and cost of the client's experiential avoidance, would then swoop in and attempt to rescue the client from any discomfort this revelation had evoked. Sometimes this rescue attempt included offering a solution to the man-in-the-hole metaphor (see example 1 below); sometimes it involved presenting ACT as a strategy itself (example 2); and often it included making some other move that served to create distance from the affective experience that had been so carefully contacted (example 3). I don't mean to suggest that the rescue attempt ruined the session or blew the therapy (otherwise we'd all be in trouble), but rather to make the point that the prevalence of this tendency demonstrates the degree to which the philosophy of ACT departs from what we have learned as humans and as therapists. It reveals how very strong (and sneaky) experiential avoidance can be. There we are, minds focused on our clients and this therapy we believe in, fully intending to move along a particular path, while what we are actually *doing* is stepping off that path and onto the very one we are pointing out as problematic! I think the observation I'm making here is best used as a "heads up" for therapists, an indication of the pervasiveness of our own experiential avoidance. It is a reminder not only that internal discomfort—ours and our clients'—is an inherent part of the therapy, but also that doing ACT well requires our own willingness to simply be with, rather than fix, that discomfort. It is a reminder that we will need to be wary and very tuned in. The very challenge provided by CH offers ACT therapists the opportunity to get squarely positioned in a stance of willingness at the outset of therapy—a stance that will be repeatedly tested as sessions unfold.

There is an inherent difficulty in offering the following examples. That is, the function of the sorts of exchanges described below depends upon their context. While a certain therapist response might serve one function in one scenario, the same response could function differently in a different context. So though I offer them as ways to explore the tendency of therapists to get out of, or try to resolve, the discomfort that can often show up in a CH session, that does not mean that the responses below would always be functioning in that manner, or even that this needs to be the primary concern. For example, while a soothing therapist response could be seen as moving away from discomfort, it could well be that the therapist determined it was important to validate the client in that instance. Or perhaps the therapy is occurring in a setting where time is an issue, and moving forward is what is called for, even if it moves away from the emotions evoked. Nonetheless, in my experience therapists often make moves in their CH sessions that are more about their own cognitive fusion and avoidance, and that is what I hope to point to here.

Example 1. Scenario: Working together, the therapist and client have clarified the various unwanted thoughts and feelings the client has tried to avoid and the various strategies she has been using in that effort. The therapist is now just completing the man-in-the-hole metaphor.

Therapist:	"…So you're in this hole and you're digging away, digging here, digging there…but what is happening? What happens when you are in a hole and still digging?"
Client:	"The hole just gets deeper."
Therapist:	"Ah. But you really want out of there! So you keep on digging."
Client	*(dejected):* "I guess that's what I've been doing. I just keep trying the same things over and over and putting myself in a deeper hole." *(Heavy sigh.)*
Therapist:	"It's not your fault that you fell into a hole—you were blindfolded. And all you had was a shovel, so you've been digging. The thing to ask is whether you're willing to drop that shovel and do something else."

While the content of this response—the actual words—seems congruent with ACT, the therapist's intention may be inconsistent with the model. That is, "it's not your fault" may be an attempt to make the client feel better because the therapist is uncomfortable. Another thing to consider, especially at this early point in the therapy, is whether suggesting that if the client drops the shovel she can do something else might be received as yet another control or fix-it strategy. Notice also that this response moves both therapist and client away from the affective experience of struggling and being stuck in a hole to "what's next?" An alternate response would be to simply sit compassionately for a bit with the client in whatever she is experiencing before moving on. This is, after all, the reality of her life. The sort of struggle she has been engaged in is painful indeed. Since a major thrust of the therapy is to help her shift from working to defend against unwanted thoughts and feelings to being willing to simply experience them, you could use this opportunity as a way to begin that work now.

Example 2. Scenario: The therapist and client have worked through the problem the client is presenting with ("depression"), extrapolating unwanted thoughts, feelings, and sensations, and have completed an extensive list of the various ways in which the client has attempted to control or avoid these internal experiences.

Therapist:	"What I hear you saying is that depression has really stood in the way of what you are wanting in your life. The sorts of thoughts that you have during those times, the low energy and feeling down, all that keeps you from doing the things you want to be doing, like getting into a relationship, doing your job well, or

getting exercise." (*Note that the therapist, while temporarily going with the client's use of the term "depression," also breaks that label down into some of the thoughts, feelings, and sensations experienced during such times. This will be a more useful way to work with the experience of depression than aligning with the client's view that depression is a thing that is in him, or that lands on him.*)

Client:	"Yeah."
Therapist:	"And we just created quite a list of the various things you've tried to make that stuff go away." (*Long, thoughtful pause.*) "And yet, here you are...."
Client:	"Nothing has helped, not really."
Therapist:	"What if what your experience is telling you here is really the case? What if all these attempts to make it go away haven't worked because they don't work?"
Client	(*clearly dismayed*): "So what do I do?"
Therapist:	"Well, that's what we're going to be working on in here. ACT is about finding another way to deal with this stuff—with unwanted, painful thoughts and feelings."

As in the earlier example, it is worth slowing down in moments like this to consider what might best move the client forward. For example, the client's question about what to do could be in the service of solving the problem of unwanted thoughts and feelings—both those they have been discussing and those occurring in the moment. By immediately responding and presenting ACT as the solution, the therapist could potentially (a) reinforce the idea that the discomfort being experienced needs to be resolved, and (b) support the notion that there is a fix for unwanted internal experiences.

Example 3. Scenario: The therapist and client are nearing the end of the session, after having revealed the client's experiential avoidance and control efforts, and pointed to the ultimate unworkability of the control agenda via discussion and use of the man-in-the-hole metaphor.

Client:	"So I guess I'm supposed to accept this stuff."
Therapist:	"And what would that do?"
Client	(*hesitates*): "I was going to say make it better but I guess that's a strategy too...."
Therapist:	"It's great that you see that. Yeah, accepting so that it goes away is just another strategy to try to get rid of it."

(*Pause.*)

Therapist	(shifts in her chair a bit, indicating that time is up, and says brightly): "So next week we'll talk more about this and where to go from here; how does that sound?"
Client	(hesitantly): "Okay."
Therapist:	"I have an opening at ten o'clock on Tuesday; will that work?"
Client:	"Yes."

or:

Client:	"So I guess I'm supposed to accept this stuff."
Therapist:	"And what would that do?"
Client	(hesitates): "I was going to say make it better but I guess that's a strategy too...."

(Both are silent.)

Therapist	(shifting in her chair a bit, asks solicitously): "So how are you doing with all this?"
Client:	"I don't know. I don't really know what to think."
Therapist:	"Yeah. This therapy can be really confusing at the beginning, but things eventually come together."

or:

Client:	"So I guess I'm supposed to accept this stuff."
Therapist:	"And what would that do?"
Client	(hesitates):" I was going to say make it better but I guess that's a strategy too...."

(Both are silent.)

Therapist	(shifting in her chair a bit, indicating that time is up): "Well, it looks like time is up. That went fast!"
Client:	"Yeah, it did!"
Therapist:	"So same time next week? By the way, how's the house hunting going along?"
Client:	"We're making headway...."

When the above examples were examined closely, it was revealed that in all the scenarios the therapists were attempting to bring their clients and themselves out of discomfort. They were hoping to make things feel more comfortable, to end on an "upbeat note" or to simply provide relief from the affective intensity of the session. We can also imagine the same content serving a different purpose. That is, "Shall we meet at ten o'clock next week?" can function very differently when asked in a way that reflects, rather than attempts to alter, what is actually happening in the moment. The distinction is whether the therapist's tone, pacing, and overall demeanor fit with what is occurring in the moment, or whether they are in the service of creating a different experience in the room. This distinction explains why self-awareness is so key. Only you, by tuning in to what is occurring for you in the moment, can determine what your intention is. Paying attention to the effects of what you do will help illuminate how that intervention functions in the session. By the way, one of the blessings of ACT is that acceptance of what is includes the therapist's experience as well. By this I mean that your thoughts and feelings are just as acceptable as your client's—the key is what you do with them. When we tune in we can use even those moments when we have stepped off the path in an effective way. For example:

Client:	"So I guess I'm supposed to accept this stuff."
Therapist:	"And what would that do?"
Client	(hesitates): "I was going to say make it better but I guess that's a strategy too...."

(Both are silent.)

Therapist	(shifting in her chair a bit, asks solicitously): "So how are you doing with all this?"
Client:	"I don't know. I don't really know what to think."
Therapist:	"Yeah. This therapy can be really confusing at the beginning, but things eventually come together."
Client:	"Okay...."

(Both sit looking at each other.)

Therapist:	"You know, I just realized something."
Client:	"What's that?"
Therapist:	"What I just did there. When I made that comment how things come together."
Client:	(Listening.)
Therapist:	"I just realized that I said that to try to take away what you were experiencing right then. Or at least what I thought you were

experiencing. My mind was handing me stuff about your reaction to this—worries about what you were thinking and feeling about this session, about me, about ACT—and I was wanting to fix it."

Client:	"I was just thinking about how different this is from what I thought it would be. I don't know whether it will help me or not."
Therapist:	"Yeah. And when I picked up that you were uncomfortable or unsure about all this, I got uncomfortable too, and then tried to rescue us both."
Client:	"That's okay. It's natural, I guess. But I'm okay. I mean, I don't get where all this is going but I'll be here next week."
Therapist	*(smiling):* "And was that a very nice effort to make *me* feel better?"
Client	*(laughs):* "Yeah, guess so."
Therapist:	"This is a great example of what we do. It is 'natural,' as you say. At the same time, it supports the idea that somehow you and I are going to dissolve if we don't get out of being uncomfortable, ASAP."
Client:	"Yeah, okay. But are you saying we shouldn't do that?"
Therapist	*(pausing to really consider):* "I'm really just pointing out how strong that pull can be. Even now, I can feel both our minds trying to wrap this up, make sense of it—all that stuff that makes us feel more comfortable. I wonder if we might just sit with this as it is for a moment…just notice what we're experiencing right now, without trying to resolve it somehow."

In sum, fears about how the client is feeling, about what he is thinking about the session, about us as therapists, or about ACT itself are simply difficult to sit with, and are particularly strong at the end of a CH session. Again, I do not mean to say that offering an explanation would always be problematic. I am pointing out how automatically we defend against internal discomfort. This response can be a problem if it has the effect of reinforcing the very client behaviors we are hoping to decrease, and it's something to watch out for. To simply end the session without attempting to alter your or your client's authentic experience could well be a more effective move.

You Do What?!

I have conducted many ACT workshops and have been struck by the negative reactions some participants, often very seasoned clinicians, have to the CH component.

Comments reflect a range of reactions, from shock to flat-out dismay: "Are you saying you just *leave* them with that [the realization that they've been pursuing an unworkable agenda]?" "I can't imagine doing this with one of my clients! I'd worry what they'd do once they walked out my door!" "Why would you want someone already in trouble to feel even more hopeless?" Such comments reflect very understandable concerns, and they underscore the degree to which ACT departs from other, more traditional therapeutic approaches. However, rather than serving as reasons to stay away from CH, these sorts of concerns can actually be used to inform our approach to CH with a particular client. We can examine the function and validity of the concern, and use that information to guide us through this challenging piece of the therapy.

FRAGILITY OR FUSION?

Earlier in this section I observed that one of the reasons therapists struggle with CH is their own experiential avoidance. However, it certainly wouldn't be fair to suggest that is the only reason therapists step out of CH or choose to stay away from it entirely. Genuine concern for the client's well-being is obviously a significant consideration. The important thing for therapists to discern is whether their concerns reflect a belief that the client cannot *technically* handle what might be evoked during or after a CH session, or whether the issue is that the client is too fused with his thoughts to remain safe. As I have often heard said in the ACT community, "Thoughts or feelings never killed anybody." It is the client's *fusion* with thoughts about his experience ("I can't take this anymore;" "I should kill myself") that poses the risk, not the thoughts (or feelings, or physical sensations) themselves. So it is one thing for the therapist to assess that the client, due to his *fusion* with these sorts of thoughts, is in too risky a place to attempt a CH session, and another for the therapist to also align with the idea that the client is so fragile that he cannot handle the ideas presented in CH. This is another easily missed distinction that, if not caught, can play an influential and problematic role throughout the therapy. It is extremely difficult to effectively and consistently convey the idea that there is a self that is intact and larger than the thoughts and feelings of the moment if you do not fully believe it yourself. This particular issue—the actual versus perceived power of thoughts and feelings—will be in play throughout much of ACT, and being clear on the distinction will help you navigate often tricky terrain. I also cannot overemphasize the power of nonverbal communication in ACT, or in any therapy. That is, when the therapist firmly holds the belief that her clients are fundamentally whole and acceptable, that surety is conveyed even while moving through very distressing content. The therapist's willingness to step into uncomfortable terrain, to unflinchingly join the client in the present moment, to serve as compassionate listener and witness without attempting to fix the client—all serve as powerful lifelines regardless of subject matter.

It has been my experience that when we defuse from our worries about the fragility of our clients and move boldly into CH, our clients can handle it just fine. To put this in perspective, for many years the majority of those with whom Robyn Walser and I conducted ACT were female military veterans who not only had experienced extensive childhood physical, emotional, and sexual abuse, but were then revictimized in the military. Many had war-zone trauma added on top of these injustices. All were diagnosed with severe PTSD, and many fulfilled Axis II diagnostic criteria as well. In short, in terms of self-concept, distress tolerance, and emotional avoidance, these women were the definition of "fragile"—*perceived* fragility, that is. Believe me, early on I really struggled with the idea of suggesting to such clients that they weren't going to be fixed, and that all their desperate attempts to not have such painful memories, thoughts, feelings, and physical sensations were for naught. But here's what happened: No one fell apart. No one ran out of the room never to return. My greatest surprise, although it makes sense to me now, was the *relief* that we would frequently encounter. You see, at a very deep level, many of these women already knew that more therapy, this thing called "ACT," wouldn't fix them. They already knew in their core that even a cutting-edge treatment at a well-known and difficult-to-get-into residential treatment program wasn't going to fix them. Hence the palpable feeling of relief I would often sense when the unworkability of the fix-it idea was put so unapologetically on the table. Not only was there no need to hide their secret fear that they would not be fixed, the failure might not even be about them! Perhaps we've *all* been deluded! What a relief indeed.

I want to stress again, though, that the sorts of concerns we have been exploring are important. It would not be wise to ignore them, and fortunately we do not need to in order to conduct ACT with fidelity. Rather, as I said, we can use these concerns about how clients will respond to the ideas in CH to guide us in session. We can hold them and learn from them while steadfastly steering in an ACT direction. In fact, as we will explore in the following sections, it is the very honoring of these sorts of concerns that will help us be successful.

ONCE AGAIN, THE IMPORTANCE OF STYLE

I mentioned earlier that timing is one of the reasons why therapists can struggle with CH. Coming at the beginning of the therapy, a CH session is often the client's first impression of the therapy and therapist. A challenge with CH is that, along with building rapport, therapists are tasked with popping any pink bubbles the client may have around being fixed. While hoping to build a positive relationship, the therapist is also saying something the client does not want to hear. And yet, as I pointed out earlier, there is a big opportunity in this moment, as well. Here is an opportunity to be the one who points to the elephant in the room and says, "Look at that elephant!"—the opportunity to be the one who is willing to be unpopular in the service of being straight. That is someone to trust, and it has been my experience that even while upset or thrown by the concepts conveyed in CH, clients also respond positively to its direct-ness. As I mentioned, there are also many nuances in how the therapist relates to the client while working through CH—nuances that make all the difference in how the session goes. I've made a list of some I have found to be key:

Joining, but not aligning

Bold, but kind

Honest, but not glum

Uncompromising, but compassionate

Let's take a look at these nuances and how they come into play with therapists as they work with clients on CH (and throughout the therapy).

Joining, Not Aligning

In chapter 3, I explored the distinction between being "supportive" and aligning with the client's cognitive fusion or experiential avoidance. When it comes to CH, the struggle centers around feeling pulled to align with the client around how much she is needing to be saved (from her despair, pain, anxiety, and so on) and feeling as though it is unkind, or unsupportive, or unsafe to challenge the idea that she can control or escape unwanted internal experiences, especially so early in the therapy. What can really help with this dynamic is to understand that just because you choose not to align with the client's fix-it agenda, it does not mean you have to let go of an ounce of compassion. In fact, it could be argued that in truly seeing that agenda for the terrible bind that it is, and in understanding that there is no ultimate fix, we are more able to find true compassion for the struggle of being human. By extending the client's struggle to a human nature problem (in other words, how we have all learned to regard unwanted private events as intolerable and abnormal and try unsuccessfully to rid ourselves of them), we are joining with the client, while refraining from further endorsing a problematic, language-derived control agenda.

Bold and Yet Kind

ACT is a bold therapy and CH is a bold way to begin. You are taking a stand, in many ways directly contradicting what the culture has been teaching the client since she could first talk. You are daring to point out that elephant. However, boldness does not eliminate gentleness, kindness, awareness, or humility. Earlier, when discussing therapist style in chapter 3, I mentioned we often incorrectly think that as therapists we have to choose between option A and option B when, in fact, we can put both A and B right out on the table. So when sitting with a client, debating whether or not to say what you are thinking, or whether or not to point something out, you don't have to choose between being bold or being kind. Remember also that transparency can be very helpful in ACT.

Scenario: The therapist and client, both female, have been exploring various ways the client has attempted to eliminate or avoid distressing memories, thoughts, feelings, and physical sensations. They have compiled an extensive sampling of strategies, listed on a whiteboard, which they are now contemplating:

Therapist:	"What comes up for you when you look at all this?"
Client:	"What a mess! My god, I'm such a disaster."
Therapist:	"Are there feelings that come along with those thoughts?"
Client:	"Just…hopeless. I feel hopeless."
Therapist	*(just sits with this for a few moments, thoughtfully considering the list):* "When I look at this I feel…hmmm, very moved. I mean, I see so much struggle here. You have really been in pain."
Client	*(tearful):* "Yeah!"
Therapist:	"I'm noticing wanting to make it better for you, wanting to ease your pain, but I also know that would just be another thing to add to the list."
Client:	"What do you mean?"
Therapist:	"Well, there's no lack of effort here on your part! No lack of ingenuity. You have tried practically everything, it seems, and yet here you are."
Client:	"Are you saying there's no hope for me?"
Therapist	*(very thoughtfully):* "I'm saying that there's something fishy going on here. That despite all these different strategies to not have those painful thoughts and feelings they are still here."
Client:	"Yeah, I just can't seem to move on."
Therapist:	"And I bet you've told yourself that one too, that you just need to move on."
Client:	"Oh, countless times. That's what my husband tells me, too—to just get over it, you know?"
Therapist:	"And has that worked?"

Client:	"No."
Therapist	*(adding "get over it" to the list on the board):* "Yeah. And here I am, on one hand really feeling for the struggle you've been in *(nodding at the board)*, and on the other, knowing that anything I would do to try to take that away would just be another unworkable strategy too."
Client:	*(Silent.)*
Therapist:	"On one hand it would be nice for both of us if I could tell you I have a way to make that stuff go away, but I also know how important it is that I be very straightforward with you right now. What I want to put out there, what I want us to take a hard look at, is that this stuff doesn't work because it doesn't work."
Client	*(confused):* "What do you mean?"
Therapist:	"That trying not to have what you have, trying to make unwanted thoughts and feelings go away doesn't work because it doesn't work. Not for you, not for me, not for anyone. You've been thinking that this has been about you, that there's something wrong with you because you haven't been able to 'get over it.' I'm suggesting that trying to get over it doesn't work."

The conversation would then continue, with the therapist working with whatever the client brings into it. It will be important to continue to look for avoidance and control strategies, as they will likely show up here and can be used as effective examples of the ongoing struggle. Continuing to normalize the struggle, the ubiquity of human suffering, will be important as well. At some point it might be effective to move into the man-in-the-hole or a similar metaphor to continue to loosen the grip of client's fix-it agenda.

In the above exchange the therapist is direct about the ultimate futility of experiential avoidance, but has likely increased the client's receptivity to this message by joining with her, in sharing some of her personal reactions in the session and normalizing the struggle, and by explicitly expressing her compassion for the bind the client has been in.

Here is another brief example of this "A plus B" strategy that is effective during CH as well as at any point in the therapy:

Therapist:	"I'm wanting to point something out here, but find myself worrying how you will receive it."
Client:	"Huh. Well, I can't really help you with that."

Therapist:	"No, you can't! *I* can't help me with that. But I can, out of respect for what we're about here, choose to head in there even if it means getting a little uncomfortable."

or

Therapist	*(very kindly):* "I've been sitting here as you've been talking, feeling really moved. I guess the word would be 'compassion'— I'm feeling a lot of compassion not just for you but for us human beings. Because a lot of what you said just now went right back to wanting to control. You so desperately want to not have what you have. And I know that struggle. I know how painful it is and how much it costs, and…here it is again."

Honest, Not Glum

Just because we are pointing out that there's no fix for the pain of being human doesn't mean we should pull our hair or rend our garments. There is a fine line between refusing to align with the nirvana notion and conveying that there's no point in anything. Now, if the client is glum, there's a usefulness to helping him notice that and experience glumness without defense. I'm talking about your own demeanor. This (CH) may be unwanted news; it may be uncomfortable or surprising or disturbing news; but it's not bad news. I'm not suggesting you be cheery, but guard against conveying a sense of doom that also doesn't fit. It is helpful throughout CH (and the rest of ACT) to remember that in revealing the unworkability of the fix-it or control agenda you are offering your client an opportunity to walk away from a fight that can't be won. You are opening the door to a life that is about living according to the values your client holds most dear. Who knows what possibilities await?

Uncompromising, Yet Compassionate

Similar to the idea about joining versus aligning explained above, it is consistent with the model to be fully on board with the idea that experiential avoidance is unworkable while still having compassion for the struggle, as seen in the earlier dialogue. I draw upon this idea again and again, especially when struggling to be straight with a client rather than aligning with a problematic idea or agenda. I remind myself what we are shooting for in ACT and why, and how backing off of that would be more about my own experiential avoidance. Here's a sort of style mantra I hold front and center when working on tough stuff with clients:

Be *unflinching*—regarding what is there to be seen or to be had.

Be *kind*—in tone, in demeanor, in my choice of words. (Direct does not mean brusque.)

Convey *confidence*—that this willingness stuff is doable. (Note that I don't attempt to *feel* confident. That is, I'm confident in the model, in the therapy, while *feelings* of confidence come and go.)

Be *humble*. (I'm in this soup, too, and my work isn't about having the right answer; it's about offering an alternative, from one human being to another.)

That very pull to rescue your client can be used to communicate just how very much you can relate to the desire to escape discomfort. You can allow your empathy for your client to infuse your work with kindness. In those silences when you simply nod in understanding, as opposed to rushing in and fixing, much compassion is conveyed. I find it fascinating how positively clients respond to a truly compassionate therapist who is, at a verbal level, frustrating them beyond belief. It's as though there are two communications going on—that of the actual dialogue; and another, which, if there *were* words, would consist of a being-to-being communication along the lines of "I, too, am like you. I, too, struggle and have pain, grief, fear, and despair. I'm here with you—and look, we're still okay. We can do this."

OTHER STYLISTIC MISSTEPS

The previous section highlighted some nuances of the therapist/client relationship that can either further or hinder CH (or any other part of ACT). I would like to also mention a few "style types" I have seen that tend to not work so well with this therapy and that really falter in a CH session. These are:

Agenda-driven

Apologetic

Persuading

In the following sections we'll explore these types and how they can lead to difficulty during this part of the therapy.

Agenda-Driven

A recurrent theme of this book is the importance of approaching ACT from the process level, rather than as a collection of techniques. Being content-driven leads therapists to prioritize their session agenda over the behavioral processes that impede or further the development of psychological flexibility. In CH, being agenda-driven manifests as essentially checking off the various content pieces of CH—the identified problem and unwanted private events, the list of strategies, the man-in-the-hole metaphor, the unworkable agenda comments, and so on—rather than thoughtfully exploring these ideas with the client while prioritizing and responding to the core processes that pertain to what is happening in the moment. To repeat myself, this sort of strategy is not consistent with ACT. Moreover, it is a distortion, and it sucks the humanity right out of the message. Being compassionately *with* the client in the *experience* of CH is essential to having it be received in a way that will further the work.

Apologetic

There is a difference between being compassionate and being apologetic. I have often observed or heard therapists work with CH as though they are somehow injuring the client. Observations are offered up hesitantly, as though the therapist is anticipating that the client is going to be upset (and that is bad). There's a tentativeness that sends the message that something problematic is happening, rather than conveying that whatever is happening in the moment is yet another experience to be had. If you find yourself doing something along these lines, the question to ask yourself is what exactly are you sorry for? For pointing out that the client is in a trap? For not going along with the idea that he can be fixed and arrive at happiness as a destination? When you're on board with the theory behind ACT, it is much easier to move from apology to compassion. That is, if you are clear that aligning with any part of the client's problematic belief system is in fact doing him a disservice, you are much more able to work with that system in a way that is unapologetic while still compassionate. Rather than being sorry for popping the fix-it bubble, you have compassion for the desperation driving that desire. You have compassion for how painful it can be to realize you have been in a trap of your own making. I have come to believe that when therapists are firmly grounded in the theory of ACT, the "hard" news they deliver in CH is actually reassuring (or arresting, at the very least) in its authenticity. I can also offer that I have seen many, many clients, representing a wide range of backgrounds and presenting problems, respond well to this component. By that I mean that they "get it," and that getting it really paves the way for the difficult work to come.

Persuading

At the other end of the spectrum are therapists who have bought fully into the philosophy of ACT, and believe with all their heart that ACT is *the* answer for their clients. This idea can lead to the pitfall of arguing with the client, or attempting to persuade him to see things in a certain way. It can be tricky to refrain from persuading while also being direct about what you are seeing. Pointing out that the client's experiential avoidance seems to be keeping him stuck, for example, can easily turn into trying to get him to agree with you (which is one reason why ACT therapists will often explicitly tell clients they are not asking them to just accept what they are saying but to check their own experience). However, I am not suggesting you be disingenuous. The idea is to be up front with your belief that there is an alternative to the control agenda that you feel will prove helpful. At a meta level, you are there to offer that alternative and help the client shift from experiential avoidance to willingness and valued living, *should the client choose* to make that shift. This purpose is one of the reasons why the horizontal relationship discussed in chapter 3 is so very important. If we remember that ACT is based on functional contextualism, which prioritizes workability, we can remember that there is no inherent "truth" that needs to be proven in ACT. There is no inherent rightness to valued living. If you can remain very clear that the client has every right to remain stuck, to hang on to the notion that there is a fix or any other notion, no matter how problematic, you will be better able to refrain from falling into a persuading or cajoling role.

THE HEART OF THE MATTER

A major objective in CH is to flush out the client's experiential avoidance. Sometimes this task can be a little tricky, particularly when the avoidance is cloaked in what the client has identified as a different sort of presenting problem, such as marital problems or inability to find work. Frequently, though, experiential avoidance is playing a role in keeping the client stuck, and the challenge is to work together until this role has been revealed.

Scenario: The therapist is conducting an initial session with a twenty-four-year-old female client, and has just asked her why she is seeking treatment.

Client:	"I have relationship problems. Nothing ever seems to work out and I'm tired of it."
Therapist:	"Are you in a relationship now?"
Client:	"No, not now. I was, but we broke up last month. He broke up with me, actually."
Therapist:	"Hmmm. Is that what you mean by 'relationship problems?' That this relationship didn't work out? Or are there other relationship issues going on as well?"
Client:	"I thought everything was fine, but this keeps happening to me."
Therapist:	"'This'?"
Client:	"Guys breaking up with me. I'm sick of it." (*Starts to cry.*)

(Therapist sits quietly for several moments.)

Therapist: "This is really painful."

Client: "Yeah, it is!"

(Therapist just holds the moment.)

Client: "I just want to figure this out, you know? What am I doing wrong? I get close to someone, things are great, then wham! They're out the door."

Therapist: "What do you think figuring it out would do?"

Client: "What?"

Therapist: "You said, 'If I could just figure this out…' What do you think that would do?"

Client: "Well, I could just, you know, stop doing whatever it is that I'm doing to drive guys away." (*Cries harder.*)

Therapist   (*again making room for the emotion, eventually continues unhurriedly*): "I can tell this is really important to you. There's obviously a lot of pain here. So I want to really have a good understanding of this—I need to keep asking you stuff to get a good handle on what's happening for you, okay?"

Client   (*sniffs*): "Okay."

Therapist: "Can you say a little bit about what being in a relationship does for you?"

Client: "What do you mean? I mean, why wouldn't I want to be in a good relationship?"

Therapist: "It's important for me to understand what being in a relationship means to you."

Client: "Well, it means I'm not alone. I get to, you know, share things with somebody, do things together…."

Therapist: "So having someone to do things with, to share your life with?"

Client: "Yeah!"

Therapist: "And it sounds like there's an aloneness that you deal with, that being in a relationship seems to fix?"

Client:	"Well, sometimes. Not always."
Therapist:	"Tell me more."
Client:	"Sometimes I still feel alone. My boyfriend—ex-boyfriend—told me I was too needy and needed to get a life…." (*Cries again.*)
Therapist:	"So there's a feeling of loneliness that you have struggled with, that being in a relationship sort of helps with, sort of doesn't."
Client:	"Yeah. But I feel even more alone now!"
Therapist:	"How long have you been struggling with this loneliness?"
Client	(*shrugs*): "Forever, probably."
Therapist	(*nods, communicating that she understands the pain and weight of what the client is saying*): "Are you experiencing it right now?"
Client:	"Yes."
Therapist:	"Help me understand what this is like for you. Can you describe the feeling?"
Client:	"It feels hopeless, like something's wrong with me."
Therapist:	"Got it. Those sound more like thoughts, though—the sorts of thoughts that come up when you're feeling lonely. You have the thought that something's wrong with you. Can you tag any emotions that are in there?"
Client:	"I feel…ashamed somehow…really sad. I just don't want to feel this way anymore!"
Therapist:	"And one way you have tried to fix those painful thoughts and feelings is by being in a relationship."
Client:	"Which only makes it worse when it doesn't work out. As usual."
Therapist:	"What else have you tried?"

In this example, the client began by stating that the problem in her life was the absence of a romantic relationship. While this is a meaningful issue, the therapist is working with her to uncover the larger issues that are at stake. This is not to suggest that the client's desire for a relationship is ignored, but rather that it is important to get at what might actually be going on such that relationships have been problematic. It would seem there are many other avenues of inquiry that would prove useful in this case. For example, the therapist could get a sense from the client of what she perceives a "good" relationship to be, and what has stood in the way of having that. The key would be to follow that line of inquiry while looking for the role that experiential avoidance might be playing, thereby shifting the focus to the client's behavior and what has been standing in the way of how she would ultimately like to be relating to others.

IT'S ABOUT THE LARGER AGENDA

One of the ways I have heard therapists get sort of stuck when doing CH is when they fall into examining the relative merit of every strategy the client introduces. That is, when compiling the list of various strategies the client has employed to get rid of or to control unwanted private events, they assess whether each is a "good" or "bad" strategy, whether it works all the time, some of the time, or just a little, and so on. You can do this, but it isn't really necessary and can result in some stickiness. For one thing, strategies aren't inherently good or bad; they are good or bad in terms of workability. So if the client is doing something that helps ("I take my mind off it by going for a run," for example) and that isn't costing her something unacceptable (to her), there's no problem here. Fortunately, we do not need to evaluate the merit of every little method the client has used to deal with challenging thoughts, feelings, or sensations. Rather, we are focusing on the overarching, highly problematic idea that we are *not supposed to be uncomfortable* inside, that something wrong is occurring if we are experiencing uncomfortable thoughts, feelings, or physical sensations. Fusion with that overall idea, and the resultant battle we wage against ourselves when discomfort is present or even on the horizon (and what we tell ourselves it means when we fail to vanquish discomfort), is what we are focusing on here. It's not whether or not an individual strategy has been useful 5 percent of the time, 10 percent, or 85 percent. While clients will often present a given strategy as either good or bad, the therapist can simply note that it is a strategy and add it to the overall list, paving the way to make the larger point that an overarching control agenda could be keeping them stuck.

When It Is Not the Right Time to Do CH

At the beginning of this chapter, I stated that there are times when it doesn't make clinical sense to do the CH component of ACT with a given client. You may have a client who is so highly emotionally avoidant, for example, that it is challenging to get her to stay in the room, much less confront her belief that she can be fixed. In a case like this you might choose to gain some footing before heading into such terrain (validating but not fusing with her experience, building her ability to be present, and so forth). Another example is someone who recently suffered a loss—for example, a mother coming for treatment after the death of her child. While ACT holds promise for someone in this sort of situation, timing will be important. It would seem that simply being fully and compassionately with her in her grief is what is initially called for on the part of the therapist—which, of course, is experientially working with the processes of being present and willingness—rather than going after a possible fix-it agenda right off the bat.

There are also clients (such as the individuals who have hit the "rock bottom" so often mentioned in the addiction literature) who are already in a place of openness when they present for treatment. That is, they already know and accept that what they've tried hasn't worked and that it is time for something new. It remains important to poke around, though, because the fix-it idea is often still lurking. That is, though humble and completely open to doing something different, such clients may well be thinking that the "something different" will nonetheless fix them. Same for "hopeless" clients. Although it might seem unnecessary to go further into the futility of various fix-it attempts with clients who clearly state they are already there, hopelessness itself (thinking, "I'll just stop caring and that will make things less distressing") can be a costly strategy. Similarly, some clients who present as hopeless hold the notion that the problem is specifically them—in other words, that there is a happiness place out there for others but just not for them. In all these cases, it is important to make the point that part of being human is to experience pain, that internal discomfort is a part of living, and that the feel-good agenda itself is specious and ultimately unworkable.

CREATIVE HOPELESSNESS LITE

I was first introduced to the term "creative hopelessness lite" by Robyn Walser. In various workshops we introduced this as a strategy wherein the basic points of CH are made without going into the depth of a more typical CH session. For example, we found it helpful with young veterans who had very recent trauma experiences to spend much less time on the various strategies employed in the service of experiential avoidance. These individuals hadn't had the time or opportunity to develop a bunch of strategies or to experience their eventual futility in getting rid of aversive private events. Enough time hadn't elapsed to clearly demonstrate that the various efforts to escape or avoid unwanted thoughts, feelings, and sensations don't ultimately work. In fact, we found these individuals to be quick to point out how certain strategies (such as exercising, using distraction, and drinking alcohol to take the edge off) seemed to be helpful. In these cases we found it fruitful to head more quickly into the idea that the control agenda is problematic—an idea that would typically follow CH—because regardless of how recent their difficulties, these clients were invested in the idea of control being a solution. So we would get clear on what the client was hoping for in therapy, highlighting the degree to which getting rid of unwanted internal experiences played a role in their perception of "getting better." We would then move more generally into the paradoxical effects of control and how that agenda has its own cost.

I'm sure you can think of other examples—with some of your own clients, perhaps—in which it would make clinical sense to start somewhere other than with CH.

The beauty of a principle-based treatment is that we can tailor what we do to what is needed. As we become facile with the core ACT processes, we can work with them according to our best clinical judgment in each particular moment and with each individual client. The key is to be aware of your own process and what is driving your clinical decision-making, so that your work will be based upon your intention with this therapy, rather than in reaction to something else.

SUMMARY

In this chapter I have examined CH, what it brings to ACT, and the ways in which it can be challenging. While recognizing that CH is difficult to do well, and may not always be what is called for, I have found it to be a powerful way to begin the therapy. I also believe there is something important to consider if you are refraining from doing CH due to your own experiential avoidance or fusion—if you don't want to overly upset the client, for example, or to experience the discomfort of confronting the fix-it ideal head on. And that is simply that these issues will most assuredly show up again. And again. What will you do? The client either is or is not fundamentally okay. Thoughts and feelings either are or aren't in charge. The Self either is or is not larger than the internal phenomena of the moment. Moving around on this (for example, by avoiding discomfort in one moment while working on willingness the next, or by helping clients contact self-as-context while "protecting" them from too much pain) is simply that: moving around—even stepping back—rather than moving forward, step by sometimes painful step.

I confess my hope that this chapter has provided food for thought for those who have opted out of CH for other than purely clinical reasons. I also suggested that the discussion points raised by this component are applicable throughout ACT, and I hope that you agree, regardless of whether or not you do CH in your therapy. Finally, for those readers who do work with CH, my hope is that you have found an idea or two that will help you further optimize what this interesting and powerful component can bring to the therapy.

CHAPTER 8

Barriers to Treatment

The focus of this chapter is on barriers to treatment. By barriers, I mean behaviors that impede therapeutic progress, as opposed to more external developments such as unexpected crises or treatment limitations. (Those sorts of challenges will be examined in chapter 11.) I will be emphasizing client behaviors that pose difficulty, but in the course of exploring these I will also discuss therapist responses that help or hinder the therapy.

It might be useful to begin with an invitation to shift from viewing barriers to treatment as problems (if you are), to seeing them as simply part of the process—as other aspects to work with, neither good nor bad. Although our minds will continue to hand us all sorts of evaluations about our clients—or perhaps our clinical skill—when barriers arise, it is useful to observe, rather than buy into, these sorts of thoughts, as they don't tend to increase our effectiveness. When we are fused with judgment, we can become behaviorally bound up in what our mind hands us about how things are going. When we can defuse and see the situation more broadly, we can better see where there might be room to move. To remake an old point, it is important to make room for both our responses and our clients' responses to the therapeutic process taking place. Doing so helps us remain in a compassionate stance toward our clients as well as ourselves, ultimately enhancing our ability to recognize and work with barriers to treatment as they arise. So instead of viewing the presence or absence of barriers as some sort of indicator of whether the treatment is working, the focus shifts to simply recognizing these behaviors as they appear, considering how they are functioning in the session or therapy overall, and then working with them in a way that moves things forward.

HOW TO SPOT BARRIERS

Some client behaviors that stand in the way of progress are both obvious and frequently encountered during a course of ACT. Repeatedly canceling sessions, not following through on behavioral commitments, and hanging on to a victim role are just a few examples that we will be exploring in this chapter. In actuality, there are myriad ways in which clients can put on the brakes, even if it's a just a light tap on the pedal. Even those light taps often reflect behaviors that keep the client stuck in her daily life, so it is important to look for these and work with them in an ACT-consistent manner.

The crucial first step in identifying treatment barriers, particularly those more subtle taps on the brake, is being present with your client. It has been my experience that when therapists make room in their awareness for what is actually happening in session, they are quite good at picking up whether something is standing in the way of forward movement. As I mentioned in the first chapter of this book, one cost to prioritizing an agenda over what is happening in the moment is that important clinical opportunities are missed. As it pertains here, therapists can be so focused on the idea or concept they are hoping to impart that they miss the fact that their client is not on board. I have also found that therapists are often aware that something is off, but rather than leaning in, they engage in a control strategy. They might work harder to convince the client, for example, or move on to something they think the client will find more palatable. In other words, they respond to what they are picking up, but in an indirect way that is geared toward eliminating, rather than working with and learning from, what is happening. Although this response might ostensibly be in the service of moving forward, the therapist is missing a clinical opportunity and often adding to the problem. That is, this sort of control move tends to strengthen, not lessen, the behavior that is posing a problem. At the very least, behavior that is representative of how the client gets stuck in her life remains unaddressed.

Aside from obvious signs such as your client scowling at you or offering up some direct argument or protest, behaviors such as sighing, avoiding eye contact, shifting in the chair or other restless movement, glancing at a clock or watch, changing the subject, or getting very "heady" (talking at the level of ideas rather than engaging in a more authentic exchange), as well as incongruence between verbal content and behavior (such as smiling or laughing when it doesn't fit)—all are possible indications that something is going on that could block forward movement. Your own reactions are excellent informants as well: Are you working too hard? Trying to manage your own anxiety? Getting distracted? Becoming angry? Intellectualizing with the client? Moving on too quickly? Or trying to cajole, persuade, or appease the client? All these responses may indicate there is something clinically important going on in the room that should be explored. As I said, most therapists I've worked with pick up on these sorts of signals. What can sometimes be lacking is then drawing this perception into full awareness and making it a focus of the session.

WHAT TO DO

In the scenarios and example dialogues that follow, you will likely notice a common strategy in working with various barriers to treatment. Primarily, it is one of leaning in and directly addressing whatever is occurring in a way that is consistent with ACT principles. This strategy involves a consideration of function, recognizing and working against any avoidance of the issue (yours and your client's), and speaking to what is occurring in a transparent fashion. As mentioned above, a common misstep is when therapists ignore or try to override client behavior that poses a problem, often continuing with this strategy until the behavior in question has grown to the point where all forward movement has ceased. While such a situation can be overcome, it can be more effective to proactively attend to those "light taps on the pedal."

Scenario: The therapist and client are following up on a topic the client introduced during the previous session, which was whether or not to accompany his wife to her company party—something he was not keen to do. The client has just stated that he went to the party and that it was "boring as hell, just like [he] knew it would be."

Therapist:	"Wow. So this is where willingness comes in. You chose to go with your wife to her party even though you didn't really feel like it. Sounds like your mind continued to hand you stuff about how boring it was going to be, and how you don't like to try to make small talk and all that, but you opted to go anyway."
Client	*(unsmiling, looking away):* "Yeah, well, what was I gonna do?"
Therapist:	"Do you mean what were your choices?"
Client	*(long sigh):* "I guess. I mean, I either had to go and be bored out my skull or have her be all pissed off...."
Therapist:	"So either way you were looking at some probable discomfort. And you made the choice to go with her to the party."
Client	*(sighs again, folds his arms, and looks bored):* "Yep."

(Here is where I have seen therapists plow on, despite many indications that the client is not where the therapist is hoping he will be. That is, the client doesn't seem much invested in the ideas being discussed, and his wording, tone, and nonverbal behaviors suggest he is not taking the same positive stance as the therapist regarding his decision to attend the party. It can be tempting in these situations to try even harder to put the client where you want him, but doing so would likely result in further truculence. Likewise, it would be a misstep to simply accept his "yep" as acquiescence and move on. That sort of move would miss the clinical opportunity presented here. Let's pick this up again:)

Therapist:	"So either way you were looking at some probable discomfort. And you made the choice to go with her to the party."
Client	*(sighs again, folds his arms, and looks bored):* "Yep."
Therapist:	"Can you tell me what that sigh was about?"
Client:	"Huh?"
Therapist:	"Just now, when I pointed out how you made a choice to go to the party, you gave a big sigh."
Client:	"Huh." *(Sighs again.)*
Therapist	*(smiling gently but leaning in):* "Right there. What is that sigh saying?"
Client	*(shifts impatiently):* "I dunno. Just tired I guess."
Therapist:	"Hmmm." *(Pauses as he allows himself to really contact the moment.)* "You know, it feels like something else to me. I mean, not to say that you aren't tired, but it feels like there's something else going on in here." *(Client is silent).* "Is there anything that is not being said right now?" *(Waits.)*
Client:	"I dunno. I'm just not that into it today, I guess."
Therapist	*(long pause, considering):* "Yeah." *(Still thinking it over.)* "For me it feels like I'm trying too hard. Like I keep pointing to something I think is important, trying to get you to see it that way too. And I'm realizing that just because I think it's important doesn't mean you will."

(I admit this is a little bit of a tricky move. That is, the first couple of sentences are pretty transparent, with the therapist modeling experiential acceptance by getting present and articulating his own experience. The last sentence, while arguably "true," has multiple functions. It continues to speak to what is happening in the room, but also is aimed at disarming the client. When I find myself in a bit of a power struggle with clients, I simply hand the matter over, whatever we are supposedly struggling about—in this case, whether or not his decision to go the party was significant. Quite often the client responds by dropping the struggle as well. In other words, there's no longer anything to push against. The remark also points to the idea that the client and no one else is in charge of his life—an idea that will be extended shortly.)

Client	*(hesitates):* "I guess I just don't know where all this is going. So I went to the party, big deal, you know? It didn't change the fact that I hated every minute of it."

Therapist	(nods, listening attentively and holding the moment): "Yeah." (Pause.) "Thanks for sharing that with me, by the way. It helps." (*This comment is aimed at reinforcing the client for moving into what is happening rather than avoiding it. Remember that whether or not this statement functions as intended, however, depends upon its actual impact. If the client then more frequently expresses himself in such moments, the statement functioned as a reinforcer. It's possible that the client would experience such a statement as aversive, and be even less likely to share what was really going on with him in the future. This is why it is important to observe the actual effect of interventions, regardless of intention. The "it helps" is aimed at remaining out of a power struggle and is part of the ongoing effort to level the playing field between therapist and client. Similarly, how this comment functions depends on its actual impact on the therapy.*)
Therapist	(continuing): "Is it kind of like, 'If these decisions don't result in me being less miserable, what's the point?'"
Client:	"Exactly."
Therapist:	"I see." (Pause.) "And of course, only you would have the answer to that one." (*With this comment, the therapist remains steadfastly out of a power struggle. He is refraining from teaching, telling, or persuading the client, while also baiting the hook.*)
Client:	"What do you mean?"
Therapist	(taking his time): "Well, as we just recognized, it certainly isn't going to work if I'm trying to convince you to value something. In this situation I see a great deal, but in the end this is about *your* life. Only you can determine if there is, in fact, a point to the choice you made." (*The therapist continues to steer clear of a power struggle while being up front about having a point of view. The message is also directly given that the client is fully responsible for his life—his actions, and what he chooses or doesn't choose to value. This last objective stems from considering the overall function of the client's behavior so far in the session. A hypothesis is that the client may be pushing against the therapist and ACT itself as an avoidant strategy. That is, as we will be discussing shortly, there can be something disquieting about being able to choose in this way, and the client may be pitting himself against the entire idea. He may be pushing against the implications of the idea being discussed as well as the emotional discomfort he is experiencing in the moment. Rather than letting this avoidance strategy work, the therapist steps out of the struggle and*)

leans in to the present discomfort, while also leaving the client with the dilemma of personal responsibility.)

Client   (*considering*): "I just…I really hate that kind of stuff, work parties…."

Therapist: "I get it! And I wonder if you were hoping that this therapy would change that somehow."

Client: "I guess so." (*Pause.*) "But I really don't see that changing."

Therapist: "Well, it hasn't so far."

Client: "And I don't see my wife changing, though that would be nice. It would be great if she could just do her thing and let me do mine."

Therapist: "And how likely do you think it is that your reactions to her when she's disappointed or mad at you will change?" (*It is very important to keep the focus on the client—his reactions, his responses—rather than on something external, such as his wife's behavior. The client wants his wife to change so that he doesn't experience his reactions to her displeasure or disappointment. When it's set up this way, he is dependent on her changing, as opposed to seeing that he can make value-driven choices regardless of his wife's behavior or his own internal discomfort.*)

Client: "Not very likely—been like this for almost twenty-two years…."

Therapist: "So that leaves you in a bind. The same bind we talked about when you first came in. You're in a hole, and either direction you dig you just make a bigger hole."

Client: (*Sighs.*)

Therapist   (*leans in*): "This is where all the things you and I have talked about come into play. And what is happening for you right now is extremely important. It highlights both what's possible for you and what can stand in your way." (*Having defused the power struggle and undermined the avoidance occurring in the session, the therapist cuts to the chase.*)

Client: (*Listening, quite focused now.*)

Therapist: "We've talked a great deal about the control agenda—the struggle to not have uncomfortable thoughts and feelings—and how that agenda has stood in the way of some of the things you deeply want for yourself. One of the first values you mentioned was having good relationships and especially a loving, vital marriage. Last weekend you made a choice that—from where I'm sitting, anyway—took you closer to that particular value. But it's as though you are saying you only want to take that step if it feels good. You are right back in the service of the control agenda, rather than in the service of your values." (*So, there are times— when you and your client have fallen into a power struggle, for example—when it is effective to emphasize that you realize he gets to be however he is and make whatever choices he makes. However, you as the therapist also get to have your own opinions and observations. Not only that; as the therapist it is important that you share these— the client has come to your therapy room for a reason, after all. When the timing is appropriate, I find it most effective to state these sorts of observations plainly and unapologetically.*)

Client   (*thinks*): "Huh. Yeah, I see that. At the time I wanted to make her happy, but then I got pissed off when the party really did suck."

Therapist: "Yeah! It would be great if every time we made a move toward our values we were rewarded with wonderful thoughts and feelings, but that's not the case."

Client: "No, I guess not. Then again, I probably would have felt even worse if I'd stayed home. Guilty or something."

Therapist: "That may be the case. But truly, from where I stand, it's not about the feelings. Feelings come and go. This is about not being enslaved by the thoughts or feelings of the moment, or trapped in the struggle of trying to avoid uncomfortable thoughts or feelings. This is about making choices based upon intention, on how you want to be in the world. This is about how you want to be in your marriage."

(*I have seen many therapists miss this one. That is, there is a tendency for us beleaguered therapists to jump onto a statement like the one the client just made about feeling worse if he chose not to go, thinking that will facilitate value-driven choices in the future. Example: "Yeah! You might have felt even worse staying at home than you did by going to the party!" But this statement supports the idea that feelings are what matter and that positive feelings are the goal—a big part of what has been keeping the client stuck. Better to maintain focus on making value-driven, not feeling-driven, choices. Notice also that in the last couple of exchanges, the therapist subtly qualified his observations [for example, "from where I'm sitting, anyway" and "from where I stand"]. This is a way to be very real and direct while acknowledging the client's own, perhaps different, perspective. It helps sidestep a power struggle and also serves as a reminder to the therapist that there*) is no ontological truth that needs to be proven here [there is no "right" perspective], which in turn helps therapists walk the fine line between offering straightforward observations and persuading or arguing with clients.)

Client: "Yeah, okay."

Therapist: "And this was why I was excited by what I saw in this situation. That you chose to go to the party, taking all the stuff you had around it right along with you." (*Still being very up front and authentic, and tying it all together.*)

Client: "Yeah." (*Hesitates.*) "I was just still mad, I think, when you asked me about it."

Therapist: "Yeah, and you get to be mad about it! You get to be bored at the party, and mad about being bored, and bored with being mad, and still see that you have the ability to make a choice."

Client   (*laughing*): "Yeah....It all sounds sort of silly now."

Therapist: "We are silly beings. We are also very powerful beings." (*Irreverence both disempowers and normalizes these kinds of evaluations. There is both compassion and excitement here, an underscoring of what it is to be human.*)

Client: "Yeah...no kidding."

So being in touch with the present moment is invaluable in helping you recognize client behaviors that can stand in the way of progress, especially if you are careful to include your own experience in the picture. Once you are in a stance of noticing both the client's behavior and your own, you can begin to consider its function, which in turn guides your response (and the impact of that guides your next response). In the next section we will explore some of the more common client behaviors that can stand in the way of clinical progress, with the idea that familiarity with these will help you tag and work with them should they arise. However, continued awareness of, and moving toward, whatever is happening in the session at a process level will continue to be your best guide.

COMMON BARRIERS TO BEHAVIORAL CHANGE

The innumerable behaviors that can impede therapeutic progress are as varied as are people themselves. Nonetheless, there are a few particular client behaviors that seem to show up frequently in ACT and that are quite challenging. In the following sections we will examine some of these behaviors and explore ways to work with them that keep things moving forward.

REASONS AS CAUSES

Any ACT therapist can speak to how steadfastly clients can cling to their reasons. In fact, this tendency is one of the chief culprits standing in the way of clients applying ACT in their daily lives. However, a common misperception by ACT therapists is to see "reasons as causes" as always problematic. In many cases, it is useful to frame things in this way (for example, "I can't go for a run today because I sprained my ankle," or "I am going to apologize to my brother because I value relationships.") What becomes unworkable is when clients find reasons in terms of their psychological experiences (such as "I am not feeling motivated") and turn these into causes for unworkable behavior (for example, "I don't have enough confidence to apply for that promotion"). It is this tendency that we target in ACT. In the following sections I'll highlight some of the factors that can contribute to clients' unwillingness to let go of this problematic notion.

TIMING

As discussed in chapter 4, the timing of an intervention plays a significant role in its effectiveness, often determining whether the intervention will serve its intended purpose, or even whether it will be received at all. I have observed that clients' receptivity to the idea that reasons are not causes is particularly sensitive to when this concept is introduced, a point I also mentioned when discussing language in chapter 6. It may be the therapist has simply introduced this piece too soon, with the result that the entire concept falls flat, the main point does not seem to land or is misunderstood, or the whole idea is flat-out rejected by the client. In many instances it isn't so much that the client isn't following what the therapist is attempting to explain, but that the response to it is a "Yeah, but…" To reiterate points made in chapter 6, helping clients learn to observe and defuse from thoughts, and building skill in accessing self-as-context, really helps them wrap their minds around the notion that such reasons are not causes. When they realize that there is a Self that is intact and larger than all the stuff their minds are handing them, clients have less need to cling to reasons as justifications for unworkable behavior. The reasons aren't needed in order to be "okay." Once that self-as-context piece begins to fall into place, even if only a little, clients are more open to the idea that the behavioral choices they make (and have made) are not actually tied to all their reasons.

NOT CAUSAL VS. NOT REAL

A common sticking point around reasons-are-not-causes is that a client can hear the idea of defusing from thoughts as the same as saying that the thoughts didn't occur. The client is caught up in the awareness of having had "real" thoughts and feelings about something (for example, that he was so down about losing his job and feeling so low energy that all he could do all week was sit on the couch and watch TV) and hears "reasons are not causes" as an invalidation of that very real experience. He essentially checks his memory, recontacts that experience (including what his mind handed him around it), and holds that as "Truth," rather than considering that there might also have been something else to be seen in that particular moment. As in the above example, we are striving for the client to understand that although he was indeed feeling down and listless, and though his mind was indeed telling him he was too depressed to do anything but sit on the couch, that thought was not *literally* true. He could, in fact, have engaged in other behavior. This confusion around what is real versus what is literally true is why I encourage ACT therapists to tackle the distinction directly when working with their clients on reasons-are-not-causes. I suggest that they make sure to explicitly state that the thoughts, feelings, or sensations in question are *very* real, often very painful experiences, regardless of the degree to which they represent literal truth. This approach typically lessens clients' need to defend their reasons, as their experience has already been validated by the therapist. Subsequently they are more willing to make room for the idea that there is something else to be seen beyond what their minds are telling them.

THE BURDEN OF FREEDOM

Over time I have observed that many clients get a certain look when they begin to grasp that thoughts and feelings are not in charge—an expression best described as dismay. There is real significance to this reaction. That is, it is powerful, is it not, to decouple our behavioral choices from all the mind-generated reason-giving? Is it not liberating to understand that we aren't actually tied to everything our minds tell us about why we can or can't do this or that, or how this or that caused us to do X, Y, or Z? So why, rather than excitement or relief when faced with this realization, do so many clients react with alarm, wariness, or even flat-out reluctance? The term "burden of freedom" always comes to mind at such times, although I am using it a bit differently than as originally meant by Fromm (1941). For me, "burden of freedom" perfectly points to the dilemma of being fully responsible for the choices we make. Every choice. On one hand this realization is freeing; on the other it means we are fully on the hook for our lives. Reasons and excuses, while convenient, are not actually to blame. Bummer!

On top of this rather existential dilemma, many clients are fused with very painful thoughts about their own worth or basic competence, so that the idea of being behaviorally free in this way comes hand in hand with the possibility of failure. For these clients, *being* stuck can seem preferable to *feeling* incompetent. Another way to say this is that these individuals have been experiencing reinforcing aspects of unworkable behavior, while not giving themselves the opportunity to experience the rewards of value-driven behavior.

There are a few things I have found helpful in dealing with this one. One is to put the burden of freedom conundrum right on the table, giving voice to what might be going on for the client in a way that normalizes and defuses the fear. Doing so can pave the way for exploring how the client's behavior may be functioning as avoidance (in other words, pushing against the idea of being free to choose). Another is to revisit the costs of being fused with reasons-are-causes, being sure to make this an open discussion rather than one in which you are trying to convince the client. Building the client's behavioral repertoire (to that "larger pattern of committed action") is a gradual process, so it is important to help clients to make even small steps in valued directions, and then to explicitly highlight what they are actually doing in those moments—in other words, that they are not being driven by thoughts and feelings but rather acting with intention. Finally, to maintain my own compassion, it has been helpful to remind myself of how very terrifying it can be to let go of what we hold to be true, even if that very "truth" has made our lives small.

This Is Too Hard

ACT takes a lot of our preconceived ideas and turns them on their head. And not the little ones, mind you, but the biggies: what it means to be human, what is "normal," what constitutes a good life, and the like. Clients are disabused of the notion that there happiness is a destination out there they can reach if they can just get things together. They lose their (psychological) reasons as justifications for unworkable choices and are left squarely on the spot for determining who they are going to be in the world. Whew! This can all seem overwhelming, especially considering that all this upheaval occurs over a short span of time relative to that spent receiving very different messages. Clients can sometimes feel as though it is all just too much.

I have found it helpful to point out some of the many ways in which clients already make valued choices in their lives. I might ask, for example, if they've ever had the experience of the alarm going off in the morning and wanting to toss it in the trash and keep sleeping. (They have.) I then point out that if they, in fact, rose and got out of bed anyway, thoughts and feelings must not be in charge. Similarly I might ask if they've ever felt like not coming to therapy (they have), and point out that when they choose to come anyway it is in the service of a larger value—what they are about in therapy—as opposed to the thoughts and feelings of the moment. Clients who are in recovery from addiction, in particular, have experiences of making value-driven choices despite the presence of uncomfortable thoughts and feelings (such as urges to use), often on a daily basis. In short, clients have often not translated these sorts of day-to-day actions into ACT terms, and therefore haven't made the connection that their ability to move through these processes (acceptance, being present, and choosing a valued action, in short) is applicable in all areas of their lives. I also make sure to make the point that they already have everything they need to live a vital, meaningful life. Not a single thought has to change, not a single feeling. They do not have to be more, better, or different after all. Even though this last message is an inherent part of the therapy, I find it useful to pull it out again explicitly when moving into committed action. It is not unusual to be able to see this piece actually slide into place for the client.

Once, in a moment of clarity, I realized that I simply needed to be willing to pay the "discomfort toll" in order to live the life that I envisioned. For some reason this notion stayed with me and I find myself passing it on to clients and other ACT providers. Perhaps it is helpful because it demystifies and simplifies what is needed to live a valued life, bringing it down to the moment-by-moment choices that will continually present themselves. The following dialogue illustrates how you might introduce this idea:

Client:	"Yeah, I really want to stop procrastinating with the school stuff. Applications are due this Friday!"
Therapist:	"What do you think is needed? What are you hoping will change around procrastinating?"
Client:	"I just want to be able to dive right in, you know? Just get it done."
Therapist:	"And what is stopping you from doing that?"
Client	*(pauses):* "Well, probably nothing, when I think about it."
Therapist:	"It seemed like you were about to say something else."
Client:	"Well, I was going to give you all this stuff, like reasons why I don't do it, but that's just what my mind hands me, as you would say. I probably have been waiting for my feelings about it all to change so that it isn't so damn hard."
Therapist:	"How awesome that you see all that! You have to be able to defuse from your thoughts to see them so clearly."
Client	*(half laughs, sighs):* "Yeah, well, if I'm totally honest I just don't want all this anxiety. School has always been such a loaded issue for me."
Therapist:	"Well, your mind certainly hands you a load around it, that's for sure."
Client	*(laughs):* "Yeah."
Therapist:	"In terms of the anxiety, it comes down to whether you're willing to be uncomfortable in order to get that degree. You will come up against that choice again and again. We all do. It's like you're

driving in the direction of your values, and up comes a tollbooth. The toll, the price you are being asked to pay, is comfort. Are you willing to give up being comfortable in order to move ahead? Or will you choose to be comfortable even if that means standing still or even turning around?"

| Client: | "I've had enough of standing still. It sucks." |
| | |

Client: "I've had enough of standing still. It sucks."

Therapist: "Yeah, that's the thing. Even if we choose to turn away from something because it's uncomfortable, that doesn't mean discomfort doesn't find us anyway."

Client: "I may as well go in the direction I want."

Therapist: "That act of *choosing*, of moving with intention even if discomfort comes along, is a powerful move."

Client: "Yeah!"

The point I am hoping clients will see with this simile is that ACT is not about having some grand new plan or algorithm for life. It is about the moment-by-moment process wherein clients, if they are present and paying attention, will know in what direction their values lie. In that moment, they will choose either to pay the toll required to head in that direction or not. The really good news is that values are inviolable. They stand, fully available, whether they have never been pursued or whether they have been followed every moment of every day. Just as we can, in any given moment, choose to remain comfortable, so we can choose to accept what moving forward may bring. Values cannot be taken away, and fortunately for us this particular tollbooth is open 24/7.

Feeling Wronged

I have had a lot of time to contemplate what is often referred to as "hanging on to the victim role," since a chunk of my career has been in the service of treating survivors of interpersonal trauma. These individuals have indeed been victimized and the effects have been devastating. They have every reason to feel wronged, as they have experienced a terrible injustice—in many cases several, piled one on top of another. For a long time I struggled with how to reconcile my awareness of this fact—that these individuals had been significantly injured by another—with how clearly the subsequent tendency to hold on to "I was wronged" or "I am injured" stood in the way of living a good life. The corpus delicti analogy, detailed in earlier texts (Walser & Westrup, 2007) is a powerful way to connect with clients on this issue. That is because it frames the functional aspect of being a victim (in other words, the purpose it is serving for the client) very compassionately yet clearly. The client's need for the injustice(s) to be "seen" is portrayed as completely understandable, in turn creating room for frank discussion of what "being the evidence" is costing the client. Once the corpus delicti analogy has been introduced, it can repeatedly be called upon as a reference point when identification with being a victim shows up.

Therapist:	"Do you watch *CSI*?"
Client:	"What? The TV show?"
Therapist:	"Yeah."
Client:	"I've seen it...."
Therapist:	"Have you heard the term 'corpus delicti'? It comes up now and then in crime shows."
Client:	"No...."
Therapist:	"It refers to needing a body in order to prove that a murder was committed. *Corpus delicti* is Latin for 'the body of the murder.'"
Client:	"Oh. Okay."
Therapist:	"The idea behind corpus delicti can come into play when you have experienced a trauma, especially an interpersonal trauma." (*Client is listening.*) "Sometimes, when something has been done to you that is not okay, it can seem like there needs to be a body to prove that it happened. Like if there's no body, no evidence, it didn't happen, or maybe it wasn't so bad."
Client:	"Yeah!"
Therapist:	"And especially if there was a sense that there was no reckoning, no justice served, the desire for there to be some sort of evidence or 'body' can be huge."
Client:	"Yeah, I can relate to that."
Therapist:	"So that fits for you? Can you think of ways that you have been, that you are being, the 'evidence' for what happened to you?"
Client:	"I'm not sure...."
Therapist:	"There's one that occurs to me. That is, you've been pretty clear that you can't trust people anymore because of what happened. In that sense 'no more trust' could be serving as evidence of what happened."

Client:	"Yeah. And how I can't be in a relationship anymore."
Therapist:	"Yeah, exactly. That's some major evidence there."

And so on. By using this analogy, the therapist is directly pointing to the function of the client's self-concept as victim. But far from painting this self-concept as pathological—as is often the case with "hanging on to a victim role"—the response is framed as understandable, even "normal." The way has been paved for direct discussion of what the response is costing the client, and the stage is set for work on defusing from this idea and other relational frames (for example, that living a good life means the trauma didn't happen or wasn't that bad, or that living a good life lets the perpetrator off the hook, which in turn means that the trauma didn't happen or wasn't that bad). Once this corpus delicti stake in the ground has been set, it can be repeatedly yet compassionately pointed to when identification with being a victim shows up.

BEING RIGHT

This barrier is quite similar to the "I was wronged" idea just discussed, and also to the "seductiveness of 'should'" barrier explored in the next section. That is, all three represent fusion with unworkable rules or self-concepts. For this reason I'll not go into a lot of detail here, as you should approach all three similarly; but I do want to share a couple of thoughts on how to work with a client who is very fused with the importance of being right. Most of us would agree that the experience of being right can be very reinforcing. Helping clients come into contact with the costs of this behavior and how it might move them away from their values is a key strategy. Many clients also view moving off this being-right position as concession, as a devaluing or lessening of themselves. While obviously defusion and self-as-context are important processes to target when working with such individuals, I have also found it helpful at times to come at this another way.

Scenario: The client, a very opinionated man, has been telling the therapist how much of a jerk his brother-in-law is.

Client:	"...But Jack takes the cake. My god, you should listen to him! That guy's got an opinion on everything. That's why I don't go over there anymore. Not even holidays. In fact, they asked me over for Thanksgiving last month and I was like, 'I'll pass!'"
Therapist:	"So the whole family got together for Thanksgiving except for you?"
Client:	"I assume so."
Therapist:	"If I've got this right, you can't stand your brother-in-law, so you stay away from get-togethers that include him?"

Client:	"That's right. Last time we were together we got in a huge argument over same-sex marriage. It got ugly—everybody got all mad at *me* when I didn't even start it! Like I said, the guy's an idiot."
Therapist:	"What a drag. Is this your younger sister, the one with twins?"
Client:	"Yeah, Jennifer. She's cool—in fact, we've always been the closest of us kids. And Ryan and Brianne—the twins—are great. Too bad they've got such an a-hole for a father!"
Therapist:	"So if he weren't there, or if he just didn't say or do stuff that drives you nuts, you would spend time with your sister and her kids?"
Client:	"Sure! When he was overseas it was great, but he's back for good now. Too bad!"
Therapist:	"Yeah! For me the toughest part about this is that he has so much power!"
Client	*(taken aback):* "What do you mean? What power? He doesn't have power over *me*, if that's what you're saying!"
Therapist:	"You were just saying that whether or not you spend time with family—family you seem to value quite a bit—depends on your brother-in-law's behavior. Whether or not you spend time with your sister and her family depends on whether he's going to be there or not. How and what he says determines whether you engage in a destructive argument, even whether you go at all."
Client:	"Okay, yeah, I see that. But he doesn't know how to leave well enough alone! He deliberately baits me. And he has no idea what he's talking about. None."
Therapist:	"So because he baits the hook, you have to bite. That's what I mean—his actions seem to determine yours. It sounds like you need him to be a certain way so that you don't feel upset, and your actions then depend on whether or not he does that."
Client:	"So what am I supposed to do? Just sit there and take it?"
Therapist:	"Hmmm. Maybe it would be useful to talk about how you might take your power back here. And that's not going to be about your brother-in-law. He is who he is. But wouldn't it be cool if, no matter what he said or did, whether he were there or not, *you* were being how *you* want to be? What would it be like if you had

the power to make moment-by-moment choices that are in line with your values, rather than being in reaction to whatever he's doing or not doing?"

Rather than working with the many examples of fusion in the above exchange (for example, that the client can't tolerate his brother-in-law) the therapist targets the larger issue of how notions of right and wrong likely function for the client, at least in this relationship. That is, being right is likely a way to feel in control—to feel okay—and the client's investment in this feeling could stand in the way of working productively with the issue. By turning this strategy on its head and pointing out that rather than being in control, the client is being controlled, the therapist creates an opening for the other work. She can then wind back around and work more productively on defusion and self-as-context, having framed value-driven action as a way to be in control rather than controlled. You can imagine meaningful and hugely freeing work being done around the idea that the client is still okay even if he feels wrong, not in control, vulnerable, and so forth. Put simply, sometimes it just works well to redirect the client's desire for control to a domain (in other words, his behavioral choices) where he might actually succeed.

The Seductiveness of "Should"

I once read a horrible story about how hunters used to trap raccoons. They would drill a hole in a log, put something shiny in the bottom of the hole, and then pound nails in diagonally so that the sharp points were at a downward slant around the hole. The coon would reach in to grasp the shiny object, its small paw easily evading the nails on the way in, but once it held the object there was no way to pull out of the log without being impaled by the nails. Instead of dropping the desired object and freeing itself, the coon would hang on tight, self-trapped until the hunter returned.

I am sorry to pass such a sad tale along to you! But the image has really stayed with me, a graphic parallel to what I've seen clients (and myself, actually) do again and again. That is, we cling to what we want, all the "shoulds," even though doing so keeps us painfully stuck. One reason for this self-defeating tendency has already been explored, which is fusion with reasons as causes. There is another element to this, though, which is simple desire. We *want* it to be so. We want that shiny object! We *want* to feel good; we *want* there to be some magic key to a magical life; we *want* life to be fair, to be orderly; we want, want, want. And so, our minds insist, it *should* be so! I have found it helpful to talk about this thought process directly with clients, agreeing wholeheartedly how things "should" be, and then pointing out who is ultimately paying the price here. There are lots of metaphors that can be used to highlight this trap: it's as though the client is standing beside the road with a big "It shouldn't be this way" sign as life rolls on by, for example. It is important not to fall into attempting to eliminate or tweak the content of the should (getting the client to change his sign, in keeping with the metaphor) but to stay at the level of function—how it's the standing with the sign, at the cost of moving forward, that is so problematic. The client can carry the same sign, while moving on to do what works.

The Homework Problem

A common therapeutic struggle is around homework. I'm referring to ACT-related worksheets or questionnaires, exercises such as daily mindfulness practice, and "bold moves" or other applied behavioral commitments—in other words, any agreed-upon behavioral task that is to occur outside the therapy room within a specified time frame, most typically before the next therapy session. Although the word "homework" might never be used, I use that term here to capture the idea that this is work to be done outside of the session, and is intended to facilitate therapeutic progress.

A common challenge therapists face is when a client does not do the agreed-upon homework, or does not complete it. Clients provide many reasons for not following through, many of which exemplify the thinking that has kept them stuck in their lives. The most common misstep I have observed therapists make around the issue of homework is to unintentionally collude with the client, supporting behavioral processes that decrease psychological flexibility. This collusion can take many forms, including sensing that the client has not completed the homework and therefore not asking about it, inquiring about the homework then quickly backing off when the client reports it wasn't done, working to make it okay for the client that the homework was not done, or quietly dropping the entire topic of homework and not bringing it up again for the rest of therapy. I see all these responses as potentially problematic, for reasons that you can probably guess at this point: In essence they can support a costly system, a system that doesn't ever fully go away and that will continue to threaten value-based behavioral choices. That is, while reason-giving will certainly continue, buying reasons as causal (as in "I need to feel motivated before going to the gym") in many instances functions as a significant behavioral constraint.

When working on a homework issue with a client, I keep the above points firmly in mind. Chiefly, I remind myself that it will not serve the client well to align with unworkable reason-giving or experiential avoidance. That said, as always in clinical work, other considerations are involved as well—such as whether to fight this particular battle at this point in time. I know of many therapists, myself included on many occasions, who choose not to assign formal (that is, structured or more specified) homework assignments during the therapy for various reasons. While it might be interesting to explore the efficacy of such decisions, the point I want to make here is that if you and the client *have* made a commitment to do a particular homework assignment—to carry out some behavioral task—it is important to follow through in a way that is consistent with the model (in other words, that supports rather than works against psychological flexibility).

Scenario: The therapist and client have just completed a mindfulness exercise to begin the session.

Therapist:	"So…let's start with talking about the willingness sheets I gave you at the end of last session—how did that go?"
Client:	"You mean those worksheets?"
Therapist:	"Yeah, the two willingness worksheets."
Client:	"I started to do them…."

(Therapist waits.)

Client:	"I don't know. I just don't like doing that sort of stuff very much. Reminds me of school and homework or something."
Therapist:	"Were these sorts of thoughts showing up at the time? Not liking it, the homework thing?"
Client:	"Um, well, I was putting it off, then when I picked it up I was noticing how much I don't like doing that kind of stuff."
Therapist:	"I see. So there was that dislike sort of feeling….Any other thoughts or feelings that you remember?"
Client:	"Just, I remember thinking it was sort of stupid….Sorry."
Therapist:	"What are you sorry for?"
Client:	"I don't know….I know you're just trying to help. I've just never done well with that type of stuff."

(Therapist sits quietly, thinking this through.)

Client	*(smiling nervously):* "What are you thinking? Am I a bad client?"
Therapist:	"I'm just noticing all the stuff that shows up for you around this. That last question, for example—whether you are a bad client."
Client:	"Well, I feel like a kid or something. Like I've done something wrong."
Therapist:	"Yeah, so there's some more—feeling like a kid, thoughts that you might be a bad client, worry that you've done something wrong by stating how you feel about it…."
Client:	"Yeah, see? This is why I hate it!"
Therapist:	"Yeah, you are really working hard right now—can you feel that?"

Client	(pauses, gets in touch with her feelings a bit): "Yes!"
Therapist:	"Let's see if we can bring that awareness even more front and center. In other words, let's just notice everything going on right now—all the thoughts showing up, the emotions, even physical sensations."
Client	(sits): "Wow, I am really tense. Like I have a big rock in my stomach or something."
Therapist:	"Perfect. Yeah, just notice that—see if you can breathe in around it, sort of hold it gently."
Client	(breathes): "Okay."
Therapist:	"I notice some tension in my body, too. A kind of ratcheting up of energy."

(Both sit and breathe.)

Client:	"So, what now?"
Therapist:	"Can you get at what you are after with that question?"
Client:	"What do you mean?"
Therapist:	"When you asked me, 'What now?' I wonder if you were trying to get out of the moment a bit."
Client:	"Yeah, I guess so! I feel weird."
Therapist:	"Yeah."

(Both sit.)

Therapist	(eventually continuing): "It's interesting how you sort of looked to me to help get you out of it."
Client:	"What do you mean?"
Therapist:	"When you asked, 'What now?' I felt pulled to give you an answer. Like I needed to get us moving forward and out of what was going on right then. Was that going on for you?"
Client:	"I suppose...."
Therapist:	"I noticed something else here; did you?"
Client:	"Notice what?"

Therapist:	"Well, something funny seemed to be going on around the whole homework issue. Something about this feels off." (*Considers*). "You know, when you were talking about how you felt you were in school or something, and when you apologized to me for not liking it—even now, when you asked if you were a bad client—all that sort of suggests that this was something coming from me. Like I was making you do homework or something."
Client	(*thinks it over*): "Well, I know you aren't *making* me do it. I do feel like it's something you want me to do, though."
Therapist:	"Hmmm." (*Thinks this over.*) "Yeah, that's fair. I mean, I have found that when clients do these sorts of worksheets outside of session it helps move things forward. So in that sense I'm for it. But I don't think it will work too well if doing things like that isn't something you've bought into."
Client:	"Yeah. I just don't like them."
Therapist:	"So what do you want to do?"
Client:	"What?"
Therapist:	"So there are the thoughts and feelings you have around them, but those feelings and thoughts aren't in charge. That is, you could conceivably decide that there was some point to doing them, and choose to do them, even if dislike or whatever showed up." (*The therapist is being very careful not to take responsibility for the client's choice by asking the client what she wants to do with this, and yet manages to make the important point that the client has the option to make a choice based on something other than the thoughts and feelings associated with doing homework.*)
Client	(*thinks*): "Yeah, I guess so."
Therapist:	"I think it's important to be intentional about this, whatever you decide—that is, to be clear that you are choosing to work on something specific outside of session, or to be clear that you are choosing not to go that route."
Client:	"Okay." (*Pause.*) "I think I'd rather not do the homework thing."
Therapist:	"Okay. And, if that changes at some point, just let me know."
Client:	"Okay."

Therapist	(upon reflection): "You know, I'm realizing that this is something that will come up again, especially as we are further along in the therapy. That is, this therapy is about getting moving in your life. There's not much point to it if it doesn't extend to your life outside the session. In that sense, it's all about the 'homework.'"
Client:	"I understand that. I just don't want to be filling out sheets and stuff like that."
Therapist:	"Got it."

Although it is quite possible that this sort of direct conversation around homework might end up with the client opting to continue working with worksheets and the like, I wanted to demonstrate another possibility—that the client could opt out. Again, remembering that this whole therapy/life thing is by choice—the client's choice—helps therapists refrain from stepping into persuading, arguing, or trying to convince the client. Those approaches pull for clients to fuse with a therapist-provided "should," which in turn detracts from the ultimate goal of increased psychological flexibility. This is not to say that the therapist needs to somehow be out of the picture. I have consistently found that when therapists allow themselves to claim their own opinions and feelings about what is happening with homework, they are better able to maintain a therapeutic stance around the issue. Some of the tension around homework comes from therapists trying to outmaneuver clients—to somehow get the client to want to do homework while attempting not to convey any sort of personal investment. It can be more effective to go with transparency here. The therapist demonstrates being able to hold it all: her desire for the client to do ACT-related work outside of session, her reactions when assigned homework is not done (or is), and her recognition that clients get to choose what they do with their time.

In short, remaining steadfast within the ACT model will help you refrain from colluding with a client's avoidance and other unworkable behaviors around homework. Your clinical judgment will continue to guide you as you work with each unique client from within that framework. For example, while in the above scenario the therapist appears to have felt it beneficial to accept (for now) the line the client was drawing around homework, it is also quite possible that an effective move would have been to confront the fusion going on even more directly. The following exchange, using the same situation, demonstrates pressing a bit more.

Therapist:	"I think it is important to be intentional about this, whatever you decide—that is, to be clear that you are choosing to work on something specific outside of session, or to be clear that you are choosing not to go that route."
Client:	"Okay. I think I'd rather not do the homework thing."

Therapist:	"I want to be careful here not to fall into trying to persuade you, because as we've just said, that starts to feel like I'm making you do something, rather than it coming from you. At the same time, there is something to see here that seems important."
Client:	"Okay...."
Therapist:	"On one hand this might not seem like a big deal, whether or not you fill out some worksheets, but on the other, it represents both the trap and the possibility you will encounter your entire life."

(Client seems a bit dubious but is listening.)

Therapist:	"It's not so much about the worksheets. It's about you buying what your mind is handing you. All the reasons for not doing them. Completing or not completing a worksheet might seem like no big deal, but it's the same mind—your mind, handing you some of the same reasons, for not living the way you say you want to be living. For not finishing that degree, for not reaching out to that friend, for not applying for that job."
Client:	"Yeah...I know."
Therapist:	"So while doing a worksheet like that might clarify something we're working on in here, which in this case happens to be exactly what we're discussing—willingness—the more significant message for you is to see that you have the *ability to choose to do it*. That because of some larger commitment to yourself, a value around what you're doing here, you choose to push through, you *can* push through."
Client:	"Okay. I hadn't thought of it that way, but I get it." *(Pause.)* "Let's keep doing the homework."
Therapist:	"Of course I'm glad to hear you say that, but I need to check to see if this feels like it is coming from you or if you are doing it because I want you to."
Client:	"Can't it be both?"
Therapist:	"Bravo! Absolutely. In fact, I see that question was me trying to get rid of anxiety I have around being too pushy or something. But yeah, exactly—you might have a bunch of reasons both to do it and not to do it, all sorts of feelings. The bottom line is that you make a choice because you can."

The following exchange highlights what has been said many times now: One of the nice things about an acceptance-based therapy is that even when therapists step off the desired path, they can simply acknowledge that, and in so doing step right back on the path, in the direction they wish to be heading.

Therapist: "I want to start by talking with you about something I realized during the week."

Client: "Okay."

Therapist: "I realized that at some point in our work together, I completely dropped the homework thing."

Client: "Yeah, I noticed that you haven't asked me about it in a while."

Therapist: "When I think about it I realize it started with not bringing it up—not asking you about homework because I was afraid you hadn't done it."

Client: "You would have been right."

Therapist: "What was going on with you?"

Client: "Huh?"

Therapist: "Why didn't you bring it up?"

Client: "Um…probably because I didn't do it."

Therapist: "Yeah, looks like we were both big-time avoiding."

Client: "That's fine with me!" (*Laughs.*)

Therapist: "I don't think it's fine with me. I think I'm doing you a disservice by avoiding something like that in order to be more comfortable. Especially since we've been working on living life according to our values. I have a value around what we do here, and skipping over important stuff because it's uncomfortable doesn't mesh with that."

By resisting the pull to avoid an uncomfortable discussion around homework, the therapist tags clinically important behavior and also establishes a productive way to continue work with the issue over the course of therapy.

Scenario: The therapist and client have been working toward the client's value around work, specifically his goal to apply for a job. (Completion of this goal has proved to be a bit of an issue so far.) At the conclusion of the previous session the client committed to filling out a particular application and bringing it into the session.

Therapist:	"Do you want to start with the job application? We can take a look at it together."
Client:	"It's in the car."
Therapist:	"Do you want to go and get it?"
Client:	"No, I didn't do much with it anyway."
Therapist:	"Hmmm." (*Sits silently.*)

(*Client gives a big sigh, shifts, and folds his arms.*)

Therapist:	"Let's really bring our attention to this moment." (*Pause.*) "What do you notice going on for you right now?"
Client	(*sighs again, looks angry*): "Just…here we are again. I don't want the session to be about this again. I didn't come here for this, you know?"
Therapist:	"This sounds important—like there's lots of information here for us. Let's start with just getting present and noticing."
Client:	"I feel bored. With this whole thing."
Therapist:	"Bored….You actually look and sound angry—or at least frustrated."
Client:	"I am frustrated. I'm tired of talking about this."
Therapist:	"Yeah, I can tag that going on for me a bit, too. Frustration that we're here again, worries about whether you'll get fed up and leave therapy, all that." (*Pause.*) "But I also have a larger value around this. I have hopes for what this therapy might offer you, so I'm going to hang in there with you on this and invite you to hang in with me as well."
Client	(*a bit more engaged*): "I know….It's just…when you ask me about it, it just makes me not want to do it even more."
Therapist:	"Yeah. When I ask you about it I feel like a parent or schoolmarm or something, rather than…a comrade in arms."
Client	(*sighs, finally looks directly at the therapist*): "It's not your fault. I should just get my ass in gear."
Therapist:	"That's a good one. How do you do that exactly?"

(*Both laugh.*)

Therapist:	"What do you think would happen if we started the session by you bringing up the issue? That is, you initiate the discussion—whether or not you did whatever you committed to do that week."
Client:	"I could do that. I'm not sure it would change whether or not I do it, though."
Therapist:	"I'm thinking more about this dynamic. Whether or not you complete what you committed to doing is one thing, but having it be clearer to both of us that this is coming from you seems important. You're pursuing therapy for a reason. You committed to some action to take outside of session for a reason. This is your life and you're in charge of it."
Client:	"I like that."
Therapist:	"Now, one thing I could see happening is you not bringing it up for some reason, like if you didn't do what you had set out to accomplish."
Client:	"Well, if that happens just remind me."
Therapist:	"That could turn into the same thing. That is, it could function the same way as me asking you about your homework."
Client:	"Yeah, right." (*Thinks.*) "Well, let's try it and see what happens."
Therapist:	"You're on. And if you choose not to do the homework, simply notice what comes up for you. There's good information for you there as well."

This exchange involved an important shift in responsibility from the therapist to the client, culminating in the client's assertive "Let's try it and see what happens." The therapist continued to use language that highlighted that the client is in charge of things here ("you didn't do what *you set out to accomplish*," "if *you choose* not to do the homework"), keeping the responsibility firmly on the client. Transparency was effectively employed in the service of moving out of an oppositional dynamic to a more collaborative one. (In other words, the therapist's "realness" forged a more authentic, in-the-moment connection with the client.) Finally, key points were established (those "stakes in the ground") that could prove useful in future discussion if what happens subsequently does, in fact, mirror the original dynamic (if, for example, the client "forgets" to bring it up and is reminded by the therapist). At the very least, both therapist and client have moved out of a power and control dynamic to a more productive way of working with this issue.

WHEN CLIENTS DON'T PROGRESS

One day many years ago, I went to my friend Robyn Walser, oft-mentioned in this book, to consult her about a client I had been seeing. The client, a thirty-eight-year-old woman presenting with depression, had received the full course of ACT, grasped everything that was important to grasp, and—as far as I could tell—applied almost nothing. "Robyn," I began, "I have tried everything. The client seems to get it. She is the first to say that as it stands, her life has little meaning, and she agrees that she actually has the ability to change that. But then she doesn't make a move. It seems like every week we start over with everything that's wrong in her life, then work through how she is still able to make valued choices and what might be standing in her way....I don't know what to do." Robyn paused in her thoughtful way, then simply said, "Well, maybe she hasn't cooked enough."

Recalling this comment makes me smile. Those few words served as an important reminder of the distinction between my client's life and my role as her therapist. In other words, what my client does with what I offer is not ultimately up to me. ACT is not some magical therapy that will always "work," and ACT therapists are likewise not responsible for whether clients make changes in their lives. Perhaps there are times when we must content ourselves with having pulled the veil from our clients' eyes—that is, having illuminated the ways in which they have been (and are) stuck and presented an alternative, a possible way to move forward, regardless of whether they choose to explore it. It may well be that some clients have not cooked enough, that they haven't stewed enough in the soup of their lives to decide to start making behavioral changes.

I find myself wanting to say something along the lines of how this doesn't mean we don't try our damnedest to help clients move through such barriers, but hopefully all that should be clear by now. Rather, it is time to speak to the difficult part of any therapist's professional life—when our clients simply do not improve. Here is where it is so important to compassionately hold our experience as therapists while also seeing with acuity what can be learned from the situation. If there were things you could have done better, allow that knowledge to be there along with the feelings that belong to that awareness. That means all of it—whether it be anger, resignation, defeat, discouragement, frustration, or sadness. It is *hard* to watch someone turn away from living a more vital and meaningful life, to remain stuck while the precious minutes tick, tick away. The experience of defeat is a testament to your desire to improve the human condition. The frustration tells you how deeply you care about your work and about your clients. Regret—even shame—about something you did or didn't do speaks to your caring and is a feeling to be honored. Check to see whether resignation doesn't harbor a deeper sorrow that you can also hold with compassion. If you find yourself not caring as much as you "should," notice that thought, and perhaps look to see if the dispassion might be functioning as a way to keep something more uncomfortable at bay. You can hold these reactions gently and without defense, while also seeing with clear eyes what is there to be seen.

The final point I'd like to make here is a reminder that ACT is always part of a larger process. It sits in the context of the client's life, a context that will continue to unfold long after the therapy has ended. Who knows what will or won't stick—what little seed might be quietly germinating only to bloom in a different time and place? Many, many times, I have learned that something said or done in therapy, some concept or intervention that appeared nonproductive in the moment, actually burst into fruition at some later point. This is why, when in a situation where the client seems determined to remain stuck, I aim for clarity. Regardless of the choices the client will ultimately make (including choosing nonaction) she will be very clear it is a choice she is making. My clients will leave therapy with the veil lifted. My hope, of course, is that such clarity will help them eventually make at least a tiny move toward the life they say they wish to be living. Who knows what will happen next?

SUMMARY

This chapter has approached barriers to treatment—those inevitable and challenging behaviors that show us exactly how our clients stand in their own way. The chapter is far from an exhaustive accounting, and only touched upon some of the barriers that can appear over a course of ACT. My own ability to work with barriers continues to develop, and I am quite sure there's no mastery to attain here. At the same time, it seems safe to say that what doesn't work is to avoid, ignore, or try to override or otherwise control problematic behavior. Regardless of the form of the behavior in question, three clinical guidelines—getting present, leaning in, and illuminating function—have served me well and will hopefully prove as trustworthy to other ACT providers.

CHAPTER 9

The Conundrum of Self-as-Context

Standing in a checkout line the other day, I found myself thinking about a girl I had known in seventh grade. She sat next to me in social studies and never said a word. I never saw her talking with anyone, actually. She was very pale, and would spend the class picking at her skin. Another image quickly followed, this time of a boy in kindergarten whom everyone avoided because of the strong smell of urine that came from his clothes. We kids couldn't believe he wore the same stained clothes to school day after day. Standing there, I had a startling thought: those kids could have been abused. Sadness washed over me, mixed with outrage and regret. And then I was through the checkout line.

These relational networks are really something, aren't they? When I went back over my thoughts, I realized that absent-mindedly scratching a small bump on the skin of my arm had made me think of the girl in social studies. Or rather, relational framing had derived a relation between that behavior and this girl, something I tapped into thirty-plus years after the fact. Relational framing further linked two people I had encountered years apart. That is, I derived that both were potentially members of a class—in this case, abused children. This derived relation was connected with the relational network I have developed around being a parent, which had already been added to the vast relational network developed in the course of my clinical work. Transformation of stimulus functions brought forth the emotions evoked by such experiences and there I was, standing in a checkout line with brand-new derived relations and a lot of painful feelings.

Relational framing is obviously a potent process. In pondering the plight of the little boy and girl just mentioned, what is most tragic is the self-concept that likely developed as a result of their experiences. Just as I and others quickly defined who they were based on how we framed their behavior or appearance, they too were deriving their very identities based on our reactions.

Putting this phenomenon into words seems to diminish its importance. The way in which we experience and label ourselves is arguably the most influential aspect of our lives. It determines the very quality of our existence. It influences our interpersonal behavior, so our self-concept has a ripple effect on others that just continues to extend. It can serve as a significant behavioral constraint or it can help us be present to, and vitally engaged in, our lives. It's a big deal.

Through the study of thinking and language acquisition, we are gaining insight into how self-concepts are formed. This has major implications for that boy and girl, for all the clients like them, and for us as therapists. By observing and coming to understand the process of developing self-concept, we see that our self-identity is actually a product of language. We have formed it. We have been taught who we are by others (just as they were taught), and by the relational frames we have derived. In that sense it's all a selected, construed reality. But how can we get past all the relational framing to help clients see that?

This question will be a central topic in this chapter concerning the self-as-context dimension of ACT. I will first revisit the experience of self as viewed in ACT, touching upon the role of relational framing. I'll then spend a bit of time on what we are ultimately after in the therapy and how the model proposes to help clients in this area. And then I will get into some specifics of some key self-as-context interventions. As always, I'll be pointing to various difficulties and missteps I have encountered, the objective being to help therapists optimize this piece of the therapy.

THE STRUGGLE

Whenever I ask therapists what part of ACT they find most challenging, they invariably point to self-as-context. When I observe ACT sessions, it is the self-as-context piece that clients struggle with most. So we have a problem in that both therapists and clients have difficulty with one of the key processes in ACT.

In the first chapter of this book I suggested that an understanding of the behavioral learning principles informing ACT is clinically helpful. I think self-as-context is particularly aided by some understanding of relational frame theory. Most essentially, it helps us be more informed regarding the processes we are aiming for. Being more informed not only assists our efforts to flush out those processes but also promotes clinical flexibility and creativity. Rather than simply relying on particular self-as-context exercises or metaphors to work on self-as-context, for example, we might think of novel, in-the-moment ways to further that ability. There is also a very thin line between the clear, practical work (such as helping clients notice that they are having a thought or feeling) and more complex ideas (such as "Who is this Experiencer?" and "Are we talking about the soul here?"). In other words, we can quickly find ourselves on unsure footing with clients. I will restate that in ACT it's okay to be unsure, so long as you respond to that uncertainty in a way that is consistent with the model. That is, as ACT therapists it wouldn't be consistent to avoid the uncertainty, or to jump in with inconsistent solutions to fix it. So let's move to what RFT has to say about the experience of self.

WHAT IS THE SELF, EXACTLY?

One way therapists get stuck is by not being clear that ACT defines three functionally different ways of experiencing the self. As I mentioned when reviewing the core processes in chapter 1, they are the *conceptualized self, self-as-process,* and *self-as-context.* It is not uncommon for therapists to get tangled up in the terminology here. "Self-as-*context*" and "self-as-*concept*" sound a lot alike, for example, but are different in essential ways. Self-as-*concept* refers to self-identity. It is the constructed self, made up of a series of evaluations and categorizations. Girl, boy, Caucasian, Hispanic, brainy, awkward, different, unlovable—through languaging we learn to apply these terms to ourselves. What's more, we relate to these concepts as though they *are* us, rather than the results of our relational framing. It's as though we *are* a word, a label, a constructed story. In contrast, self-as-context is the sense of self that has been there through time, the context in which experiences (including a self-labeling process) occur. Through the contributions of RFT, we are coming to understand this very awareness, this locus of perspective, as a learned behavior. That is, self-as-context is not a *thing*, but rather an ability that is learned over time. This has real implications in the therapy room, for when we understand the particular abilities that are thought to be at work we are better able to tease those out and strengthen them in a way that benefits our clients.

Before heading into this more fully, let me mention that I have also seen therapists miss the distinction between self-as-*process* and self-as-*context*, treating them as one and the same. Self-as-process is more about the ongoing *noticing* of internal experiences, whereas self-as-context is about *awareness* of the noticing itself. (This is why we often say that with self-as-context we notice that we are noticing.) Self-as-process refers specifically to the ability to flexibly bring attention to the thoughts, feelings, and bodily sensations of the moment and is therefore key to being present.

HOW DOES SELF HAPPEN?

I've mentioned that, as a clinician, there are certain theoretical takeaways of RFT that help me in the therapy room. The main one concerning self-as-context has been to understand the experience of conceptualized self as a learned behavior—and further, that the ability to contact and observe our experience and self-descriptions can also be learned. Being very clear on this idea helps me detach from the conceptualized self and help others do the same.

For me, this is not the same as saying that we learn who we *are*. In fact, one thing I've come to realize is that I don't know what I am constructed of (some miraculous combination of energy and matter, I suppose). I only know how I *experience* my Self. This requires not only a certain perspective, but the ability to identify that perspective. In RFT this ability is called *deictic framing*, briefly mentioned in chapter 1. There I provided an example of how easily my daughter could develop an identity around being the "worst dancer" in her class. Through derived relations, "worst" means something that is then related to something else, which is then related to something else, and so on. But this explanation doesn't address how my daughter even knows to think of herself as an "I" (as in "I am the worst dancer"). This was also learned. But how?

What we have learned through many years of applied research (and some ingenious research designs) is that it is only over time and many repetitions that we learn to identify the locus of perspective called "I." Furthermore, we must learn it from others. We have to learn from somewhere what it is that we are experiencing. We have to be taught to identify that particular perspective and to call it the "I." This is tricky because it is our perspective and we are the only ones who can experience it. That is, no one can point to it and say, "This is your perspective." But when those around us repeatedly refer to this locus of perspective, we gradually deduce what it is that they are referring to. We have learned to identify the "I."

For example, when a parent asks, "Why are *you* crying?" or "Do *you* like that?" or makes such statements as "*You* just spilled your milk," there is one common denominator. Through many such examples the child learns that the "you" being referenced is the locus of perspective that was the common thread throughout these experiences. Gradually, a distinction is made between the entity experiencing this perspective and others. Deictic framing refers to this derived relation (for example, "I" versus "you"), as well as to the related frames of "here" versus "there," and "now" versus "then." These frames are related because they require that same locus of perspective. Just as we need a certain locus of perspective to distinguish between "I" and "you," we need it to distinguish between "here" and "there," and between "now" and "then." It is one common locus of perspective that experiences "I/here/now" as distinct from "*you*/here/now." It is that same locus of perspective that can distinguish between "I/there/then" and "*you*/there/then" (or "other/there/then").

There is another sort of framing thought to be going on here: *hierarchical* framing. This is the ability to relate things as being part of a class, such as my daughter's ability to lump peas and other yucky foods into the class called "vegetables." This ability allows us to identify all the different experiences, observations, and awarenesses as viewed from one locus of perspective as belonging together. All the observed and felt experiences have been experienced from an I/here/now perspective and thus in a sense "belong" to this locus of observation (I am not my thoughts, feelings, and emotions; I *have* thoughts, feelings, and emotions). So self-as-context can be seen as a "conceptualization of the self based on deictic framing and hierarchical framing, in which the continuous perspective I-here-now and the psychological processes there-then are conceived as a container and a content" (Villatte, 2013).

For me, an interesting implication of all this is that while we do our best to find ways to describe, interpret, and otherwise work with the experience of being human, we aren't even close. Whatever labels and deictic frames we have come up with are at best representations of aspects of being human. While it may seem that we are learning more and more about ourselves when we learn to apply such terms as "girl," "daughter of Mary," "sister of Tom," "brunette," "tall," and so on, we actually make ourselves (whatever that is) smaller. Each description draws an ever-narrowing boundary around the mysterious combination of energy and matter we have learned to experience and identify as the "I." In recognizing this process, particularly by detaching from the conceptualized self, we can come closer to freeing ourselves from these verbally created constraints. In recognizing that our self-identity is a luck-of-the-draw construction (we could have been taught that we are worthless, or we could have been taught that we are magnificent), we are free to decide who we want to be in this moment and the next.

This approach to the experience(s) of self suggests ways to work with these processes. As therapists we can use these same language processes to help clients defuse from rigidly held, unworkable self-concepts (such as "I never finish what I start") while strengthening the link between behavior and more workable self-concepts (such as "I am someone who values good parenting"). We can help clients build self-as-process such that they are in contact with the contingencies of their lives (not just what their minds hand them) so that they might move away from unworkable behavior toward behavior that brings meaning and vitality to their lives.

IS THE SELF THE SOUL?

This is an example of the sort of question therapists might dread if they are feeling uncertain about the self-as-context piece of ACT. I have watched therapists struggle to answer this and other existential questions. And while relational frame theory, particularly deictic framing, offers a behavioral interpretation of the experience of self—including a transcendent self—remember that as ACT therapists we don't have to have the "right answer" to these sorts of questions. We are not pursuing some sort of truth. In fact, it would be important to assess how this sort of question is functioning for the client and in the session. I have heard these and similar questions posed by clients who are prone to intellectualizing at the cost of being actively engaged in their lives. It can also be said that sometimes the pursuit of such answers is in the service of being fixed (similar to asking "why" things are as they are in order to figure things out, so that they can then be fixed). If the question is functioning to move the client off of discomfort, or is in the service of a control strategy, you may want to work with it accordingly. For example:

> *Client:*   "So is ACT like Buddhism? Like having no ego? Or do you mean like Christianity, like the soul that 'moves on' after we die?"

Therapist:	"That is an interesting question! Let me ask you something: Do you have any sense of what having the answer might do for you?"
Client	*(a little stymied):* "Well, you are talking about the Self here. So I'm wondering what ACT would say about that."
Therapist:	"Like ACT has a 'right answer' to this one?"
Client:	"I guess."
Therapist:	"Well, let's say that it does. Let's say that I've just come back with 'Yes, the observing self is the soul.'"
Client	*(short laugh):* "Well. That doesn't do much."
Therapist:	"Yeah, what happens?"
Client:	"My mind just immediately comes up with 'and how does *he* know?'"
Therapist:	"Exactly."
Client:	"So what you're saying is…that there's no point in asking this?"
Therapist:	"We humans have been asking these sorts of questions for a long time. Pondering the 'mysteries of life' is part of the human experience. A rich part. It's more that this therapy isn't about having *the* answers to those sorts of questions. You have your own relationship with 'the soul' and what that means to you. In ACT we might look at what that relationship means in terms of how you live your life."
Client:	"Yeah, okay. That makes sense."

In the above example the therapist directly explored the function of the client's question. In doing so he gently pointed to the client's desire to get to right answers. He also emphasized the client's "right" to hold whatever beliefs he has, as well as ACT's emphasis on workability. Of course, should you determine it to be clinically appropriate (for example, if the client is simply working to understand), you can always respond to the content of the question.

Client:	"So are you talking about the soul? Is the 'Observer self' the soul?"
Therapist:	"Some people might call it that. There can be a limitless, boundary-less quality to it. When we contact that self that's always been there, that's distinct from all the thoughts going on, all the feelings, all the ideas about ourselves, we sense a self that

is not bound by that stuff. We are aware of the experience of self that has been there all along, is there in this moment, and will be there in the next."

Client: "Cool."

WHAT ARE WE AIMING FOR?

Are we aiming to get rid of the conceptualized self? This question makes me think of the spiritual awakening described by Eckhart Tolle (1999). As he recounted in *The Power of Now*, Dr. Tolle experienced a sudden, fundamental shift from fusion with a conceptualized self (although he used different words) to self-as-context. In a sudden epiphany he recognized the distinction between Thinker and thought, and made what sounds like an immediate shift to a transcendent experience of self. According to Tolle, this drastic shift in self-experience was not fleeting but stable for a period of five months, after which it "diminished somewhat in intensity, or perhaps it just seemed to because it became [his] natural state" (1997, p. 4). Indeed, Tolle reported that following his epiphany he spent two years camped out on a park bench in a state of total bliss. (I was horrified and immediately put down the book.) Even if self-as-context as a stable state were possible for us ordinary folks, this is not quite what we are working toward in ACT.

ACT's focus on psychological flexibility points to what we are after when it comes to self-as-context. We aim to help clients flexibly access different dimensions of self-experience such that they can be present to their lives and engaged in activities that bring vitality and meaning. This ability is at work in other key processes targeted in ACT—such as mindfulness, acceptance, and defusion. A recently elaborated definition of self-as-context points to this: "Self as context is the coming together and flexible social extension of a cluster of deictic relations, (especially I/here/now) that enable observation and description from a perspective or point of view. Self-as-context enables or facilitates many different experiences, including theory of mind, empathy, compassion, self-compassion, acceptance, defusion, and a transcendent sense of self" (Hayes, 2011).

Note also that this definition points to the importance of this ability in relating with others. "Flexible social extension" refers to the idea that the same skills that help us see things from the I/here/now perspective enable us to imagine being behind the eyes of another person. This skill is critical in developing empathy, among other important abilities.

It might be timely to remind ourselves of the functional contextualist approach to behavior. There is no one "right" self-experience. Rather, we want to develop our clients' ability to access them all in a way that is workable. A personal example: My self-concept as someone who is "determined" and who "gets things done" has helped me achieve things in life. It is helping me complete these pages with a deadline looming. However, rigid attachment to this self-identity can also lead me to drive myself silly keeping the house shipshape, the laundry done, and paperwork filed while under a deadline—even when I and those around me suffer from the resulting stress. A more flexible response involves defusing from thoughts and getting present to self-as-process: "I am having the thought that I have to make the bed," "I am experiencing anxiety and tension," "I am doing something I don't need to be doing." I can recognize the conceptualized self as such (as in "I *don't* actually have to get everything done"), and recognizing it empowers me to make more workable choices. Self-as-context allows me to observe the entire process with understanding and compassion, to desist from cleaning, and to use the experience as an example in this chapter.

Fusion with self-concepts such as "loser," "screw-up," "unlovable," and the like can lead clients to behave in ways that support such labels and identities. Even if very painful, their self-concept is all they've got, in a sense. Since that's *them*, they'd better hang on to it no matter how harsh. Letting go can be terrifying and is therefore avoided at all costs. This is why helping clients access a self that is larger than such identifications is so key. Recognizing that there is an Experiencer there who is doing all the noticing, thinking, and feeling helps clients see that there is something to stand on should they detach from their self-concept. The ability to bring awareness to the ongoing flow of internal experiences is clearly vital here. So the processes of self-as-context and self-as-process support and extend each other, and both enable detachment from the conceptualized self.

A final comment about the conceptualized self: Therapists get a firsthand view of how attachment to certain self-identities can limit clients in painful ways (for example, "I can't get close to anyone because I was raped and am therefore defective"). And as we know, in ACT we aim to develop abilities that help clients detach from such self-concepts. As a result, some of the therapists I have encountered have the perception that conceptualized selves are undesirable. This is not so—rather it is the *attachment* to a conceptualized self that is problematic. If it is rigidly held, a client's self-concept can prevent her from more flexible responses based on what is currently unfolding in her life (for example, "I was raped and have the thought that I'm defective, but that does not mean I cannot form a meaningful relationship with this person"). While rigidly held self-concepts can be problematic, self-concepts per se often function in helpful ways. In fact, self-concept is basic to the values work in ACT, which intentionally links self-as-content with behaviors clients find meaningful and reinforcing. We encourage clients to get clear on what they want to stand for in life, who they want to be in the world, and so on. This is a powerful use of relational framing in the service of vital living.

SO HOW DO WE GO ABOUT IT?

The previous discussion helps us understand the key objectives in ACT when it comes to the experience of self. We want to help clients build their ability to access the different senses of self in a flexible manner, according to what will help them move forward at a given point or moment in their lives. In this particular domain we want to (1) help clients defuse from the rigidly held conceptualized self, (2) build clients' ability to experience self-as-process, and (3) build clients' ability to experience self-as-context. To accomplish these objectives, we will be targeting specific abilities: getting present, willingness, defusion, and, of course, self-as-context. Three specific tools are useful here.

First is promoting the use of defusing language. We use the language of defusion to further all three objectives. For example, when we model and encourage clients to phrase experiences as "I am having the thought that…" or "I am noticing the feeling of…" we are working toward all three objectives. We are helping to develop ongoing awareness of the flow of internal experiences, which requires defusing from those experiences. We drive a verbal wedge between the client and the constructed identity (for example, "I am *having the thought* that I'm a loser," versus "I *am* a loser"). And the language serves as a reminder that this experience of self is the result of an activity (in this case, perspective taking based on I/here/now).

Second, metaphors come into play. Metaphors are used to help clients make the distinction between these different ways of experiencing the self. We use metaphors because they are efficient. As nicely explained by Ramnero and Törneke (2008), when we use a metaphor (for example, the client is like a chessboard), we connect one relational network to another. Certain functional qualities of one (in this case, the *board's* ability to hold things, its strength and wholeness) are transferred to the other (the *client* is able to hold things, is strong and whole). In this way a new perspective is taken and relationship to self is potentially altered.

Third, we continue to provide clients with the experience of self-as-context via mindfulness work and experiential exercises. I am never more appreciative of this aspect of ACT than when working on self-as-context. When conveying a metaphor or guiding a client through an experiential exercise, we are harnessing language processes in a way that helps clients move toward psychological flexibility. Such techniques can help clients *experience* themselves differently—for example, as being larger than the internal phenomena of the moment.

Self-as-Context Master Plan

So here's my general strategy for working with clients on self-as-context: In essence, I deliberately pull out all the stops and use everything ACT has to offer—language use, metaphors, experiential exercises, and general discussion. The work begins immediately in terms of language use as discussed above. That is, from the outset of therapy I demonstrate self-as-process and self-as-context when talking about my own experiences in session and when reflecting back to clients what they have said. When it comes to talking more explicitly about self-as-context, I like to make the soil as fertile as possible. Ideally, my client demonstrates some ability to defuse from thoughts, and some willingness to be present to the moment rather than engaged in a control/avoidance strategy. For this reason I often head into self-as-context after having worked with clients on willingness and defusion.

Mindfulness is central to self-as-context and is something to pull in from the beginning of the therapy. In fact, mindfulness meditation has long been thought to help humans contact the transcendent self. With mindful awareness of the moment, specifically awareness of our ever-changing thoughts, feelings, sensations, evaluations, judgments, and so forth, we learn experientially that everything changes. We learn that the internal phenomena of the moment are transient and part of an ongoing flow of experience, and we become aware of the Observer watching the flow. We build awareness of the Experiencer that has thoughts, feelings, sensations, and so on, but is distinct from those internal experiences. In mindfulness meditation, we learn over time and with much practice (at defusing and simply noticing) that we are more than these experiences.

As previously discussed, regularly incorporating mindfulness into your ACT sessions is helpful on many levels. Therapists are able to regularly assess clients' abilities in several core processes: getting present (which requires willingness), defusion, and self-as-process/self-as-context. Building clients' abilities with self-as-process paves the way for explicit work on self-as-context. I have found it both a natural progression and effective to begin explicit self-as-context work with the "Observer exercise" (sometimes referred to as the "Continuous You" exercise). This exercise was first introduced by Hayes, Strosahl, and Wilson (1999) and is geared toward helping clients access self-as-context. In this guided imagery exercise, clients are asked to remember what they were experiencing at different points in time (for example, that morning, at some point during the previous week, during the previous summer, during high school, or as a child). Clients are cued to revisit these points in time as fully as possible, and to notice the attendant internal events (for example, "What thoughts are you having at this moment?"). The therapist draws a continuous thread through these points of time, helping clients see that there is a locus of perspective, a "continuous you" that is constant throughout. Clients are guided to become aware of this continuous locus of perspective (the "Observer" noticing those experiences), as well as what is unfolding in the present moment. (For more detailed examples see Hayes et al., [1999] and Walser & Westrup [2007]).

It is important to check in with clients following this exercise. I have seen clients experience epiphanies, really contacting the "self that is continuous and larger than thoughts or feelings." It is also not at all uncommon for clients to report something along the lines of "I don't get what you mean by the 'self'." I like to use such opportunities for in-the-moment work:

Me: "So, are you aware that you are sitting there, looking at me?"

Client: "Yes...."

Me: "And did you hear yourself say 'Yes'?"

Client: (Nods.)

Me: "And were you aware of yourself nodding?"

Client:	"Yeah."
Me:	"And are you aware of your body in the chair?"
Client:	"Yeah."
Me:	"And can you catch any thoughts you are having? Like maybe thoughts about what we're doing right now?"
Client	(slight laugh): "Yep."
Me:	"And check in for a moment—you don't need to answer. See if you can identify any emotions that are showing up right now." (Pausing for a few moments.) "Did you notice any?"
Client:	"Yeah."
Me:	"So that entity doing all the noticing? That's the self we're talking about here. The self that is aware of being in this moment, that can notice the thoughts, feelings, and sensations of the moment. That's the same observing self that was in those different situations we just went through in the exercise—that self that knows you are here in this moment, that knew you were there in those moments."

I cannot recall a situation in which this sort of in-the-moment work has not helped clients recognize the conceptualized self. A typical move at this point would be to move from this sort of discussion to a metaphor or additional experiential exercise. I really try to come at self-as-context from a variety of directions to solidify and fill out this process for clients.

Now enters the chessboard metaphor, a key intervention. There are several useful metaphors for self-as-context (such as "house with furniture" and "box with stuff in it"). However, the chessboard metaphor is a powerful classic. Since first presented in the original ACT book by Hayes, Strosahl, and Wilson (1999), the chessboard metaphor has been one of the central interventions in ACT. It is a personal favorite simply because I have found it to be effective; it is often the chessboard metaphor that helps clients finally understand what we mean when we talk about the "self that is larger." (Note the hierarchical framing involved here: that even while recognizing a self—a locus of perspective—that is distinct from or larger than present thoughts or feelings, we see that they belong together. The experienced thoughts, feelings, and sensations belong to that larger self.) Yet I have found the chessboard metaphor to be the hardest of the commonly used metaphors for therapists to do effectively. The idea may seem straightforward, but execution can be a bit tricky.

Most of the difficulties have to do with setup. I'll talk about setup again in the next chapter when discussing general ways to maximize ACT metaphors and exercises.

Before you begin here, it is important to get clear on just what it is that you hope your client will take away from the metaphor. Let's apply this goal to the chessboard metaphor specifically:

Main process being targeted: self-as-context (contacting the self as the chessboard)

Other processes facilitated: defusion (from the chess pieces as thoughts/feelings), willingness (simply holding the pieces), committed action (the board moves with the pieces)

Supporting points: chess pieces cannot be removed from the board (history is additive), there's no winning (since pieces can't be removed), the board contacts all the pieces (this is not a strategy), the board is intact (the self is distinct from the pieces), being the board is different from feeling whole and intact.

In identifying these various clinical objectives, therapists are guided to set up the metaphor in a way that will help them convey these points. A central strategy in optimizing ACT is to use every available opportunity to further psychological flexibility. In other words, although you may be targeting a particular process, why not further other abilities as well, if the opportunity is there and your client seems ready for them? While the chessboard metaphor is geared toward self-as-context, there is rich opportunity to make headway in willingness and committed action, for example. There is another significant opportunity as well. When clients learn to operate at "board level," they see that they are whole and intact regardless of the pieces they carry.

In chapter 6, I stressed the importance of word choice in ACT, stating that even small wording differences can have important implications. As it applies to the chessboard, sometimes therapists don't specify, when establishing the metaphor, that the board "extends in all directions" (that there are no edges to the board). The client then does not understand why individual chess pieces must remain on the board. As another example, many therapists support clients in evaluating their experiences by labeling pieces as "good" or "bad," rather than taking the opportunity to help clients defuse from such thoughts.

I have seen therapists set themselves up for a struggle with this metaphor when they set the stage in an overly elaborate manner. That is, they get caught up in detail that doesn't really add anything clinically. One consequence is that they open themselves up to a complicated discussion that is off point. They can get bogged down in some detail of the metaphor rather than focusing on the processes being targeted. Another consequence is that the main point is diminished. I have seen cases where the therapist put so much into the setup that the client had lost interest by the time the "you are the board" point was reached. So the point is not "the story of the chessboard." The metaphor is meant to illuminate a *process* (self-as-context), and it's advisable to get there as cleanly as possible. Keeping the intended function of the metaphor firmly in mind will help you determine how much detail—and which details—to provide. Consider keeping it concise.

These are finer points that don't necessarily make or break the metaphor. Again, it's about facilitation and optimization. I try to choose words that help make the main point as well as further other important abilities. I also strive to make this metaphor as experiential as possible, and as personally relevant to the client as possible.

Application of the Chessboard Metaphor

Before offering a detailed example, I'd like to stress that applying the chessboard metaphor is not about having a script. What I hope to demonstrate here are ways to highlight certain points and ways to add some affective oomph. When reading the following, please keep in mind that the pace is relaxed and unhurried. The therapist is carefully assessing (analyzing the function of) the client's reactions as she goes, attentive to what is happening in the moment.

"In this metaphor, it's as though your life is a chessboard." (Therapist puts a chessboard or something representing a chessboard on the floor or table.) *"So imagine that this is your life. In this metaphor, though, there's no edge to the board. So imagine the board as extending in all directions, like an infinite plane. Can you picture that?"* (Client nods.) *"As you're moving through life, you are picking up pieces."* (Therapist begins placing pieces somewhat randomly on the board.) *"Every thought, every feeling, every memory you've ever had is a piece on your board. And remember, this board extends in all directions. There's no edge to it. So just like your own history, once a piece is on your board it's on your board. There's no way for pieces to fall off or get knocked off once they're on. Are you with me so far?"* (Client nods.) *"Some of these pieces are really pleasant* (holding one up piece before placing it on the board). *Some are neutral; others are not so pleasant* (picking up a different-colored piece). *In fact, some of these are downright painful."* (The therapist picks up a few pieces that are the designated "not so pleasant" color and places them next to each other on the board.) *"Do you notice something here?"* (Client is silent, considering the board.) *"The pleasant and uncomfortable pieces sort of hang out together. We could call this one the trauma you experienced in ninth grade* (picking up a large 'unpleasant' piece), *and these are all the painful thoughts and feelings that come along with that* (bunches them together on the board). *And here are pieces that come up around your grandson* (bunches a bunch of 'pleasant' pieces together and pauses for client to take this in). *And, as we've talked about a lot in here, what we humans do is try to win this game! We try to make the pleasant pieces win. We try all sorts of things to vanquish the pieces we don't want to have* (moves pieces around randomly). *But we've got a real problem."* (Therapist pauses for a moment or two, joining with the client in simply pondering the board.) *"What's the problem with all this strategizing, with all this trying to win, when there's no edge to the board?"*

Client   *(after a moment)*: "There's no way to get the pieces off."

Therapist	(moving pieces around urgently): "But you want them off of there!"
Client:	"Just don't think about those pieces."
Therapist	(moving one of the "unpleasant" pieces on the board): "Yeah, so that's a move."
Client:	"Oh. Yeah." (Pause.) "I don't like this game."

(The therapist silently picks up one of the pieces that hasn't yet been placed on the board, shows it to the client, and puts it on the board.)

Client	(laughs a little): "Yeah, okay."

(Therapist waits silently.)

Client:	"So we're stuck with it."
Therapist	(picks up another "unpleasant" piece, shows it to the client, and comments casually): "We're stuck with it." (Places that piece on the board while continuing.) "Yeah, there's no way to win this game. But that doesn't keep us from trying, does it? We're like this piece here (picking up a piece), fighting the good fight. We move, countermove…move, then countermove (demonstrating this with the pieces). Round and round we go."
Client:	"It's a stalemate."
Therapist:	"Yeah. Not to mention that it takes a lot of effort and energy." (Pause.) "So it seems we agree that there's no winning this game. There may be something else to see here, though. Sticking with this metaphor, what if we are something besides all these pieces moving around?"
Client:	"What?"
Therapist:	"If you weren't the pieces, what else might you be—sticking with this metaphor?"
Client	(thinks for a bit, then asks hesitantly): "The player?"
Therapist:	"Seems like that's something you've tried. To be the player. Adding more pieces, moving them here and there.…Again, staying with this metaphor, if it doesn't work to be the pieces or the player, what else might you be?"
Client:	"The board?"

Therapist	(leaning in): "Ah. Now that's an interesting idea! What if you were the board?"
Client:	"I would just have all the pieces up there."

At this point the therapist is well placed to work on the main ideas conveyed by this metaphor. I really lean in as soon as clients arrive at being the board, emphasizing that what we are on to now is something major. It would be important to talk about how the board is in full contact with the pieces, because clients can quickly turn being the board into a control strategy. That is, it isn't about not being affected by the pieces. It's about the awareness of being distinct from the pieces and about simply holding and experiencing them rather than getting pulled into battle. I like to (carefully) pick up the board and move with it across the room, inviting the client to notice how the board can move, with all its pieces, in a valued direction.

I tend to save the most (in my view) significant implication of this metaphor for last. After the above points have been made, I ask the client a final question:

Me:	"What else do you notice about this board?"

(Client looks puzzled, is silent.)

Me	(slowly and deliberately knocking on the board): "What do you notice about this board?"
Client	(beginning to see): "It's strong!"
Me:	"It is strong! It's intact!"

(Client sits smiling, gazing at the board.)

Me:	"This board is intact. This board is fully capable of holding these pieces and all the pieces to come."

I also use the opportunity to assist clients in making the distinction between *being* the board and *feeling like* the board. Individuals who are fused with very negative self-evaluations can quickly reject alternate perspectives. They turn to their experiences, their thoughts and feelings, as guides to reality. When told that they are actually not to blame for being victimized, for example, or that they are, in fact, acceptable as they are, they immediately check their internal experience. When they find their experience to be incongruent with what they are being told (in other words, they do not *feel* okay) they reject the contradictory input wholesale. Trying to change these sorts of self-concepts can result in the client feeling even more unworthy. Her "bad" self-concept is further evidence of her flawed nature. In other words, such fix-it efforts tend to extend existing relational networks in problematic ways. I usually put pieces on the board to represent these evaluations, and point out: "Even if you have never had the *experience* of being whole and intact, even if those pieces have never been on your board, you are still the board."

As I said, the intention in providing this detailed example is to demonstrate how, via thoughtful language and engagement with the client, we can maximize the potential of this and all such metaphors. It is so very important to add heart—that is, *being* with the client in the experience and allowing yourself to feel the process as it unfolds. I have witnessed really elegant verbal explanations of this metaphor that go absolutely nowhere. The client "understands," but something vital is missing. The client processes only part of what is before her. It's as though she gets the idea but not its implications—she certainly isn't having a "board level" experience. It is pretty clear when this metaphor lands. If there is no "Aha!" there is more work to be done.

If you're working with the processes sequentially, it can take two or more sessions for clients to really contact self-as-context. As I just described, I have often found that starting with the continuous you, processing that with in-the-moment work, then pulling in the chessboard metaphor makes a good "first run" at self-as-context. I recap these exercises and then introduce additional experiential work, such as the label parade (see Walser & Westrup, 2007, for a detailed example), in subsequent sessions. Once self-as-context has been specifically worked on, it makes sense to explicitly incorporate this key process (including the pertinent exercises and metaphors) in every remaining session.

Clients vary greatly in their ability to grasp the distinction between the conceptualized self and self-as-context, and in their ability to begin to access self-as-context. A consultee I once worked with had a client who just could not make the distinction between his thoughts and the Thinker having the thoughts. The therapist kept at it, though, and was finally able to help him get there. After having tried various interventions, she had a very direct conversation with the client about how there was a particular thing—the "Self that is larger than thoughts and feelings"—that she had been trying to help him see, and how she felt they hadn't gotten there. As an example, she talked about the "Continuous You" exercise. (They had done it, but the client hadn't grasped the idea of the continuous you.) And she spelled out in very clear language what the exercise was meant to get at. She then redid the exercise having laid this explicit groundwork, and the client got it. Once the distinction was made, my consultee was able to build upon it by revisiting related metaphors and exercises.

OTHER PERPLEXITIES

In the course of exploring how we further self-as-context in ACT, I have mentioned ways in which therapists can set themselves up for difficulty. Now I'll highlight some other missteps I've observed that can make this part of the therapy challenging.

First, it is not about the parts. That is, sometimes therapists, while working on building self-as-context, will suggest that the client needs to go with (as in attach to or buy into) a different self-perspective—as though the point to flexible perspective taking is to select a "better" perspective. While some such perspectives might indeed prove beneficial to the client (for example, "I *am* somebody who can ask a girl out"), this approach does not get at the distinction between that particular thought and the locus of perspective having that thought. In terms of maximum flexibility, experiencing oneself as a context offers more.

As another example, while doing the "box with stuff in it" experiential exercise (in which thoughts and feelings are likened to the stuff and the client is likened to the box), one therapist pointed to the box and said, "You are the totality of all that." Not quite. What we are after, according to this model, is the idea of self-as-*context* for these internal experiences. We are the box holding the stuff.

Finally, I have also known therapists to stop short of working explicitly with self-as-context. What typically happens is they help clients build self-as-process by way of mindfulness exercises, or help clients learn to defuse from thoughts, but stop there. The therapist doesn't work to help the client see the larger implications of self-as-process, for example. I see this as a real misstep, as a major gift of this therapy is developing self-as-context. This is where clients have an opportunity to experience a self that is whole, strong enough to hold experiences past and present, and well beyond any sort of evaluations or categorizations our human minds can invent. I have watched this realization spread over the faces of clients who have never in their entire memory had the experience of being fundamentally okay. It's huge.

The importance of this piece isn't just its subjective implications (in other words, what it's like for clients to have a different sense of themselves than as fundamentally flawed). It's also that the ability to access self-as-context facilitates other important processes. Clients no longer need to cling to restrictive self-concepts. They no longer need to ward off or defend against uncomfortable thoughts or feelings. They are freed up to be present in their actual lives, engaged and making value-driven choices.

I certainly cannot claim that every ACT client I have had or have been involved with via supervision has come away from the therapy with this realization. I wish that it were so. In actuality there have been times when I have had to accept that a particular client was just not going to get there. Fortunately, it is more often that eventually—and often only by pulling in many different examples, exercises, and modalities—clients *do* learn to experience themselves this way. (Also see the section on the corpus delicti metaphor in chapter 8.)

SUMMARY

I'm sure this section has revealed my feelings about the self-as-context piece of ACT. As a fellow therapist, it is likely you, too, have looked in the eyes of a fellow human being who is 100 percent convinced she is worthless. You, too, have encountered the difficulty of making any sort of meaningful chink in that self-concept. And you have also witnessed the detrimental effects of moving through the world in that way. I have found that the approach to self-experience promoted in ACT can help even these clients contact a self that is whole and intact. I have seen how doing so helps them to finally step out of the internal battle they have been waging and into living their lives.

Nearly every time I delve into the various ACT materials around self-as-context, I come away with something useful. I find that small but important pieces slide into place, strengthening the work I do with clients. I have attempted to slide some of these pieces over to you, and I hope they prove helpful in your work on this important piece of the therapy.

CHAPTER 10

Optimizing Your Secret Weapons

ACT incorporates experiential exercises and metaphors as a way to further targeted processes while not extending problematic verbal networks. If you have ever tried to simply tell a depressed client that she might benefit from regular exercise, for example, it is likely that you observed this sort of instruction to be ineffectual. In fact, it is quite possible that your client agreed with you, then added her failure to exercise to the list of things wrong with her. Our clients—and we, as well—can get so caught up in the content of our minds (who we should and should not be; rules about what will or won't happen; what is, or is not, tolerable; our reasons and self-concepts) that we lose sensitivity to the often contradictory information provided by our environment (for example, that we can go for a walk when experiencing depressive feelings, that doing so can result in an increase in energy and a sense of well-being). So rather than simply utilizing verbal rules, ACT therapists use metaphors and experiential techniques to help clients contact their direct experience.

The fact that exercises and metaphors are an established feature of the therapy does not mean they are optimized, however. I mentioned earlier that when first learning ACT, I was surprised to discover that my readily "getting" a metaphor didn't mean that I was able to convey it meaningfully to clients. Similarly, reading about, or even observing, another therapist do an experiential exercise did not directly translate into effective delivery on my part. In fact, I found it surprisingly difficult to work with exercises and metaphors in a way that really benefited the client. As a supervisor and consultant I have now had hundreds of opportunities to observe and work with therapists as they tackle the more commonly used ACT exercises and metaphors, and have found my experience to be very typical. At the same time, the use of experiential exercises and metaphors is an intentional and powerful part of the therapy, so it is important to drill down and take a look at what might prevent therapists from taking full advantage of this component of ACT.

WHY SO HARD?

In this section I'll take a look at some specific aspects of working with metaphors and experiential exercises that ACT therapists have found challenging. While there are, of course, any number of things clients can do with metaphors or exercises that flummox therapists, in this section I will focus on ways in which therapists can reduce, constrain, or otherwise limit what this piece can ultimately bring to the table.

Content vs. Core Process

The importance of working with ACT at the level of behavioral principles is a familiar refrain, isn't it? Nonetheless, I bring it up again because approaching the therapy as a set of techniques, or as a bunch of information that needs to be taught, can really wreak havoc when it comes to implementing experiential exercises or metaphors. It's as though the therapist approaches the metaphor (or the exercise) as a script that needs to be memorized and delivered, rather than keeping its intended purpose front and center. A problem with approaching metaphors and exercises as scripts to follow, rather than as a means to illuminate and work on the core ACT processes, is that the therapist is set up for difficulty if there is some deviation from the script. If the therapist flubs his lines, for example, or the client has an unexpected response, they are now suddenly off-script and it can be hard to regroup. When the therapist is clear on the process(es) reflected in the metaphor or exercise, he is better able to work flexibly with whatever transpires in session. Another issue is that focusing on content over process in this way can subvert the point of doing a metaphor or experiential exercise in the first place. That is, it is easy to turn exercises and metaphors into more elaborate forms of verbal rules such as persuading or convincing. Finally, approaching exercises and metaphors in a content-focused way creates an unnecessary constraint. That is, just as the core processes are intertwined, the common ACT exercises and metaphors reflect multiple processes and can therefore be effectively implemented at many points in the therapy. There is no one "right time" to bring in a particular metaphor or exercise. There may be multiple times and, in fact, multiple variations of the exercise or metaphor that will further the work.

WINGING IT

This may seem contradictory to my previous point about the problem with approaching exercises and metaphors as though following a script, but trying to just wing it can also be problematic, especially for therapists who are newer to the therapy. The way the chessboard metaphor is set up, for example, can either help or complicate matters. The willingness scale metaphor, the tug-of-war exercise, "passengers on a bus"—all can be unintentionally conveyed as ways to avoid or control. As with all the exercises and metaphors, even minute wording differences can determine whether you are furthering the therapy or working against yourself.

Later in this chapter I'll provide some examples of these slight yet potentially significant wording distinctions. But a preventative rule of thumb is simply to practice. Due to my own learning experience, I encourage supervisees and consultees to practice the common ACT exercises and metaphors before attempting them in session. By practice, I mean to actually verbalize them. Play with them, work with them—again, not as scripts or techniques, but in order to develop some familiarity. This rehearsal is not intended to create a smooth, artificial performance of some kind. Rather, it will allow you to discover any wording or conceptual hitches, any nuances you don't understand as well as you thought you did, and what pieces are needed to make the central point or points. As always, being present-focused in session is key.

NOT GOING FOR IT

First I pointed out how there is no one way to do metaphors or exercises, then I suggested practicing, and now I'm telling you to just go for it. Bear with me for a moment more. Practicing is helpful when you are attempting to make someone else's idea your own. That is, one of the reasons I think it can be harder than we anticipate to impart a metaphor we have read or heard about, or to conduct an exercise we saw or heard somewhere, is that it originated with someone else. It takes working with the exercise or metaphor a bit to put our own stamp on it in a way that is genuine while still consistent with the model. At the same time, there will likely be many occasions, especially as you become more and more facile with ACT, when a new metaphor or experiential exercise will suddenly occur to you. Or your client might say something that you realize is a useful metaphor for something you are working on. In other words, as ACT therapists gain experience they often find themselves doing all sorts of in-the-moment stuff that just seems to be the thing to do. Trust that! That sort of inspiration is not coming from a description in a text somewhere, a training video, or a workshop. It is a reflection of becoming adept at recognizing and working creatively with the core ACT processes, and it is worth seeing where it takes you. Remember, also, that effectiveness is not about being smooth, in control, or clever. If you find yourself in a mess, lean in to the experience and use it as a way to model for your client. There's no rule that you have to stick with it—if your metaphor is mangled, acknowledge that and move on!

Not Letting It Do Its Work

Despite the acknowledged importance of exercises and metaphors, a common misstep occurs when therapists view them as adjuncts to the therapy, as helpful support tools, rather than as having an important purpose of their own. They are both vehicles *and* mechanisms of change (Villatte, Villatte, & Monestes, 2014). Seeing them as merely ways to flesh out a point can result in their underutilization and also make therapists more likely to undermine, undo, or otherwise take away from what experiential exercises and metaphors have to offer. Put simply, the therapist does not allow the metaphor or exercise to do its work. It can be hard for therapists to move out of their own words for a moment, to prioritize *doing* or *feeling* or *being* over talking. There have been many occasions when I have heard or watched a therapist do a beautiful job with a metaphor or other experiential exercise, only to subsequently drown it in explanation and evaluation. It can be particularly easy to do this if exercises and metaphors are viewed as having supporting roles, with verbal rules holding the more important, leading role (to use a metaphor). In actuality, metaphors and exercises have key parts to play, and should not be written out, cut off, or upstaged.

Where'd It Go?

One of the more distinctive features of ACT is the incorporation of experiential work. This includes building mindfulness and in-the-moment work geared toward helping clients contact their direct experience (as in "Take a moment and notice what is coming up for you around this" or "What happened after you told your grandson you weren't coming to the game?"). The term "experiential exercise" is often used to refer to more formal exercises, such as "Take your mind for a walk," that have been around since ACT was first introduced and that remain relevant today. Along with the familiar standbys, there is an abundance of new exercises that continue to bring vibrancy to the work. Thanks to creative therapists (and clients) worldwide, therapists now have access to a wealth of experiential exercises that are described not only in the literature, but on the ACBS website and in rich exchanges on the ACT listserv. Moreover, every ACT training or workshop I have ever participated in has stressed the experiential piece of the therapy and has never failed to offer a new idea or way to approach an ACT metaphor or exercise. All this is to emphasize how striking I find it that many ACT therapists gradually move entirely away from including formal experiential work in their ACT sessions. Although my focus on individual sessions led me to initially miss the breadth of this trend, after observing numerous ACT therapists over time it became clear that this tendency was not uncommon. Many therapists who initially would include at least one or two formal experiential exercises per session would begin to implement them less and less frequently, until these sorts of exercises were altogether absent from the therapy. A meta-review of earlier supervision and consultation notes revealed the same trend. (I should note, however, that use of metaphors tended to remain strong.)

When I began to explore this tendency with therapists, it was almost always the case that they were not aware of having moved away from formal experiential work. When we looked a little deeper, however, there was often some discomfort around doing these sorts of exercises, and at an unconscious level a choice had been made to stick with more familiar dialogue. Sometimes the therapist wasn't so much uncomfortable with formal experiential work as just *very* comfortable with talk therapy. This is not to say that formal experiential exercises are the only way to go in ACT. Helping clients contact their experiences through natural exchanges in conversations can be quite effective, and I've provided some examples in this book. However, not infrequently I have heard comments regarding more formal exercises along the lines of "Doing that sort of thing is just very different from what I usually do" and "I never know how my client is going to react," or "I feel funny doing those sorts of things with my client." I can find that in my own history, too: a tendency to stick with discussion or metaphors rather than making the additional effort to come up with, or pull in, a more formal exercise. Of course, becoming present to this tendency provides the opportunity to choose differently, and I encourage ACT therapists to (1) check to see whether they are giving more formal experiential exercises short shrift, and if so (2) consider whether their inclusion might be beneficial. Not only can these exercises be clinically powerful, they are particularly helpful when working with very fused clients.

YOU, BUT NOT ME

Aside from underutilization, another common misstep I have observed with experiential exercises is when therapists do not join their clients in an exercise that would benefit from mutual participation. In the "lemon, lemon" defusion exercise, for example, I have often seen therapists instruct the client to repeat the word over and over again, and then simply observe rather than join in. When the function of this choice is examined closely, it is frequently the case that the therapist was simply more comfortable in the therapist role, "expertly" instructing and observing the client, rather than joining in this rather weird experience in a human-to-human way.

I have seen therapists maintain distance even in the most intimate of exercises, such as "eyes-on." This is the willingness exercise where the therapist and client (or participant pairs, if doing a group) sit knee to knee and give each other their attention without speaking. It is an intentionally evocative experience that provides a clear and accessible opportunity to experience the desire to avoid and the ability to remain engaged despite discomfort. It is typically a pretty intimate experience. But I have observed that after concluding the exercise, many therapists do not share what they experienced. That is, they keep the focus solely on the client—as in "What did you notice during that exercise?" Given the intensity and mutuality of the exercise, this approach represents possible avoidance on the therapist's part that is worth taking a look at. It is also a real missed opportunity. These sorts of exercises hold tremendous promise for authentic connection, for modeling, for demonstrating the horizontal therapy relationship, for creating that clinical oomph that brings important points home. Again, getting present to your own experience in the session is a good place to start. Notice your reaction to the idea of doing an exercise with your client, and notice what you do with that. As always, the beauty of ACT is that whatever our response, it also reflects core ACT processes and is excellent fodder for the work.

Therapist:	"I want to share something with you."
Client:	"Uh-oh. What is it?"
Therapist:	"It's just something interesting I noticed. Last week I had planned to do an exercise with you and then ended up not doing it."
Client	*(somewhat uninterested):* "Okay."
Therapist:	"The thing is that I sort of bailed on it. That is, I think it could be a powerful exercise for you, but I was worried that you wouldn't like it, and I also wasn't completely confident that I would be able to do it well, so I just skipped it."
Client	*(surprised):* "What was it?"
Therapist:	"Well, let's do it now, shall we? I can just sort of hold my worries and anxiety about it and head in there, if you are willing."
Client:	"Sure."

Basic How-Tos

Let's talk for a moment about using metaphors. I pointed out in chapter 1 how we humans naturally conduct functional analyses and utilize basic learning principles as we make our way in the world. I suggested further that awareness of these principles and clarity regarding how they function assists our ability to work with them toward therapeutic ends. Similarly, the use of metaphors is so embedded (to use a metaphor) in our daily language that we don't even notice them. Increasing our awareness of how metaphorical language functions will also help us optimize its use in the therapy room. Matthieu Villatte, Jennifer Villatte, and Jean-Louis Monestes (2014) offer this nice explanation as to what metaphors bring to the therapy, worth quoting in full:

> Metaphors make abstract concepts concrete and memorable by providing a rich verbal context that evokes the same types of thoughts, feelings, and behaviors as the client's actual situation.
>
> The story-like quality of metaphors has the advantage of providing instructive lessons that are rich in emotional and perceptual detail, mimicking direct contact with the environment and making the experience more memorable. Metaphor create a verbal world where clients can explore new behaviors and discover the contingencies for themselves, circumventing the

verbal traps of learning by instruction. Metaphors also draw attention to salient features of a situation that may go unnoticed in the client's real-world environment, thus liberating them from the cage built by language. (16–17)

Do you remember the earlier discussion about transformation of stimulus functions? That an important feature of relational framing is how the qualities of whatever is being related—how it functions for us—is transformed from one to the other? (Think of how the "yick" of peas is now related to all "vegetables" according to my daughter, or how for the trauma survivor the shame and horror of being raped was connected to her notion of herself, with the idea of men, with intimacy, and so on.) Metaphors utilize this principle quite effectively. That is, the function of one idea or situation (as depicted in the metaphor) is applied to the client's situation with the goal of transforming how something is functioning for the client. Consider a client with a history of childhood abuse and neglect, whose life continues to be about attempting to receive love and validation from her still-abusive mother. While working with such a client I found myself thinking about how basic that need for validation is, and yet how tragic it is to spend one's life trying to get love from a dry source. A metaphor came to mind that I have since come to use frequently:

Me:	"Imagine that you are terribly thirsty, and you have come upon a water well. Luckily there's a bucket there on a rope, and so you lower it down (*acting this out*). You pull it up....There's no water! So you lower it down again." (*Pausing, then acting out the following.*) "You pull it back up again—there's no water! But this is a well! It's supposed to have water! So you lower it down again." (*Pausing, continuing to mimic dropping and pulling up the bucket.*) "You pull it back up. No water." (*Pause.*) "But you're *really thirsty*! So you drop down the bucket. You pull it up again. Guess what?"
Client:	"No water."
Me:	"But you're *really* thirsty! You need water! Everyone needs water! So you drop the bucket." (*Long pause.*) "You pull it back up again. No water. So you dr—"
Client:	"You need to find another well."
Me:	"But this is the well you know! It's the one that's here. And it's *supposed* to have water (*mimicking dropping down the bucket*)."
Client:	"But it doesn't. You can't just keep trying to get what's not there."
Me:	"But you need water." (*Pause.*) "You *need* love and validation—we all do." (*Mimics dropping it down again.*) "And mothers are supposed to do that! So you keep dropping the bucket."

Client	(long pause): "I see. I've been trying to get water from a well. A very dried-up well."
Me:	(Silent.)
Client:	(a bit tearful): "I think it's time for me to move on."

In this case, noticing the functional sequence among the events in the metaphor (the futility of seeking water from a dry well) allowed for a transformation of the way the events in the client's situation are perceived (in other words, seeing that seeking love and validation from a source where it is not forthcoming is futile). The client was able to contact her direct experience—including the unworkable consequences—around her behavior with her mother. Other features could be transformed as well, such as by validating the need itself (water, love), demonstrating how "should" can keep us trapped (a well should have water, a mother should love), and confronting how scary it can be to leave the known and venture into the unknown.

When we understand the change mechanisms thought to be at work in metaphors, we are guided as to how we might optimize their use in therapy. In essence, we use words to increase the experiential aspect of the intervention, as doing so "makes interaction with the elements of the story more concrete, emotionally evocative, and memorable" (Villatte et al., 2004). For example, the indicative present tense was used to give the metaphor oomph: "...But you're really thirsty! And so you drop the bucket down." This sort of verbal cuing helps clients experience the metaphor in a way that is more immediate and powerful. Also, rather than directly stating the relationship between the metaphorical situation and the clinical situation (for example, "trying to get love and validation *is like* trying to draw up water from an empty well"), the therapist linked the scenarios in a way that highlights experiential learning. ("But you need water....You *need* love and validation—we all do....And mothers are supposed to do that! So you keep dropping the bucket.")

So far I have pointed out a few ways in which therapists can prevent themselves from fully capitalizing on what ACT metaphors and experiential exercises offer the therapy. I have also examined the processes thought to be at work in the use of metaphors as a way to help maximize their use in therapy. The following checklist is offered as a basic guideline for maximizing the effectiveness of metaphors and exercises:

✓ When planning ACT therapy sessions, proactively consider which metaphors and exercises might further the core processes you hope to advance.

✓ Know the purpose of your metaphor (or your selected experiential exercise). What points are you wanting to make? What core processes are in play?

✓ Have the metaphors and exercises ready to go. That is, practice actually doing them if you haven't already.

✓ When working with a client in the moment, look for ways to experientially demonstrate what you are working on. That includes going with metaphors that are most likely to be particularly relevant to the client, or using ones that naturally arise in the course of conversation.

✓ Take a chance! It's okay to be messy.

✓ Don't let the "story" override the present.

I have found the above guidelines to be useful as a general approach to ACT metaphors and exercises. I would also like to point interested readers to a recently-released book, *The Big Book of ACT Metaphors: A Practitioner's Guide to Experiential Exercises and Metaphors in Acceptance and Commitment Therapy*, which includes the chapter by Villatte, Villatte, and Monestès that I've cited. This text promises to be a significant resource for optimizing your clinical experiential work. In the following sections I will offer some additional considerations in working with this component of ACT.

TIMING, YET AGAIN

When exploring timing in chapter 4, I mentioned as an example that I generally save the passengers-on-a-bus metaphor until the later stage of the therapy, having found that it does a great job of pulling together the various ACT processes in a way that makes sense to clients. I also suggested there, and in chapter 9, that in order to maximize the chessboard metaphor it helps to wait until the client has certain skills (such as being present and defusing) at least partly under his belt. Once again, considering the timing of an experiential exercise or metaphor on the basis of the behavioral process(es) you are targeting will help you make this determination. If you are fairly early on in the therapy, it makes sense to use exercises and metaphors that really flesh out particular processes. For example, the "take-your-mind-for-a-walk" exercise, in which therapist and client take turns enacting each other's minds as they physically walk around together, homes in on cognitive defusion. The "anxiety machine" demonstration, in which the client is metaphorically hooked up to a machine that senses even the tiniest blip of anxiety, homes in on the paradoxical effects of control. That is, as clients are instructed that their only task is to not have any anxiety, they quickly realize that the more they try not to be anxious, the more anxiety will register on the machine. When beginning to work on a particular core process with a client, I like to use more simple metaphors or exercises that illuminate that process particularly well.

Toward the end of therapy, I move to more elaborate examples that pull together multiple processes. For example, I like to bring in the passengers-on-a-bus metaphor when most of the involved processes have been explored and the emphasis is on committed action. (To recap: The client is told that his life is like a bus that is constantly picking up passengers. Every experience he has—every thought, feeling, and memory—is a passenger on the bus. So some passengers are quite pleasant; others are quite unwanted. The client is reminded of the various ways in which he struggles with unwanted passengers, trying to get them to leave, sit still, keep quiet, and so forth. Of course it doesn't work, because we can't get rid of such passengers in life. As the driver of the bus, though, the client has the choice to drive in a valued direction. If he is willing to let the passengers be, he can get behind the wheel and drive in whatever direction he chooses.) This metaphor is a particularly good one for demonstrating self-as-context (the bus and driver of the bus), willingness (being willing to let the passengers be, regardless of what they are doing back there), values ("In what direction will you choose to head?"), and committed action (putting your foot to the pedal and driving in the direction of your values).

I will also use an exercise or metaphor that reflects multiple processes in such a way that just one key process is highlighted early on, and then pull it in again after additional processes have been explored. For example, the "two computers" metaphor is commonly used to introduce cognitive defusion, although like most ACT exercises and metaphors it actually reflects multiple processes: being present (to what is showing up on the monitor), defusion (observing rather than buying the text on the monitor) willingness (noticing versus going to battle with), and self-as-context (who's doing the noticing). It even points to valued action, by demonstrating that critical space between observer and program. Bottom line: It is a rich metaphor that can be used in many ways, like many of those found in ACT. I have found it helpful to introduce this metaphor early on, focusing on the defusion aspect, as it depicts this so nicely, and then refer back to it as other processes are explored.

Aside from considering at which point in the therapy to use a metaphor or exercise, it is also important to consider the timing within the session. For example, is it best to open with an exercise? Or does it work better to verbally introduce a concept, such as *control as problematic*, and then do an exercise or pull in a metaphor? Putting right and wrong aside and going with the goal of optimization, I'll share some considerations I've found helpful:

Nothing beats an epiphany. That is, if the client can have his own realization around an ACT idea, it seems to have more personal relevance and staying power than if he simply understands and even agrees with something you are suggesting. For that reason, I will often opt to go into an exercise without a lot of explanation, in the hopes the client will have his own "aha" moment. If the point of the exercise or metaphor is a new one that has not previously been explored, I will process it with the client afterward, making plenty of room for his personal experience with it while also listening to make sure he is not distorting the point (perceiving a defusion exercise, for example, as a way to control thoughts). If we have already worked with the process(es) reflected in the exercise or metaphor, or if the client's response to it is especially powerful, I will let the metaphor or exercise do the work and stay out of the way afterward as well.

It can also be quite effective to discuss a key idea or concept, and then pull in a metaphor or exercise to bring the point home. In fact, there are certain clients who may respond better to this strategy. For example, I am thinking of the highly fused client mentioned in chapter 9, who was able to grasp self-as-context only when the therapist spelled out incredibly clearly the point of the "continuous you," detailing in advance exactly what she hoped the client would gain from the exercise. I have also advised therapists to consider this approach when working with highly defended clients who are so afraid of being revealed as ignorant that they are unable to actively listen to a metaphor or participate in an exercise. That is, they are so fused with thoughts around needing to perform, or needing to have the right answer, that they are unable to be present to the exercise or metaphor. They are too busy anticipating and managing their sense of being put on the spot. With these folks, particularly if it's early in the therapy, it may make sense to go with introducing a concept straightforwardly, and letting them know what you are after with related metaphors and exercises before you do them. This is an example of picking your battles: do you target the client's avoidance (work on defusing, being present, and willingness), or is it more important at this point that she receive the information you are hoping to convey with the exercise or metaphor? Again, the key is context—where you and your client are in the therapy and what is happening in session will guide your decision-making. It may be, for example, that the client needs to understand the point of an exercise targeting defusion in advance in order to begin building that skill. Alternately, the dominance of the pathological process may be the most pressing matter. For example, defensiveness (avoidance) may be so predominant that nothing else can be accomplished until that is addressed head-on. So no right or wrong here, either—just factors for you to be actively considering when working with metaphors and exercises.

A powerful aspect of ACT is that we *can* take advantage of various learning modalities, so I try to utilize them all when working with any key principle. As ACT therapists we continually assess how interventions actually function in order to learn what seems to work best with a particular client.

Common Challenges

In the next section I'll offer some examples of common challenges faced by ACT therapists when working with some of the better-known metaphors and exercises. Although I am capturing just a smattering here, my hope is that the points raised will be relevant to the many exercises and metaphors that are used in the therapy.

WHY CAN'T THE PASSENGERS DRIVE THE BUS?

Even though metaphors are used to circumvent the potential pitfalls of verbal rules, when working with metaphors both clients and therapists often fuse with rules about what we're supposed to doing with metaphors! For example, we buy into the idea that somehow there's a truth to a good metaphor, that it needs to "make sense." This idea can best be described with an example of a common scenario.

Scenario: The therapist has just finished setting up the man-in-the-hole metaphor.

> *Therapist:* "...and the only tool you find in there is a shovel! And so you dig. Because that's what you know to do—if you're in a hole, and all you have is a shovel, what do you do with it? You dig. But what's the problem with digging when you're in a hole?"
>
> *Client:* "The hole gets deeper."
>
> *Therapist:* "The hole gets deeper! If you're in there digging, the hole just gets deeper."
>
> *Client:* "I would dig steps into the side of the hole and climb out."
>
> *Therapist:* (*Pause.*) "And before you know it you've fallen into another hole. And you start digging."
>
> *Client:* "I would take my blindfold off so I could see. That way I'd avoid the holes."
>
> *Therapist:* "The blindfold is knotted so tight you can't undo it—it doesn't come off."
>
> *Client:* "Then I would just stop walking."
>
> *Therapist:* "But then you wouldn't be living your life. You'd just be standing still."
>
> *Client:* "Then I would start crawling and feel my way."

And so on. This sort of cat-and-mouse game can occur with any of the metaphors, and probably the experiential exercises as well. For example, as implied in this section header, one way the passengers-on-a-bus metaphor can stall out is when the client questions why it is, exactly, that only she can "drive her bus." The therapist then falls into the trap of thinking this question must be answered, that there is some truth to the metaphor that must be demonstrated, that everything must make rational sense. Not so! Metaphors are used to point to something, not to prove something. Here's a way to handle the above exchange:

> *Therapist:* "...and the only tool you find in there is a shovel! And so you dig. Because that's what you know to do—if you're in a hole, and all you have is a shovel, what do you do with it? You dig. But what's the problem with digging when you're in a hole?"
>
> *Client:* "The hole gets deeper."

Therapist:	"The hole gets deeper! If you're in there digging, the hole gets deeper."
Client:	"I would dig steps into the side of the hole and climb out."
Therapist:	"In this metaphor it's not that kind of a hole. Digging just gets you in deeper."

In other words, there's no actual burden of proof on you here. Rather than fusing with the content the client has provided and thinking that you need to have an answer, you can return to the intended purpose of the metaphor. Some clients really feel the need to debate the veracity of metaphors, to point out their flaws, and so forth. There are a couple of ways to work with this. One is to provide some quick education on metaphors.

Client:	"But why can't the passengers get off the bus? And I don't see why they can't drive."
Therapist:	"That's the thing with metaphors. They aren't intended to make sense in that way. Rather, they point to something. There is a gift in a metaphor, a piece of wisdom for you if you can be open to seeing it."

After a conversation like this, especially if I think it likely the client will take an oppositional stance to a metaphor I'm about to introduce, I might preface it with a reference to the earlier conversation:

Me:	"There's a metaphor I want to share with you. As we've talked about before, metaphors do require a sort of leap of faith. You have to go along with them enough to see what piece of wisdom they contain. So I invite you to be open to seeing if there might be something in this one for you."

Another way to work with a metaphorically challenged client is to address the function of their questioning or resistance:

Client:	"But why can't the passengers get off the bus? And I don't see why they can't drive."
Therapist:	"They can't drive because only you can. You're the driver."
Client:	"But they're *my* thoughts and feelings, right? So in that sense they're me. They're parts of the driver."
Therapist	*(pausing and holding the moment):* "May I ask you something?"
Client	*(a little edgily):* "What?"

Therapist:	"Can you speak to what's happening for you right now? What are you experiencing right now, in this moment?"
Client	*(a little defensively):* "I don't know. I just don't get this stuff...."
Therapist:	"This is important, so hang with me here. What is happening—what's going on with all the questions around this bus metaphor?"
Client:	"I don't know. I'm just annoyed or something."
Therapist:	"Yeah. That doesn't mean something wrong is happening here, by the way. It's just information for us. Can you get at what you are after with all the questions? Do you have a sense of why it's important to point out flaws with this metaphor?"
Client:	"I just...I don't like it when things don't make sense."
Therapist	*(thinking it over):* "So maybe you are trying to get more comfortable in some way, or maybe it's a way to push against me or what I'm saying?"
Client:	"Maybe, I dunno."
Therapist:	"Yeah, we probably can't ever get at exactly *why* you are feeling the need to point out all the ways this metaphor doesn't make sense. But my concern is that in doing that, you are short-changing yourself."
Client:	"I'm not sure what you mean."
Therapist:	"Metaphors have been around for a long time. They're one of the oldest ways humans have passed on wisdom, and there's a reason for that. A metaphor might mean one thing to one person and hold a different meaning for someone else. The point is that there is potentially something of value in it for you, but you would need to be open to receiving it."
Client:	"It's not that I'm not open...."
Therapist:	"If you are looking for flaws, ways it won't make sense, there will be no shortage of evidence. So the question is whether you can sort of hold those observations or questions, or whatever discomfort is going on for you, and look to see what is there to be seen."
Client	*(thinks it over):* "Yeah, I can do that."

A client like this could well engage in questioning or debate when working with exercises or metaphors in the future, but now the therapist has put that stake in the ground (to use a metaphor) that will help them work together on this as it shows up.

TURNING BUSES INTO SHOVELS

One of the more pernicious and yet understandable challenges is when clients turn various ACT metaphors and exercises into control strategies. In fact, I have been awed by the ingenuity of the human mind—it's amazing how a metaphor specifically geared to target willingness, for example, can be transformed into a beautiful method of control. Therapists, too, can inadvertently distort the intent of a metaphor or exercise, sometimes sending a message that is in direct opposition to that intended. There are actually myriad ways in which a control message can sneak into a session. We will explore how this happens, and ways to work with some of the more common exercises and metaphors such that our intended message is conveyed. Although there is only space for a few limited examples, the discussion should be applicable to exercises and metaphors more generally.

Chinese finger trap. I'm starting with this exercise because it is a good example of how easily, with just a word or two, therapists can contradict themselves while doing an exercise or metaphor. I am assuming the reader is familiar with Chinese finger traps—those straw finger tubes? When someone inserts an index finger into each end and then tries to pull back out, the tube constricts, trapping both fingers. The harder the person pulls, the tighter the trap. The point of it, of course, is to demonstrate the futility, indeed the paradoxical effects of avoidance and control—in other words, not only does pulling not work, but the tube becomes tighter. This is a popular exercise due to its simple yet graphic nature, and because actual finger traps can be used to make the point experientially. However, I have witnessed many therapists wrap up the demonstration by stating that the only way one can escape the tube is by counterintuitively pushing one's fingers in, that pushing or leaning in is the only way to get out of the trap. Here you have the therapist on one hand pointing to avoidance or control as problematic (it keeps one stuck), and on the other suggesting a different escape strategy is needed (supporting avoidance and control). Am I being picky? Perhaps. But consider that your clients are likely hearing almost everything in ACT through an intractable fix-it filter. They are in all probability continuously searching for a way to escape the pain of being human. This means that even when therapists aren't subtly supporting the control agenda it is still in operation. As ACT therapists we can strive to keep from supporting unworkable strategies and look for opportunities to poke a hole in an unworkable control agenda.

Continuing with this specific example, when using the finger trap exercise I advise consultees or trainees to stick to pointing out how pulling makes the trap tighter, and how pushing or "leaning in" creates room. No need to mention escape at all. If the client goes there, you can use the opportunity to refer back to all the various things that haven't "worked," how pulling against the trap indeed keeps us stuck, and that this work is about creating some space, some room to move. For the difficult client who insists on making the point that the demonstration actually shows how one can escape, remember, it's *your* metaphor. You get to say, "The point of this metaphor is to show how struggling against something can make us even more stuck," and move on.

Two computers. Previously, I mentioned the two computers metaphor, which is commonly used to target cognitive defusion. It also gets at self-as-context. That is, it is designed to help clients learn to observe thoughts (and attendant emotions and physical sensations) as "programs" or text that has shown up on the computer monitor, rather than being fused with those thoughts or computer programs. While perhaps not explicitly explained at this point, that process requires being the Experiencer, the Observer (the locus of perspective noticing the program or text). The point is made that when we are not fused with our thoughts, when—to go with this metaphor— our heads aren't buried inside the computer monitor, we can see the program of the moment for what it is: as text, amongst more text. This perspective, in turn creates a bit of space between the Experiencer or Observer and the program. This space is not about being more comfortable, however; it's simply that in that space we have the ability to choose.

A common misstep I have observed with this and other defusion exercises (such as "lemon, lemon" and singing a troubling thought) is when therapists convey to clients that the point of defusing is to lessen discomfort. Even more often, the therapist has not actually suggested this, but it is what the client takes away from the metaphor nonetheless. Cognitive defusion may indeed reduce *suffering*, but only as a consequence of not buying into and battling with one's thoughts. Defusing used as a control or avoidance strategy per se sets the client up to remain embroiled in the I'm-not-okay-unless-I'm-comfortable business. Fortunately, it is not difficult to undermine the ongoing fix-it agenda when working with this metaphor. Simply making the point that a painful thought is a painful thought and that efforts to eliminate, or reduce, or otherwise alter text is just more text, and stressing that work with the metaphor is about creating space between the observer and the program, rather than altering the program, will help therapists steer clear of aligning with the control agenda.

One other small point regarding the two computers metaphor: I generally advise therapists to consider staying away from saying things like "You have good programs there, bad programs there…" or "That's a good thought; that's a bad thought," and so on, because good/bad evaluations are simply more text on the screen. In fact, if the client offers something like this, some comment about how a particular program is good or bad, it is important to point out how that particular evaluation would now be added to the text on her screen.

Lemon, lemon. The point I'd like to make here is very similar to the one I just made: this defusion exercise is not about lessening pain or discomfort. As discussed in chapter

6, it is about demonstrating how language functions, how we relate to language in both effective and problematic ways. In asking clients to join us in repeating a word like "lemon" or "milk" over and over, we notice the distinction between the symbolic features of language and the more direct and concrete aspects of our experiences. In other words, though we can create a virtual experience with language—"Imagine you are biting into the lemon; you can feel the bumpy, slightly cool peel on your tongue as you break the skin"—words are in fact just sounds we produce. It has been striking to me how often therapists directly or indirectly send the message that the point to defusing via repetition in this way is to lessen pain, as opposed to being able to see language (and hence cognition) for what it is, and isn't. Even if you are steering clear of this stickiness, I encourage you to look for this one; in my experience, unless this point is directly clarified, clients almost always see the exercise as being a means to control or avoid.

Oh, one more small but important point about this particular exercise: in doing the "lemon, lemon" exercise or a similar one, a common misstep is to not allow the repetition piece to go on long enough. That is, the verbal repetition should last for a while, long enough to where the function of the word is noticeably altered—the object "lemon," for example, is lost, and all that remains are some strange sounds being emitted. What often happens is that the therapist has the client (and himself) repeat the word only briefly, and then explains the point, rather than allowing the client to get into experiential contact with the fact that words are ultimately just noises we make. This is an example of what I referred to earlier—how we can optimize experiential exercises and metaphors by allowing them to do their thing rather than turning too quickly to verbal explanation.

SOME STICKINESS WITH MINDFULNESS

The ACT literature and trainings generally do a good job of clarifying what is meant by "mindfulness" in ACT, so I'll not repeat that here. Rather, here are a few of the common missteps or client challenges that are frequently faced when working on mindfulness with clients.

Mindfully controlling. Isn't it something that clients (and therapists) can use mindfulness as a control strategy? But yes, and why not? This is why it is so important that therapists clarify what is meant by mindfulness in ACT when introducing it to clients, and that they regularly check in with clients to see if and how mindfulness is being implemented in their daily lives. I frequently hear clients report proudly that they used mindfulness as a technique to distract or lessen a painful experience. The problem with this isn't that they helped themselves in a given situation—we're not trying to make people feel bad, for Pete's sake. It's that if they perceive this as the purpose of mindfulness they are missing the point and cutting themselves off from the larger offering: that they are intact, whole human beings who can observe and simply hold even the most painful moments in life. I usually suggest therapists handle this one simply by directly clarifying the distinction—pointing out how reducing mindfulness to a control method sets the client up to be not okay when mindfulness doesn't succeed in taking away pain or discomfort.

Trance-like states. I wouldn't say this is terribly common, but I have heard some clients report that they were successful with mindfulness because they put themselves in a trance. One woman told her therapist that she had "become hypnotized by watching a fan blade go round and round," for example. This is not the "ongoing awareness" we are hoping to build in ACT, but rather an example of why it is important to find out just what your client means when she says she has been practicing mindfulness.

Good leaf, bad leaf. It is not surprising that evaluation shows up during mindfulness exercises. In fact, it would be more surprising if it did not! But it can certainly get in the way, particularly when clients are highly fused. That is, it can be tricky to defuse enough from evaluations to see that you are evaluating. This is another reason to check in with clients after mindfulness exercises. If the client's experience was powerful and his take-away is in line with that intended, you can let the experience speak for itself. If, however, the client reveals some sort of difficulty or misconception, you now have the opportunity to work on that together. As applied to "leaves on a stream," clients often report having good or bad thoughts on the leaves (or the clouds in the sky, as the case may be), rather than realizing "good" and "bad" are just more leaves. With this one I have found it effective to have the therapist conduct the exercise again, this time guiding the client to place each noticed thought on a leaf (or cloud), and if an evaluation follows, to put that on another little leaf that attaches itself to the first as they go down the stream.

When a Client Has a "Bad Experience"

Not infrequently, a consultee or supervisee will report that her client had an uncomfortable experience during an exercise—as though discomfort is a problem. For example, one trainee, clearly alarmed, reported that her client had gotten very upset by the "floating above the earth" exercise. In case you are not familiar with this exercise, in it clients are guided via imagery to gradually rise above the room in which they are sitting. They are then guided to rise up until they are looking down at the building containing the room, and higher still until they are looking at the block below, then the city, then the entire state and continent, and so on. Finally, they are floating in space, observing the blue planet called Earth below. Throughout, clients are guided to get in contact with the shared humanity on this planet. That is, while guiding the client to slowly rise up, the therapist makes comments such as "You see all the people hurrying to and fro, going about their busy lives....They, too, have hopes, dreams, fears, and disappointments....They, too, feel pain, joy, sorrow...."

In this particular instance the client had become upset when, as she put it, she thought about "all the people who are feeling suicidal." My trainee was not expecting this response (most clients experience a comforting sense of connection), and her interpretation was that something had gone wrong with the exercise. It can be helpful to remember that, despite what our minds hand us in such moments, (1) unexpected does not equal "wrong," and (2) a client becoming upset does not mean something is "wrong." Do you remember way back in chapter 3, when I shared how making space at the table for the unwanted guest has been a particularly helpful message to keep in mind? So, as applied here, while the client was doing this exercise an unexpected, sorrowful guest suddenly showed up at the table. Actively welcoming this and any other unexpected, unwanted visitor that may appear during an exercise will help you maintain an ACT-consistent stance. For example, here is how my trainee could have handled the situation:

Therapist	(noticing the client seems visibly upset upon concluding the exercise): "What are you experiencing right now?"
Client	(slightly tearful): "I just…I started thinking about all the people who are feeling suicidal, even right this minute."
Therapist:	"How would you describe the feeling that goes along with that awareness?"
Client:	"Like, what's the point?! Like, just really sad and hopeless!"
Therapist:	"Does 'despair' fit?"
Client:	"Exactly. Despair."
Therapist:	"Yeah." (Just sits with this for a bit.) "So you got in touch with all the despair going on in the world—that, even in this moment, there are people having the experience of despair."
Client:	"Yeah, it's too much. I can't deal with that."
Therapist:	"Can you imagine that, even in this moment, there are people who are having that thought? That, just like you, they have the thought 'It's too much,' or 'I can't deal with that'?"
Client	(thinks it over): "Yeah, I suppose so."
Therapist	(not at all rushing, allowing the experience to be in the room): "Let's just sit with that awareness for a moment." (Eventually continues.) "So in this moment, a painful moment, there are likely others who are sharing a similar experience, feelings of despair, thoughts about it all being too much."

Client:	"Lots of others!" (*Pause.*) "But that is sort of strange to think about—it's also comforting in an odd way. I mean, I'm sad for them, for me—all of us—but it makes me feel…compassionate toward everybody in a way."
Therapist:	"Yeah, sorta like 'it's hard to be human sometimes'?"
Client:	"Exactly."

In this example the therapist is actively welcoming—in fact, leaning in to—what the client is experiencing. In so doing, she furthers the processes of getting present and willingness, while clearly conveying a central message of the metaphor. When assisted to just hold what she was experiencing, the client was able to contact the shared humanity suggested in the exercise.

Mixed Messages

It is interesting that not only it is possible to distort any ACT metaphor or exercise, but the distortion is often in direct contradiction to the model. As I described in the previous section, it is amazing how often a control message sneaks in, even when that is the last thing the therapist is intending. There are also other mixed messages that often show up with certain metaphors and exercises, and I've included a couple of examples below for readers to consider. As I've said, my hope is that by providing these examples, ACT therapists will be inspired to thoughtfully consider just what they are conveying when they work with a metaphor or exercise—even the little differences in wording can carry a lot of clinical weight.

Two Scales. I wanted to include this metaphor as there are a couple of related therapist missteps I hear rather frequently. For discussion purposes, let's imagine that the therapist has described having two scales in front of her, where one, say, measures anxiety and the other measures control. She has made the point that when anxiety is at a 10, and the effort to control is at a 10, it's as though the anxiety is locked into place. The key at this point is to make sure the client takes away two main ideas: (1) that control tends to lock in the anxiety (or grief, or self-loathing, or whatever example you are using), and (2) that willingness (introduced either by bringing a third "willingness scale" into the discussion or by converting the control scale into a willingness scale) simply means things are not locked in place. Therapists sometimes neglect to make sure the client understands this does not mean the anxiety (or whatever) will automatically go down. This is not a new form of control strategy, in other words. In my experience, it is not so much that the therapist doesn't understand this point but that he or she neglects to adequately clarify it for the client. It is important to make sure the client understands that even if willingness is at a 10, the anxiety could stay at the same level of intensity—it could even go up, or it could drop way down. The point is that it's not locked in. A related, subtle but important misstep is to swing too far with this and suggest that the client's anxiety (or grief, or self-loathing, or whatever) will never go away. How do we know that? This misstep can occur with many of the exercises and metaphors. ACT isn't about what we don't know (in other words, the future). It is about what the evidence has shown about what tends to happen when we pit ourselves against our own internal experiences, when we focus our attention and energy into not having what we have. The client can look to his own history to see how well trying not to have an unwanted thought, feeling, or physical sensation has worked. When that control agenda is replaced with willingness, we don't actually know what happens next.

Friend or foe? Of the many wording changes I have experimented with over time, one that has seemed to stick involves the way I depict unwanted thoughts and feelings to clients. That is, at some point it occurred to me that there was a contradiction in promoting radical acceptance (acceptance of even those most unwanted thoughts, feelings, and memories) and also conveying the idea that unwanted thoughts were "bullies," or some such antagonists. Antagonists are by definition something to push against. Another example is depicting unwanted thoughts and feelings as "monsters on the bus." As viewed in our culture, monsters are also antagonists and something to push against or try to escape—you get the point. But does this wording really matter if the main point of these metaphors is that even very powerful-seeming thoughts and feelings aren't in charge? If considered in the context that we all are already set up to struggle against unwanted thoughts and feelings, it may not be a good idea to support that system, no matter how subtly. More pragmatically, why not use images that promote a more accepting stance, such as the idea conveyed in the "Welcome anxiety, my old friend" meditation?

I have come to appreciate a metaphor that fellow ACT provider Jeremy Goldberg shared as a way to relate to the workings of the mind. Jeremy said he thought of his mind as an "overeager assistant," someone constantly following him around, scribbling notes, and handing him suggestions, warnings, reminders, and so on. The key is that, while misguided and a real pain at times, the overeager assistant is just doing his job. The client can pat his assistant reassuringly on the back and then make the choice that is in line with his values. Similarly, I stick with "passengers" on a bus rather than monsters, and I take care not to add fuel to the idea that these are actual foes when setting up that metaphor. It may not seem all that important, but I have seen clients visibly lighten as they consider giving a quick greeting to even the most unwelcome passenger on their bus. Such a gesture represents a radical shift in relationship with that unwanted thought (or memory, or experience). It is not a small thing when a client realizes she can give an understanding hug to the scared and vulnerable "victim" on her bus, or that she can give a quick nod to the trauma passenger seated staunchly in row 3 while firmly taking her seat behind the wheel. These are the transformative moments that really stick.

To make myself very clear here, I realize that therapists could work similarly with whatever words are being applied to unwanted private events, that a "scary trauma passenger" and "monster" are arguably similar, and all that. My point is simply this: you can aid yourself and your client by using words that are less loaded and less likely to be misinterpreted, and you can use words that maximize the opportunity to gain whatever there is to be gained.

USE WHAT WORKS

How fortunate are we that there is such a treasure trove of exercises and metaphors to use when doing ACT! While I encourage trainees and consultees to actively explore and experiment rather than unnecessarily limit themselves to what they already know and are comfortable with, this is about what works, after all. Some metaphors or exercises may just ring more true for you than others, some will work better for some clients than others, and there's no rule we need to buy into around having to do particular exercises or metaphors. However, we can also increase our effectiveness by considering just what it is that makes this learning approach effective and applying that to the context we are operating in.

It is only by experimenting and trying on different metaphors and exercises that we learn what works best for us. We learn what works best for our clients by being present and assessing how the intervention is actually functioning in the moment. You may find that some of the suggestions I've offered in this chapter do not match your own experiences with these exercises, or you may have simply discovered other ways to work them that serve you well. Perhaps, like me, you really enjoy playing with this piece and seeing how even slight changes can positively impact the work. Regardless of where you ultimately land, thoughtful assessment and experimentation with exercises and metaphors decreases the likelihood that you will step outside the model, and increases your ability to capitalize on this potent component of the therapy.

SUMMARY

In writing this chapter I realized I had *something* to say about nearly every metaphor and exercise I have encountered in ACT. I would daresay most anyone who has worked with ACT for a bit has come up with ways to tweak and refine exercises and metaphors to best suit their purposes. The idea is to be aware and thoughtful with this piece of the therapy. Not only will doing so raise the odds that your main point will be well received, but it can create opportunities for clients to receive other gifts the exercise or metaphor might contain. It has certainly been my experience that bringing real intention to this piece—considering *why* (what is it about experiential work that is effective), *what* (what processes are we targeting and which exercises or metaphors will get at that best, given this particular client), *when* (at what point in the therapy would it work best, and at what point in the session), and *how* (are the words we are using working for, or against, the model, and are the words we are using capitalizing on what the exercise or metaphor potentially offers?)—translates directly into increased clinical effectiveness in the therapy room. Plus, it's fun.

PART 3

Some Finer Points

CHAPTER 11

Curveballs and Consistency

A predominant theme of this book is that the key to doing ACT well is to consistently approach the therapy on the basis of the principles forming the model. I have also acknowledged that this shift to working consistently within an ACT framework represents one of the most challenging competency milestones of the therapy. Once made, however, it translates into increased flexibility and competency in session, regardless of what transpires. This chapter attempts to demonstrate that even when—or rather, especially when—the client throws you a real curveball, adhering to the principles of ACT will serve you well.

OH, BY THE WAY...

I find it both exhilarating and a bit frightening that there are so very many ways clients can perplex their therapists. In the following sections I relate a few examples that demonstrate the range of conundrums that can unfold, including relatively minor developments as well as some that are more challenging. The common denominator in all these examples is that the therapist approaches them from within the ACT framework.

You may notice that the example dialogues in this section are more fully drawn (that's a nice way to say "long"). I've simply decided to take the opportunity to provide that level of detail, given this book is intended for ACT clinicians (others welcome!). An inherent challenge is that in order to get at a particular idea, I must provide a scenario, when in reality, the function of the behaviors being depicted would be entirely dependent on context.

The following scenario had its genesis in a situation that happened to a consultee just as he was rolling along nicely with his client, fifty-eight-year-old Jim, who had presented for depression following retirement. Approaching the therapy sequentially, the therapist had been working with the client on self-as-context and had anticipated starting his next session with the Continuous You exercise. As it turns out, Jim had a different idea.

Therapist:	"Let's begin with a mindfulness exercise. There's a particular exercise that I thought would be a good one for us today, but it's a bit longer than what we usually do—"
Jim	*(interrupting):* "I was actually going to ask if it was okay if my wife came today."
Therapist:	"What?"
Jim:	"My wife. She's in the lobby. We were wondering if she could come to my session."
(Pause.)	
Therapist:	"Are you thinking that would be helpful for you?"
Jim:	"Yeah, my wife wants to know what we're doing in here. I try to tell her but it never seems to make sense when I try to explain it."
Therapist:	"Are you wanting me to talk with her about something in particular?"
Jim:	"Well, I just think she wants to talk to you about all this stuff. She has some questions too, I think."
Therapist:	"And what do you think?"
Jim:	"About what?"
Therapist:	"Do you want her to meet with me? This is your therapy session. Do you want to include her in your session today, or would you rather just meet with me individually?"
Jim:	"No, it's fine. Okay, I'll go get her."

You could speculate that there are some interesting dynamics going on here—for example, the way the client has introduced the idea of a joint session as coming chiefly from his wife gives rise to hypotheses about the nature of their relationship and whether there might be some passivity and avoidance on his part. The first task, however, is to determine how to respond to the immediate request. After his initial surprise and data gathering (in other words, finding out how this idea arose), the therapist's next move is geared toward several ends. As a way to honor the therapeutic relationship, he underscores the fact that the client, Jim, is his main priority. Noting Jim's use of words ("My wife wants…"), the therapist checks to see whether Jim is okay with his wife joining the session, and in doing so, points to the idea that Jim is in charge of his life—he needs to okay, or not okay, the idea. The fact that Jim does not take the opportunity to push back against what his wife is wanting does not mean avoidance is not present—that is, he may not be prepared at this point to acknowledge he is going along with this idea in order to avoid her displeasure (just one possibility). This is all conjecture at this point, but the therapist has effectively raised and addressed the issue in case it is, in fact, a feature of their relationship. One thing is for sure: any plans the therapist had for the day's session must be tossed out the window—he's got about two minutes to regroup before meeting with both husband and wife.

One option would be to bag ACT for a session and just spend time chatting with Jim and his wife, answering questions, and so on. However, it isn't necessary to do so—we can work with this situation in an ACT-consistent fashion, *if* we are approaching it from the principles forming the model rather than as a collection of techniques or ideas. Toward this end, our wise therapist uses the minutes waiting for his client to return to do some basic mindfulness: breathing and getting centered in his chair, noticing his thoughts and feelings, and focusing in on his intention to be fully present and open to what may next unfold. For the purposes of saving time and space, I'll summarize what happens next: The wife, Mary, is openly curious about the therapist and about ACT, and states that she thinks Jim is "doing better," meaning that he appears more engaged with her and with life in general. She wishes, though, that Jim "wasn't so down on himself all the time." The therapist continues to further ACT processes by asking Jim to report what he experiences when Mary says this, and by inquiring from time to time what each of them is experiencing, throughout the session. Still working with the hypothesis that there might be some avoidance going on with the client, and to further the idea that the principles of ACT apply to everyone, including himself, the therapist makes moves to avoid being the expert or "answer person" in session (a role he is being pulled by Mary to assume). For example, he makes it clear by his demeanor that he expects Jim to speak for his own therapy experience—to answer his wife's questions directly regarding what they have been working on in the therapy and why—and steps in only to clarify or flesh out key ideas as needed. Rather than attempt to introduce the concept of self-as-context, as initially planned for the session, the therapist is looking for ways to capitalize on the fact that this is now a joint session. Because the nature of a couple's relationship can either facilitate or impede a client's progress, the therapist is actively considering the couple's skill level with the core ACT processes. The predominant deficit seems to be avoidance—each looks to the other to change so that unwanted thoughts and feelings go away.

Therapist   (to Mary): "One thing that seems clear to me as I sit here listening to you is that you care a great deal about Jim."

Mary	(*tearing up instantly*): "I do! He's…well, he's my rock."
Therapist:	"And it's also clear you experience some painful thoughts and feelings around him as well. You have a lot of worries."
Mary:	"I do! It's just so hard to see him be so down on himself."
Therapist	(*speaking to Jim*): "And Jim, it's been pretty clear in talking with you today that it pains you that your wife has these sorts of worries and feelings about you."
Jim:	"Yeah, I hate that she worries so much about me. I feel guilty."
Therapist	(*to both*): "And here we have it, don't we?"

(*Both look at the therapist blankly.*)

Therapist	(*continuing*): "What I mean is that both of you want the other person to not have what they have, and you don't want to have what *you* have—worry, guilt, and so on. And Mary, although you and I haven't talked about this, I'm guessing this is something you've really struggled with—not having these worries, or trying to get Jim to change so that you don't have those worries and he doesn't have bad thoughts about himself."
Mary:	"Yes, that's true, but nothing helps."
Therapist:	"And yet you keep trying. And as Jim was just explaining, one of the things we've worked on in here is how that very struggle has its own sort of pain, and that perhaps an alternative is to step out of that struggle—to be willing to experience what's there to be had, even if it's a painful worry, or a tough thought."
Mary:	"But…" (*Stops, a bit at a loss.*)
Therapist	(*anticipating what she is struggling with*): "This doesn't mean there's nothing to be done, however. It isn't at all about being resigned or just giving up."
Mary:	"Okay…."
Therapist:	"Let me ask you something: You've said one of your biggest struggles is how Jim feels about himself. What bothers you about that? What's the problem with Jim not liking himself?"
Mary:	"It makes him unhappy."
Therapist:	"And why do you care about that?"

Mary:	"I love him!"
Therapist:	"So underneath all this worry is love for Jim."
Mary:	"Yes!"
Therapist:	"And Jim, why do you care if your wife worries about you?'
Jim:	"Because I don't want her to feel that way. To worry."
Therapist:	"Why not?"
Jim:	"Because...it makes me feel guilty."
Therapist:	"What are you guilty of—according to your mind, anyway?"
Jim:	"Making her unhappy."
Therapist:	"Why do you care if she's unhappy?"
Jim:	"Why? Because...well, because I care about her."
Therapist	(pausing and really holding the moment): "Isn't that something? What I mean is, underneath all this worry and guilt and struggle is simple caring."

(Jim and Mary both sit silently, thinking this over.)

Therapist:	"I'm wondering if you both could consider the possibility that the worrying, the feeling guilty, and so on, can just be there—that maybe it doesn't have to be fixed. It's a reflection of your caring, after all."
Mary:	"Hmm. I can see that, but it's hard to stop trying to fix it."
Therapist:	"Exactly. That's for sure, and as Jim said earlier, that's part of what we're working on in here. We're on a bit of a journey with this therapy and we still have farther to go. There are some important ideas Jim and I will be continuing to explore together. In the meantime, I'm wondering if maybe the biggest gift you can give to each other is to simply let each other have what you have. Rather than try to fix it or struggle against it, just let it be there, knowing all the while that it's a reflection of your love for one another."
Mary:	"But will it eventually change? When you're done, will we be in a better place?"
Therapist:	"There are so many ways to answer that question, Mary, but I'm wondering if you would be willing to just hold that, as an example

of what I'm talking about. Much remains to be seen for sure, but by simply holding that thought and the worry behind it, you are actually creating some space for Jim and what he's about here."

Mary: "Okay, I guess I can do that."

Therapist: "Jim, is there anything you want to add right now?"

Jim: "No. Just that…it would be nice to have a bit of space to do this."

The therapist in this example worked with the suddenly-joint session by continuing to view what was transpiring through an ACT lens, mindful of the processes he was supporting (or alternately undermining) and homing in on experiential avoidance as it functioned both individually and as a potentially pathological process in the marriage. He gently presented willingness in the service of values (in other words, loving and supporting one another) as an alternative to control. At the end of the session it would make sense to talk with Mary and Jim about their options going forward, such as participating in marital therapy (a referral to an ACT therapist would make sense, given Jim's work and Mary's apparent interest in the model). The point of this example was to show that despite the unforeseen development, it was not necessary to put the therapy on hold. Rather, the therapist used the development to further the therapy based upon the core ACT processes that most pertained to the situation.

Here is another "oh by the way" example where the therapist is faced with an abrupt change in her treatment plan. In the following scenario, the therapist has had four sessions with her client and has been exploring willingness as an alternative to control. Although the client seems to understand this idea conceptually, he continues to demonstrate a fix-it agenda. He has increased his ability to defuse from thoughts and to simply notice what is occurring in the moment, however, and the therapist has planned to continue work in this area.

Therapist: "Hi, Steve. How are you doing today?"

Client: "Well, I do have some news—I'm moving to Chicago."

Therapist: "Oh really? That *is* big news! When?"

Client: "Next week."

Therapist: "*Next week!*"

Client: "Yeah, I know. Kinda sudden."

Therapist: "I'll say! What's going on?"

Client: "Well, my buddy Rich—you know, the one who does construction? He's starting a project next week—says he can put me on the team if I get out there right away. I need the cash, so…"

Therapist:	"How long will you be gone?"
Client:	"Oh, I'm moving there for good. At least, for now. Rich says he has lots of work for me out there and I'm kinda tired of Pittsburgh, so…"
Therapist:	"I see. Wow." (*Pause.*) "So my mind's jumping all over the place with that one, but let's check first and see what's going on for you with this. What are you experiencing around this?"
Client:	"Well, it's a big change, and pretty sudden, like I said."
Therapist:	"What sorts of feelings are going on?"
Client:	"I'm psyched—I think it's gonna be good."
Therapist:	"Hmm. Well, we can definitely talk more about this and what it means for you and for our work together, but first let's begin as usual, and start with a mindfulness exercise."

In this scenario the therapist receives some unexpected news that has real implications for the therapy. She responds by finding out what led to her client's decision to suddenly move, but also notes that her own mind became very busy. This cues her to check in regarding what the client is experiencing and, in fact, to return to how she would typically begin a session—with a mindfulness exercise. This move represents defusing from the compelling content of the moment and moving to operating from the principles of ACT. She has made it clear that this situation will be viewed through an ACT lens. To continue:

Therapist:	"I'm wondering how to use this session, what will serve you best given that it's the last one we'll be having, at least as far as we know." (*Transparency, and—subtly—values on the part of the therapist.*)
Client:	"Yeah, I've been wondering about that. This has been real helpful."
Therapist:	"What has been helpful about it?"
Client:	"Just having someone to talk to, and the things we've been talking about."
Therapist:	"Well, how about we start with those things—maybe review the key ideas we've covered and see where you are with those."
Client:	"Okay."

This approach will give the therapist a reasonable idea of what the client has taken away from the therapy so far. She can then determine if it makes sense to stick with previously explored concepts or whether she might introduce more of the central principles in ACT before the therapy concludes. In other words, the therapist will consider the core processes and where the client's ability lies with these—including which of the core processes seem most important for this client, and which seem most possible to further, given the truncated time.

> *Therapist:* "It seems from what you're saying that you can really see how 'trying not to have what you have' doesn't work. That, in fact, you've spent a lot of time and energy on that, and it hasn't gotten you anywhere."
>
> *Client:* "No, like you said before, if I don't want it, I got it."
>
> *Therapist:* "It does sound like you understand how trying to not have what we have can keep us stuck. I did want to check in with you on that one, Steve, because it has seemed to me at times that you are still sold on the control idea. That you still think there's got to be some way to not have uncomfortable thoughts and feelings."
>
> *Client* (thinks it over): "Huh. I don't know. I think I get it."
>
> *Therapist:* "It may be that you 'get it,' and still want it, you know? Like I catch myself still trying various control strategies sometimes, rather than just letting myself notice and hold whatever's going on. Seems like that desire to be comfortable really never goes away." (*The therapist is making her point while normalizing.*)
>
> *Client:* "Yeah, I suppose that's true."
>
> *Therapist:* "The key is to catch *that* and then choose whether you're going to be about that agenda or something else."

At this point the therapist has essentially determined what to home in on with this client in the time remaining. That is, the hypothesis is that her client's main source of suffering has been buying in to the idea that before he can begin living life in the way he would like, undesirable internal experiences (such as anxiety, depression, and low self-esteem) have to be fixed first. This idea has kept him very stuck. If this system can be undermined, then he will be in a better position to make different choices in the future.

BAD NEWS

Sometimes therapists who are unfamiliar with ACT, or perhaps newer to the model, mistakenly think that they have to somehow overlook or ignore their own clinical judgment to conduct ACT with fidelity—as though they have to park all that experience at the door. This is far from the case. The idea is to work from within the model while using that hard-won clinical acumen. Nonetheless, it has been my observation that many ACT therapists struggle with this false dichotomy when something portentous happens with their client. In working with these situations I am often told the therapist was torn between what she "would usually do" and being ACT-consistent. These two do not have to be in opposition. Often, only a slight wording change or a slightly different move makes the difference in being consistent with the model, rather than in contradiction. Looking through that ACT lens at what is happening can actually make it easier to do what feels most clinically appropriate.

Therapist:	"You mentioned on the phone that you had some bad news."
Client:	"Yeah, really bad news, in fact. I've got cancer."
Therapist:	(*The therapist resists an immediate pull to come in with words. With an expression full of caring and compassion, she holds the client's gaze while breathing deeply. The intent is silent acknowledgment, with no rush to fix. In this instance, the therapist perceives that the client needs support and validation. By resisting the urge to verbally fix or otherwise ameliorate the situation, she is providing both while remaining consistent with the model.*)
Therapist	(*after a moment or two*): "Ah, Jen. I'm sorry to hear this."
Client:	"Yeah. Breast. Stage 3. Soooo…"
Therapist:	(*Again resists the urge to get in there verbally, but is working hard to be as fully present as possible, to convey that there is room at the table for even this.*)
Client:	"You know, I knew this would happen. My mom got it, my aunt…. I am so terrified!"
Therapist:	(*Nods and breathes deeply again.*)
Client:	"And I don't even know where to turn—there's so much to do! I've got to meet with a specialist, and a surgeon, and it's all going to be in Rochester, so I've got to find someone to take care of the dogs and—"
Therapist:	"Jen, all those thoughts running around figuring things out and problem-solving—you're going to be needing those. There's a time and place to really capitalize on that. But right now I'm really just focusing on what this is like for you right now. You've had a real blow!" (*The therapist is using her own experience in the session to*

inform her response. That is, she is aware of her desire to make this moment less painful and that this desire could mirror what is going on for the client. Her comments point to defusion and willingness— rather than try not to have thoughts run around, notice that they're there; not only are they not pathological, they are useful at times. The comment "You've had a real blow!" is more validation and is geared toward leaning in to what's there.)

Client   *(begins to cry a little):* "Yeah, I'm so scared."

Therapist   *(pauses, says quietly):* "I'm here with you." *(She is providing support and validation while remaining ACT-consistent by not trying to fix.)*

(They just sit for a while.)

Client: "Driving over here, I was thinking about what you might say, about what I should do with this. I definitely don't want this, you know? But I got it anyway."

Therapist: "Yeah. And this is a big one."

Client: "I suppose you are going to tell me not to buy all my thoughts around it."

Therapist: "Right now I am really just wanting to be here *with* you, with however you are around this news. Of course my mind is on hyperdrive too, but that's its job. I think it's more important just to make as much space as possible to let you have what you have around this." *(The therapist is being careful not to give the client more "shoulds," while modeling important processes that promote the psychological flexibility so valuable in a situation such as this. That is, she models defusion ["my mind is on hyperdrive"], rather than suggesting the client defuse from thoughts, and she models willingness by explicitly stating that she is actively making room for whatever the client is experiencing and by not attempting to ameliorate the situation or join in problem-solving.)*

Client: "But everyone says that you need to take charge of your health. Beth—you know, the one who had breast cancer six years ago? She says it's important to believe you can get better and to make that happen for yourself."

Therapist: "Jen, there are many, many ways you can help yourself in this situation. In fact, I'm guessing every skill or resource you have will be called upon in the weeks or months to come, and I have a lot of faith in your ability to do whatever needs to be done.

One thing I'd love for you to see here is that you can experience everything you have around this—the fear, all of it—and still do what you need to do."

Client: "So you're saying I don't need to fight how I feel about this."

Therapist: "We've explored that one quite a bit, what trying not to have unwanted thoughts and feelings can cost. Perhaps allowing yourself to experience whatever is there to be experienced internally will help you focus your effort and energy where it really counts, on your treatment and recovery."

Client: "Yeah."

And so on. The clinical decision-making continues as events unfold. For example, as this session nears its conclusion the therapist considers doing a physicalizing exercise with the client, with the cancer being the externalized object, but ultimately decides against it. She determines it is too soon for it, that the client might experience the exercise as a bid to "be okay with" her cancer. She files the idea away, however, as it could be a very powerful exercise later on in the therapy. As oft mentioned, simply contacting the present moment and being with your client is a fail-safe move. At times like this, when the client is being tasked to hold something difficult indeed, joining in that task could be the most powerful move you can make. Hopefully it is also clear that the therapist is making full use of her ability to sense what her client needs, while also making sure she does not work against the model. In fact, it could be argued that her intention, to provide support and validation to the client, was better served by staying within the ACT framework. That is, if she had fallen into trying to make the client feel better in some way, or joined in all the problem-solving, she would have run the risk of supporting both of their avoidance.

IN PURSUIT OF HAPPINESS

At age eight I decided I was going to be a hairstylist. I dropped that idea, however, when I realized I would not be able to choose my clients. So it's a bit ironic that I often find myself working with clients, either directly or via my supervision and consulting work, who typify "the challenging client." I have been struck by how ACT has enhanced my ability to maintain a compassionate stance with such individuals and to work effectively with what they bring to the therapy. The following scenario depicts a difficult client who identifies a goal for the therapy that is not in line with the objectives of ACT.

Scenario: This is the therapist's first session with his client, a thirty-four-year-old male who presented with anxiety and "anger issues." The therapist has been conducting an informal assessment, and is exploring where the client stands in terms of his values. The client has been testy, sarcastic, and slightly hostile so far.

Client: "What do I really want out of life? I'd like to live on the beach all by myself. Well, maybe with some babe. Yeah, a twenty-year-old babe."

Therapist: "What is pleasing to you about that idea, being on the beach with a babe?" (*The therapist chooses to take the client seriously, forming a hypothesis that the client may be making this sort of statement as a control move.*)

Client: "What, you don't get that? Oh, are you gay?"

Therapist: "I can't tell if you are seriously wondering that or not. Are you seriously asking me if I'm gay? If you are, it would be helpful to know why you are wanting to know that—what does that mean to you?" (*The therapist is transparently exploring the function of the client's statement.*)

Client (*backing down after being so directly questioned*): "Nah, I was just joking around."

Therapist: "Hmmm. Do you think that was a way to get out of this discussion—joking around, maybe the whole babe on a beach thing?"

Client: "It was just a joke. But yeah, that's what I want out of life—beach and babe. Where do we start?"

Therapist (*Just sits, looking steadily at the client*): "I'm actually feeling pretty stuck at the moment." (*Transparency, authenticity.*)

Client: (*Smirks, then looks a little uncomfortable as the therapist just sits silently. He eventually breaks the silence.*) "So, what do we do from here?"

Therapist: "Heck if I know."

Client: "Okaaaaaay."

(*Therapist sits.*)

Client: "Well, this is bogus. I mean, if we're just going to sit here, then what's the point?"

Therapist: "What do you mean, what's the point?"

Client	(*exasperated*): "What's the point to being here? Why am I here?!"
Therapist	(*looking surprised*): "Are you asking *me* that? Why *you're* here?" (*Again speaking not so much to content as to what is actually happening in the session.*)
Client:	(*Glares, is silent.*)
Therapist	(*very conversational, matter-of-fact*): "I think it's pretty clear to both of us that you are going to determine what happens here. I certainly can't take you anywhere you don't want to go, as you've just made quite clear. Fortunately, I wouldn't want to do that even if I could." (*The therapist explicitly hands over control, while establishing that both he and the client have choices here.*)
Client:	(*Silent.*)
Therapist:	"I would guess you're here for a reason—you don't quite seem the sort that would seek out something like this just because. But whether you choose to take that anywhere is obviously going to be up to you." (*Puts the client squarely in the position of choosing.*)
Client:	"Well, I want to take it somewhere. I need…I need help. I just don't want to be talking about crap like '…what do I care about in life'! I want to be happy, just like anybody else."
Therapist	(*thoughtfully*): "Hmmm, I don't know…."
Client	(*impatiently*): "You don't know what?"
Therapist	(*relaxed, taking his time, conversationally*): "I'm just noticing all the thoughts coming up around this…thinking about what you've said, what you say you want out of this. It may be that what I offer and what you want simply don't match up. I'm also wondering if they might be more aligned than it seems." (*Modeling getting present and transparency, and also baiting a hook.*)
Client:	"I have no idea what you're talking about."
Therapist:	"I don't blame you! Let me see if I can untangle it." (*Thinks.*) "It sounds like you came here for a reason—to be happy, as you put it. I would describe what I do as helping people to live well— to live vital, meaningful lives. There's a lot of good stuff going on with that, though the goal isn't happiness per se. Regardless, it would take some real working together. At the very least, it would require you being open to checking out what an alternate

approach might be like." (*Being transparent and very direct about the choice before them.*)

Client: "It's pretty hard to be open to something when you don't know what it is."

Therapist: "I agree."

Client: (Just looks at therapist silently.)

Therapist   (*after a moment or two*): "Well, there's one good thing."

Client: "What?"

Therapist: "If you did decide to explore this, you certainly wouldn't be asked to feel differently about it, or even to have different thoughts about it. That is, I wouldn't be trying to get you to suddenly be all enthused, or to not have doubts about what we're doing. That would be unnatural and wouldn't work anyway!" (*This is an important point. The client has every right to feel or think as he does. Often clients in this situation feel pressed to somehow alter how they feel and think about the therapy. So it can be a relief to be told this is not necessary. Some degree of openness, however, is critical.*)

Client: "Okay…"

Therapist: "Here's what I would be asking of you if we were to decide to work together: I'd ask that you be open to seeing if there isn't something you might learn, something new to be considered. The skepticism can be right there, too, frustration…whatever shows up. The idea is to be open to seeing if there isn't another way to work with whatever's going on with you—an alternative life approach, if you will."

Client: "I consider things. I'm open to learning."

Therapist: "Well, that would be important for sure. Because I certainly don't want to be trying to yank you somewhere you don't want to go—I don't think that would work for either one of us." (*Firmly avoiding persuading the client; pointing out again that they both have choices to make here.*)

Client: "No, it wouldn't!"

Therapist: "So anyway, that's what I was wondering." (*Sits silently, simply looking at the client. Stopping here helps the therapist continue to refrain from persuading, teaching, telling, and so on. It experientially points again to the idea that the client has a big role to play in what happens next—that is, the therapist is not filling the space with "so therefore…," but waits for the client's contribution.)*

| Client: | "So…what is this alternative life approach?" |

Therapist:
"Such a reasonable question, and yet it's not easy to give a satisfying answer! That's because this is about your individual journey. What would actually roll out here for you remains to be seen. It's almost easier to talk about what this particular therapeutic approach *is not*—for example, it *isn't* about fixing you in some way so that you're permanently happy. The short answer is that it's about stepping out of what doesn't work—by that I mean the ways we humans typically try to work with what we are experiencing—and learning how to work with what's going on with us in a way that allows us to be living the way we want to be living."

Client:
"I don't get it."

Therapist:
"I don't blame you, and let me assure you that I'm not trying to be cagey. It really is a process to experience together, rather than some program agenda I can just hand you right now. So that openness I mentioned would start right away. Would you consider being open to exploring this path, given all the unknowns and uncertainty?" (*The therapist is now being very direct with his request of the client.*)

Client
(*thinks it over*): "Well, I really don't know what we're talking about here." (Pause.) "Sure, why not see where it goes."

Therapist:
"I'm so glad that you're up for it! And you get to keep deciding, right? That is, you stay in control of this process—if you decide after a few sessions or so that this isn't for you, we can talk about other ways to go." (*The therapist reinforces the client stepping forward with transparency. His authenticity continues to undermine a potential power struggle—he is openly glad the client is choosing to continue—as does highlighting the fact that the client will always have the ability to choose to continue or not.*)

Client:
"That's right."

So a lot happened here in a very short span of time. The therapist opted to begin the therapy with some values identification. Had he been simply operating at the level of content, however, he would likely have run into problems. That is, he went to process rather than content, probing the function of the client's response and utilizing transparency regarding his own reaction. By acknowledging that he felt stuck, the therapist effectively "stepped out of the game" and modeled being present, willingness (to feel stuck), and being authentic. He then explicitly gave control to the client (symbolically, as control can't actually be passed back and forth), again undermining the client's attempt to push against the therapist as a control/avoidance strategy. In doing so, he also explicitly "leveled the playing field"—an idea central to the model, and key in developing a productive therapeutic relationship. With this and in several subsequent comments (for example, sharing his thoughts about whether it is a treatment match, making it clear that something would be required of the client) the therapist doesn't fall into the trap of persuasion, as in persuading the client to work with him, and highlights choice—mutual choice, that is, not just the client's. He offsets these sorts of "clever" moves, if you will, by readily agreeing with the client's observations and acknowledging the trickiness of what they are attempting to explore. It is likely this client will continue to use power and control as a way to avoid discomfort as the therapy progresses, yet the therapist has driven a significant stake in the ground (in other words, the agreement to be open to learning something new) that can be revisited in future sessions. The identification of values is central to ACT and certainly will not be forgotten. In this case the therapist opts to table that for now, focusing instead on laying a productive foundation for the therapy.

SUMMARY

If your experience reading these examples is anything like mine, you thought of any number of other ways to work with the depicted scenarios. Perhaps you recognized alternate hypotheses that could have been explored, identified slight wording changes that would have made things even clearer, or thought of a different tactic altogether. There is clearly no one, right way to respond to a given situation. This chapter is more about what doesn't work so well, which is to abandon the model when you're clinically thrown. It is my observation that stepping outside the ACT framework not only results in mixed and contradictory messages but makes things that much harder. Adhering to the core principles of ACT will help you navigate these sorts of situations in a way that makes sense and that actually furthers the therapy.

CHAPTER 12

Your Continued ACT Journey

I began this book by explaining why I felt the need to offer it. To come full circle, the issues raised in this book are the result of observations made over the course of my own work and in supervising and consulting with other ACT providers. I learned that there were common, even predictable, delivery challenges, some of which really stood in the way of therapeutic progress. Many if not most of these involved stepping out of the theoretical framework of ACT. Other missteps, while not critical, still served to shortchange the therapy in some way. Large or small, the result of these difficulties was that the potential of ACT was not optimized.

I also mentioned at the beginning of this book that most of the issues highlighted herein are pointed out in pretty much every ACT text—issues such as the importance of approaching the therapy at the level of behavioral principles rather than as a collection of techniques, and how to work with the core processes. I have spent some time contemplating why it is that common missteps and misunderstandings persist, given the richness and availability of ACT information. Returning to this question, I point to the challenges discussed in this book. One reason is simply that ACT is not an easily mastered therapy. Though the model can be parsimoniously presented, the core processes at the heart of the therapy are nuanced and replete with important theoretical and clinical implications. In addition, the nature of the behavioral principles upon which ACT is based means that everything applies: fidelity requires consistency throughout, so everything that occurs within (and without) the therapy room must therefore be viewed and worked with from within the ACT framework. This takes skill. Finally, the basic tenets of ACT tend to fly in the face of what we've learned as human beings and as therapists. Even if we "get" the model, we don't always realize just how deeply we might be holding contradictory beliefs and tendencies, and how these can work against the unfolding therapy.

In short, ACT is hard in some ways. There are many reasons why therapists might struggle with it or choose to not do it fully. I'll not revisit the arguments made for adherence to the model, but will simply offer again my observation, acquired from hundreds of cases now, that fidelity does indeed make a clinical difference—a powerful difference, and one that is worth striving for. I have consistently found ACT, when conducted with fidelity, to be a clinically potent therapy. So while claiming my personal agenda here, I'll move into exploring some of the barriers that I've seen stand in the way of developing competency in ACT.

CLAIMING YOUR BARRIERS

If you are with me on the idea that it is clinically beneficial to conduct ACT with fidelity—or even if you're just considering the possibility that this might be the case—then join me in pondering how we might better close the gap between being introduced to ACT and conducting the therapy according to the model. I explore this question from a position of compassion and understanding, having gone, as I've said, through my own learning curve with this stuff. As for my own path, I can see that there was far more I could have done to learn the model and to progress more quickly. For example, it took me a while to actually sit down with some of those excellent applied ACT texts. (I was busy.) It took me even longer to sit down and really acquaint myself with RFT. (I was trained in radical behaviorism and got the general idea—wasn't that enough?) I had patients to see and a program to run; that ACT reading or that workshop would have to wait. And so on. The typical life of a clinician, in other words.

As the years have passed and my supervision and training experiences continue, it seems the typical life of a clinician has only gotten faster and busier. Particularly for those providers working in institutions such as Veterans Affairs, workloads have become immense while the work itself is no less critical. For many of us, it is sometimes all we can do to show up for our sessions with our heads on straight. That said, do we stop there? Is it possible for all the above to be true and for us to still take hold of the reins here? In this chapter I hope to dig into this issue a bit. While I'll cover the usual strategies for furthering your ACT learning—workshops, readings, and the like—my hope is to delve a bit further into that place of intention from which anything is possible.

LIVING YOUR INTENTION

I have already referred to some of the barriers that can stand in the way of continuing to grow in ACT. Being busy and overloaded in general are often culprits—it is just plain hard to devote time or effort to yet one more thing. Many of the clinicians with whom I have worked have pointed out that they also have values around family and personal time—are they to spend Saturday night with their nose in an ACT book? And it could be argued that there's efficiency to just getting by, especially if it seems our clients are benefiting from what we are doing.

There are also very real logistical issues: What if you are the only one in your setting or area doing ACT? What if you've read everything out there and *still* feel you are not quite there clinically? What if you'd love to get more training but there just isn't a workshop or trainer or consultant within reach (or budget)? In a moment I'll address these sorts of concerns. First, I'd like to explore ways in which we therapists stand in our own way of what is ultimately possible with this therapy.

WALKING THE WALK

Let me start with a simple question for those readers actively conducting ACT: have you done everything you feel you can do around building competency in ACT? As you consider this question, know that I ask it sincerely. I recognize that just because for many years my answer to that would have been "no" (and actually, as I think about this honestly, I realize my answer would *still* be "no"), it does not mean that *you* have not intentionally and actively increased your competency in ACT to the best of your ability. You are, after all, reading this book. But bearing with me for a moment, what thoughts came up for you as you considered that question? Did you identify any reasons—reasons for not taking your work with ACT further? Even now, as I allow myself to really be with this question, reasons show up almost instantly: money (I couldn't afford that trip to the Sydney World Conference this year), this book (who can read when every spare moment is spent writing?), effort (I'd love to form that much-needed consultation group here in Durango, Colorado, if there weren't so many other things to do), and on and on. And yet, as I write this, there is also the recognition that I can drop down below all those reasons to the Self that is watching them and choose differently. Isn't that something? What if we can be willing to peer over the pile of baggage that shows up with this question and accept—no, celebrate—that we have the ability to choose? I could have gotten to Sydney if I had to, for example. I could make moves today to start that group. That is real freedom and it is marvelous, regardless of what I ultimately choose to do with it. What I am suggesting, to myself as much as to you, is that rather than viewing more learning as a burden, another task on our to-do list, we might recognize the opportunity to grow in ACT as possibility. This in turn might help us remember again that there is room to move forward should we choose.

Of the many enjoyable experiences I have had as an ACT consultant and trainer, my favorite has been when an ACT therapist remarks that he or she has been profoundly and positively impacted by doing ACT. While this particular feedback itself doesn't surprise me, the commonality of this experience does—it has occurred in nearly every case. It is an indication that the therapist really began to comprehend

ACT, for to understand the model is to see its applicability to oneself. It makes sense that therapists are altered by the work just as their clients are. Looking at the issue raised in this chapter, then, we might question why we are letting ourselves off the hook (if you are) when it comes to furthering our skill in ACT. Is providing excellent therapy a value? Is doing our best a value? Is ACT a therapy we believe in? If so, what is the valued choice here? Getting by? Or getting as good at ACT as we can?

I'm feeling the need to acknowledge those diligent readers who have wholeheartedly applied themselves toward this goal. If you are one, I truly respect what you have done. If not, then perhaps we can join in a commitment to take this on. ACT, we assure our clients, can help bring vitality and meaning to your life. To act with intention, to pick up the reins and drive into, then dive into, then roll around in all that ACT information out there is what I call being vibrantly alive. It is sure to bring even more meaning to our work as therapists.

WAYS TO GROW

So what, exactly, do I mean when I talk about actively and intentionally building skill in ACT? First, let's examine the ACT learning curve in general. I have conceptualized this learning curve as consisting of three steps, although in actuality they are not so clearly separated. The first step is what I will call *Introduction* to ACT. This is where the therapist comes into contact with ACT in some way, and acquires information on the theory, treatment rationale, core processes, experiential exercises, and so forth. The next step I'll call *Application*, as in the actual doing of ACT. In my view, this is the steepest part of the learning curve, as it involves translating concepts into actual behavior and moving forward right along with all the unknowns, uncertainties, and confusion inherent in doing something new. Missteps and falterings are a given. The third step I will call *Refinement*, the phase in which the therapist continues to build skill in ACT. This third step has no end point—there is no finite degree of competence that can be reached.

Before going any further, I need to direct readers to the official website for ACT—or more accurately, to the official website for the larger area of contextual science (which includes ACT). It is the single best resource for those interested in this therapy. Every piece of information I considered including here—upcoming conferences and events, how to find (or establish) an ACT chapter, available training seminars—it all is easily found on the site. You will find information on ACT camps and workshops, how to join the ACT and RFT e-mail groups (I highly recommend participating—the discussions are rich and sure to keep you current), and ways to access ACT consultation. There are listings and summaries of the latest research developments, podcasts, and so on. My problem with this website is that I can't keep up with all the information continually being added! It's an exciting community to be a part of, that's for sure. Here's the site: http://www.contextualscience.org.

Introduction Phase

There is any number of ways to acquire an introduction to ACT. Of course I am a proponent of participating in one of the ACT trainings provided by one of the many talented ACT trainers. A major accomplishment of the ACT community is how well and how widely information about the therapy is being disseminated. At this point there are opportunities to receive excellent training all over the world. But that is not the only way to acquire an introduction to ACT, of course. An assiduous student can avail herself of the rich literature and learn plenty about the model. There are several texts that provide great introductions to ACT and that also guide therapists through the application process. For example, *ACT Made Simple,* by Russ Harris (2009), offers a great introduction to the therapy because of its wonderful clarity and overall accessibility. I consider *Learning ACT: An Acceptance and Commitment Therapy Skills-Training Manual for Therapists,* by Jason Luoma, Steven Hayes, and Robyn Walser (2007), a must-read for those learning the therapy. It is thorough while user-friendly, walking readers through a basic understanding of the theoretical underpinnings of ACT to case conceptualization and how to advance the core processes while avoiding common sticking points. There are introductory DVDs that cover the therapy thoroughly and well (such as *Introduction to ACT,* with Matthew McKay and Patricia Zurita Ona, 2011). And of course, there is the seminal ACT book, *Acceptance and Commitment Therapy: An Experiential Approach to Behavior Change,* now in its second edition (Hayes et al., 2012). This is only to name the texts that are presently speaking to me from my bookshelf. I am sure that I am unintentionally slighting some that have contributed to my learning in meaningful ways. The bottom line is that there is really good stuff out there.

Other means of learning about ACT include ACT boot camps (see the website!) and working with an experienced ACT provider in a training setting, such as an internship or fellowship. Such training opportunities are becoming more and more common due to increased demand. In short, there are many approaches to gaining an introduction to ACT. It's the second and third steps that can be trickier and that are the focus of this book.

Application Phase

Assuming that you have had an introduction to the therapy, this phase is about bringing ACT into your therapy room. I want to mention two or three trajectories I've seen in regard to this learning curve. A metaphor that can be used here is the difference between diving into a pool with the intention to swim, versus playing around in the shallow end, or sitting on the edge and dipping in a toe or two. That is, I have seen how the process tends to unfold when therapists set out to "do ACT"; and I have observed what tends to occur when therapists "sort of do ACT," due to being unsure or tentative. While those diving in will flounder around a bit, they have set themselves up to swim strongly in ACT. Those at the shallow end or still testing the water can easily stay right there.

As mentioned at the beginning of this book, I sat at the edge of the pool (with my ACT dissertation and texts beside me) for some time. Many of the therapists with whom I have worked have also been sitting at the edge of the pool for a while. Many have spent quite a bit of time wading around in the shallow end (sort of doing ACT) and wondering what all the fuss is about. The good news is that nothing prevents any of us from starting to swim, no matter how long we've been sitting on the edge or playing at the shallow end. All it takes is willingness and committed action.

The central difficulty with ACT at this stage of learning is that people can't know what they don't know. In other words, many of the common therapist missteps made in ACT are not immediately obvious to the therapist. Time and time again, consultees and supervisees have been surprised to learn, for example, that they have been sending their clients control messages while overtly working on willingness. It is quite possible to work with a metaphor for years without using it in a way that maximizes its ability to promote psychological flexibility. A therapist could conceivably be following an ACT protocol to a T while supporting problematic language processes by remaining in the expert role. Also, if you've been "sort of" doing ACT without really realizing it, it can be hard to unlearn that and operate with fidelity. This is why one of the most valuable ways to increase your competency in ACT is to obtain feedback on your actual sessions.

If you have not been fortunate enough to work directly with an experienced ACT clinician, it can be challenging to obtain this sort of feedback. It is possible, however. For example, I have encouraged participants in my ACT trainings to use the opportunity to establish peer consultation groups, and I have seen it carried out with great success. Not only do such groups provide a means for constructive feedback, but there is no end to ways such groups can further their learning. For example, I know of at least two such groups (composed of private practitioners) that regularly invite a seasoned ACT trainer to provide group feedback using actual cases as working platforms. I know of individuals who sought out more experienced therapists and volunteered their time as a way to acquire experience and feedback, coleading an ACT group, for example. Some therapists have contacted a more experienced ACT colleague and arranged for direct consultation. (There are also ACT consultants such as myself who offer this sort of consultation as a fee-based service.) In short, if there is any way to obtain feedback on your actual ACT sessions, it is by far the best learning mechanism out there.

The following goes without saying, and yet it is so central that it must be said: The more open you are to feedback, the more you will learn. It takes guts to allow other clinicians a window into your actual therapy room, as in allowing them to observe or listen to actual therapy sessions. It requires a willingness to be vulnerable, in the service of optimizing what you are doing in ACT.

Aside from direct feedback, let me point you to some materials that can enhance your ability to apply this therapy. While the materials previously mentioned can continue to guide you through how to apply the therapy, there are other materials that can be particularly helpful at this stage of the learning curve. For example, *ACT in Practice*, by Patricia Bach and Daniel Moran (2008), offers a clear synthesis of the theoretical underpinnings of ACT and the role of functional analysis. The authors' guidance on how to apply functional analyses to case conceptualization can be particularly helpful at this phase of learning. As another example, *ACT Verbatim* (Twohig & Hayes, 2008) utilizes actual session transcripts to demonstrate how expert ACT therapists advance the core processes and move toward psychological flexibility. I particularly appreciated the access it provides to the decision-making process that unfolds during the course of therapy (including rich discussions around moves that might have been more effective). And I've just sat down with *Getting Unstuck in ACT* (Harris, 2013), which likely applies to both the application and refinement stages of the ACT learning curve. So far it looks to be classic Harris, tackling and demystifying some of the trickier aspects of ACT in a way that is highly accessible.

There is good literature out there that focuses on conducing ACT with different treatment populations. Similar to those already mentioned, these texts walk readers through the application of ACT, and how to look through that ACT lens while working with common clinical challenges that arise in working with a particular sort of presenting problem. Examples are *Acceptance and Commitment Therapy for Anxiety Disorders* (Eifert & Forsyth, 2005); *A Practical Guide to Acceptance and Commitment Therapy* (Hayes & Strosahl, 2010); *Acceptance and Commitment Therapy for the Treatment of Post-Traumatic Stress Disorder and Trauma-Related Problems* (Walser & Westrup, 2007); and *Acceptance and Commitment Therapy for Eating Disorders: A Process-Focused Guide to Treating Anorexia and Bulimia* (Sandoz, Wilson, & Dufrene, 2010). In this last text, for example, the authors guide therapists in assessing and intervening according to clients' skill level with the core processes. That is, interventions are designed around whether the client demonstrates an "early," "intermediate," or "advanced" skill level with the core ACT processes (such as defusing and contacting the present moment). Interventions are introduced that match the client's current ability level. Once skill is developed at that level, the therapist introduces an intervention requiring a greater degree of skill. In this way, clients are guided along a path of ever-increasing psychological flexibility.

Being able to observe an expert ACT therapist as she works with various processes and clinical scenarios can really help with the application part of the learning curve. Many therapists at this stage report that they really need to "see" the therapy, rather than do more reading about it. Fortunately, there are DVDs available that offer just this (for example, the DVD training series *ACT in Action*, 2007), and even YouTube videos (although I am not familiar enough with these to speak of them intelligently).

Refinement Phase

There is a point on this ACT learning curve where things jell. I can't say how often I have been told by a consultee that he suddenly "gets it." This level of comprehension is not actually sudden, of course. Rather, in working with the core processes with actual clients, a point comes when the therapist can see how the processes relate to one another, to the client, and to psychological flexibility overall. At this point therapists are able to work with core processes in a way that consistently moves clients forward. As their skill increases, they are increasingly able to recognize and work with ACT processes as they arise in session. Now it's about honing those skills.

One way to do that is to continue to utilize the literature. I have mentioned various texts that are great introductions to ACT and that guide therapists as they learn how to apply the therapy to actual clients. I have also mentioned texts that help strengthen therapists' ability to apply ACT with particular client populations. Now I'd like to mention some materials that offer additional ways to sharpen your clinical skills. I do not intend to rank materials by including some in this discussion and excluding others. Nor do I mean to rank them based on where I am placing them on this metaphorical learning curve. This is simply one route to building depth and breadth in this therapy, based on my own encounters with these materials.

You would think that once you've read one book on ACT there would be little else to learn. On the contrary, each treatment has added depth and dimension to my understanding of ACT, in turn increasing my effectiveness in the therapy room. I have found it quite helpful to reread texts that I initially encountered years ago. It is a different experience to digest them with some experience under my belt. This was certainly true for the original ACT text, *Acceptance and Commitment Therapy: The Process and Practice of Mindful Change* (Hayes et al., 2012). In essence, this is about gaining depth and clarity. Revisiting some of the seminal texts can bring pieces home that did not fully land at an earlier point in the learning curve. And, there continue to be additions to the literature that further deepen understanding of the therapy or a particular process. A beautifully written example is *Mindfulness for Two: An Acceptance and Commitment Therapy Approach to Mindfulness in Psychotherapy*, by Kelly Wilson and Troy DuFrene (2008).

I have been a proponent in this book of therapists acquainting themselves with the science in ACT. Specifically, I have encouraged therapists to learn a bit about RFT. A good resource is *Learning RFT* by Niklas Törneke (2010). Dr. Törneke has real skill in making this important area of scientific inquiry accessible to nonscientists. Similarly, if you are not versed in behavioral therapy—or perhaps just a little rusty—I cannot overendorse Ramnero and Törneke's book on behavioral learning principles, *The ABCs of Human Behavior: Behavioral Principles for the Practicing Clinician* (2008). Another excellent resource for developing your knowledge of RFT is the online tutorial at http://www.contextualpsychology.org/rft_tutorial. This is an excellent and affordable ($9.00) tutorial that offers six continuing education units for an additional $60.00. I have also really been appreciating *The Self and Perspective Taking,* a recent contribution by Louise McHugh and Ian Stewart (2012). As the title suggests, this book focuses specifically on the experience of the self as perspective taking, bringing readers up to date on this rapidly evolving area of study. Finally, I am excited to mention *The Language of Psychotherapy: Strengthening Your Clinical Practice with Relational Frame Theory,* by Matthieu Villatte, Jennifer Villatte, and Steven Hayes. This text, which will soon be available (if its release hasn't already beaten mine!), is about recognizing, applying, and integrating RFT principles into clinical practice. I've had the privilege of taking an advance peek at this contribution and can assure you it will not disappoint.

I hope readers will avail themselves of these materials that build important bridges between research and applied work. Contextual behavioral science is evolving rapidly and is up to some really cool stuff. We clinicians can benefit from staying current and learning how to pass what is being learned on to clients in a way that helps them in their lives. I should mention that deepening my understanding of the science behind ACT has directly translated into increased consultation and supervisory skills. I am far more able to articulate why we do what we do in ACT, and to point my trainees and consultees toward materials that further clarify the model.

LONELY IN ACT-VILLE

What if you are the Lone ACT Ranger in your setting? First, bravo! I wish you were surrounded by peers, employers, and institutions that actively support what you are doing. Getting back to reality, I urge you, if you have not already, to take advantage of the ACBS website. Access the global ACT community by getting on those e-mail lists, or getting yourself to a conference or workshop. You happen to be part of a value-driven community that is serious about openness and collaboration. Put yourself out there and see if there is someone who can join you on your ACT journey (by regular Skype calls, or whatnot). These strategies are being effectively used by others in your position, and there are likely other therapists out there who are looking for ACT peers. See if there isn't someone who might join you, even if that involves getting creative. And if you come to the next World Conference (in Minneapolis, July 2014) be sure to introduce yourself!

I don't mean to make light of your situation if you are in an unsupportive setting or do not have ready access to ACT training or consultation. It is obviously an advantage to be part of an ACT cohort in your setting or community. That said, don't let being on your own stop you from connecting with the larger ACT community. It's out there and waiting for you. This stuff can be tricky and we all can use support.

CONCLUSION

It has been such a pleasure to witness other therapists as they develop competency in ACT. I'll wrap up with a particular memory that I think of often, something a consultee said to me after conducting a powerful ACT session. This highly seasoned provider had chosen to conduct ACT (for the first time) with a client she had been seeing for several years. The session had been significant in that the client made a huge shift in how he was holding a painful experience that had been defining his life. My consultee was extremely moved. She remarked wonderingly, "I have been doing this for thirty years, and this is the first time I feel like what I do actually makes a difference!" I have heard many comments along these lines. We are onto something with this therapy.

This book is intended to help therapists optimize the delivery of ACT. A starting point has been that basic competency in ACT requires conducting the therapy with fidelity to the model. This means working at the process level and maintaining theoretical consistency with the therapeutic language and various interventions. Fidelity to the model is also reflected in the nature of the therapist-client relationship.

Optimization is about taking all this further. It is about learning how to use the principles of ACT to work with clients in a way that is powerful—both in terms of influencing behavior change and in affective quality. Of course, one way to strengthen our ability to effectively conduct ACT is to avoid missteps that can work against the therapy, so I've spent some time on that in this book. Another is to use such missteps as therapeutic fodder, and hopefully that idea has been furthered here as well. The most essential point about optimizing ACT is that there is no "optimization destination." Just as we have good days in the therapy room, we have not-so-good days. For every clinical opportunity we take, we are turning away from another choice that could have had even more utility. But there seem to be some consistent ways to work with this stuff that make a meaningful difference in the therapy room, and I have done my best to pass those on to you.

I began this final chapter by promoting "walking the walk" when it comes to working with ACT. I have taken the same approach to this book, striving to be open, willing to have whatever came up (which, believe me, was a lot), while steadily moving forward with my intention to offer something helpful to other ACT clinicians. In other words, psychological flexibility was required to do this thing. It occurs to me rather belatedly that if we gather up the various skills, tips, approaches, and stances suggested in this book, together they do a pretty good job of representing psychological flexibility. It seems psychological flexibility is a requirement in helping others develop psychological flexibility. There's something perfect about that, don't you think?

References

Bach, P. A., & Moran, D. J. (2008). *ACT in practice: Case conceptualization in acceptance and commitment therapy.* Oakland, CA: New Harbinger.

Eifert, G. H., & Forsyth, J. P. (2005). *Acceptance and commitment therapy for anxiety disorders: A practitioner's treatment guide to using mindfulness, acceptance, and values-based behavior change strategies.* Oakland, CA: New Harbinger.

Fromm, E. (1941). *Escape from freedom.* New York: Farrar and Rinehart.

Harris, R. (2009). *ACT made simple: A quick-start guide to ACT basics and beyond.* Oakland, CA: New Harbinger.

Harris, R. (2013). *Getting unstuck in ACT: A clinician's guide to overcoming common obstacles in acceptance and commitment therapy.* Oakland, CA: New Harbinger.

Hayes, S. C. (2007). *ACT in action* [DVD]. Oakland, CA: New Harbinger.

Hayes, S. C. (2011). Discussion on the Association for Contextual Behavioral Science LISTSERV.

Hayes, S. C., & Strosahl, K. D. (Eds.). (2010). *A practical guide to acceptance and commitment therapy.* New York: Springer.

Hayes, S. C., Strosahl, K. D., & Wilson, K. G. (1999). *Acceptance and commitment therapy: An experiential approach to behavior change.* New York: Guilford Press.

Hayes, S. C., Strosahl, K. D., & Wilson, K. G. (2012). *Acceptance and commitment therapy: The process and practice of mindful change* (2nd ed.). New York: Guilford Press.

Luoma, J., Hayes, S., & Walser, R. (2007). *Learning ACT: An acceptance and commitment therapy skills-training manual for therapists.* Oakland, CA: New Harbinger.

McHugh, L., & Stewart, I. (2012). *The self and perspective taking: Contributions and applications from modern behavioral science.* Oakland, CA: New Harbinger.

McKay, M., & Zurita Ona, P. E. (2011). *Introduction to ACT: Learning and applying the core principles and techniques of acceptance and commitment therapy* [DVD]. Oakland, CA: New Harbinger.

Ramnero, J., & Törneke, N. (2008). *The ABCs of human behavior: Behavioral principles for the practicing clinician.* Oakland, CA: New Harbinger.

Sandoz, E. K., Wilson, K. G., & Dufrene, T. (2010). *Acceptance and commitment therapy for eating disorders: A process-focused guide to treating anorexia and bulimia.* Oakland, CA: New Harbinger.

Stoddard, J. A., & Afari, N. (Eds.). (2014). *The big book of ACT metaphors: A practitioner's guide to experiential exercises and metaphors in acceptance and commitment therapy.* Oakland, CA: New Harbinger.

Tolle, E. (1997). *The power of now.* Vancouver, BC, Canada: Namaste Publishing.

Törneke, N. (2010). *Learning RFT: An introduction to relational frame theory and its clinical application.* Oakland, CA: New Harbinger.

Twohig, M. P., & Hayes, S. C. (2008). *ACT verbatim for depression and anxiety: Annotated transcripts for learning acceptance and commitment therapy.* Oakland, CA: New Harbinger.

Villatte, M. (2013). Discussion on the Association for Contextual Behavioral Science LISTSERV.

Villatte, M., Villatte, J., & Hayes, S. C. (in press). *The language of psychotherapy: Strengthening your clinical practice with relational frame theory.* New York: Guilford Press.

Villatte, M., Villatte, J., & Monestes, J. L. (2014). Understanding and using relational frame theory in experiential clinical practice. In J. Stoddard & N. Afari (Eds.). *The big book of ACT metaphors: A practitioner's guide to experiential exercises and metaphors in acceptance and commitment therapy.* Oakland, CA: New Harbinger.

Walser, R., & Westrup, D. (2007). *Acceptance and commitment therapy for the treatment of post-traumatic stress disorder and trauma-related problems.* Oakland, CA: New Harbinger.

Wilson, K. G., & DuFrene, T. (2008). *Mindfulness for two: An acceptance and commitment therapy approach to mindfulness in psychotherapy.* Oakland, CA: New Harbinger.

Darrah Westrup, PhD, is a licensed clinical psychologist practicing in Colorado and California with an established reputation for her work as a therapist, program director, trainer, researcher, and consultant to practitioners at various firms and organizations. She is a recognized authority on post-traumatic stress disorder (PTSD) and acceptance and commitment therapy (ACT) and has conducted numerous presentations and trainings at international, national, and local conferences, seminars, and workshops. She currently serves as an expert ACT consultant for the VA-wide evidence-based treatment rollout of ACT for depression, and has coauthored two books on ACT: *Acceptance and Commitment Therapy for the Treatment of Post-Traumatic Stress Disorder and Trauma-Related Problems* and *The Mindful Couple*.

Index

Association for Contextual Behavioral Science (ACBS), 91
authenticity, 53, 54, 55, 58
avoidance. *See* experiential avoidance

B

Bach, Patricia, 241
bailing out, 126–132
barriers to treatment, 147–174; behavioral change and, 154–172; being right, 161–163; burden of freedom, 156–157; difficulty of ACT, 157–159; explanation of, 147; feeling wronged, 159–163; homework problem, 164–172; how to spot, 148; lack of progress and, 173–174; reasons as causes, 155–156; seductiveness of "should," 163–164; timing related to, 155; working with, 149–154
behavioral therapy, 242
behaviors: context of, 12, 30; learned, 13, 109; therapy-impeding, 147–174
being present, 68–70
being right, 161–163
Big Book of ACT Metaphors, The (Stoddard and Afari), 201
boldness with kindness, 134–137
box with stuff in it exercise, 191
burden of freedom, 156–157
"but" vs. "and" usage, 106

C

case conceptualization, 38–40
causes, reasons as, 155–156, 164
centered response style, 19–20
challenging clients, 229–234
chessboard metaphor, 42, 79, 185–190; example of applying, 187–190; guidelines for setting up, 186–187; timing considerations, 201
Child exercise, 100
Chinese finger trap exercise, 207–208
clients: being directive with, 46–49; difficult or challenging, 229–234; exploring language with, 107–111; getting in the room with, 51–54; handling curveballs thrown by, 219–226; lack of progress by, 173–174; sharing stories or comments with, 54–55; therapist equality with,

49–51; unintentional collusion with, 164; wrap-up session for, 97–101
clinical acumen, 226–229
cognitive defusion. *See* defusion
cognitive fusion. *See* fusion
colluding with clients, 164
committed action, 20–21, 31, 84
comparison, relation of, 15
compassion: apology distinguished from, 139; being uncompromising with, 137–138
competency in ACT, 237–238
conceptualized self, 20, 35, 177, 182, 185
confidence, conveying, 138
consequences, learning by, 13
constructed self, 177
consultation groups, 240
contact with the present moment, 19, 68
content areas, 81, 84
context of client behavior, 12, 30
contextual behavioral science, 8–9, 243
contextualscience.org website, 91, 238
Continuous You exercise, 121, 184, 190, 220
control agenda, 22, 84, 124, 144
control strategies, 207–209
coordination, relation of, 15
corpus delicti analogy, 159–161
couple therapy example, 220–224
creative hopelessness (CH), 123–145; bailing out from, 126–132; control agenda and, 84, 124, 144; difficulty with, 125; effective use of, 124–125; experiential avoidance and, 123, 125, 126, 140–143; exploring with clients, 123–124; fragility of clients and, 132–133; fusion with thoughts and, 132; including vs. excluding, 124; larger agenda related to, 143–144; "lite" form of, 144–145; negative reactions to, 131–132; purpose of, 123, 125; stylistic missteps in, 138–140; therapist style and, 133–140; timing of, 125, 133, 143–144
crisis as content, 40–43

D

decision making, 67, 76
defensiveness, 203
defusion, 18–19; experiential exercise for, 119, 208–209; language exploration and, 111, 120–121; methods of working with, 42; observation of thoughts and, 84; promoting through language, 183;

reluctance to practice, 120; self-as-context and, 182–183; two computers metaphor for, 34, 208

deictic framing, 16, 178

depression, 105, 106, 127–128

derived relations, 15, 175, 178

description vs. evaluation, 112–120

difficult clients, 229–234

directive approach, 46–49

dirt patch metaphor, 77, 79

disclosure, 42, 50–51, 55

discomfort toll, 158–159

dispassion, 174

dry well metaphor, 199–200

DuFrene, Troy, 242

DVDs on ACT, 239

E

empathy, 138, 181

enabling style, 60

engaged response style, 20–21

equality with clients, 49–51

evaluation: description vs., 112–120; mindfulness exercises and, 210

exercises. *See* experiential exercises

Experiencer perspective, 63, 64, 66, 184, 208

experiential avoidance, 13; creative hopelessness and, 123, 125, 126, 140–143; examples of, 31, 35, 36, 140–142

experiential exercises, 193–215; challenges of working with, 207–209; client discomfort with, 210–212; concluding final sessions with, 100–101; content vs. process of, 194; control strategies related to, 207–209; in-the-moment use of, 195; key role of, 195–196; language processes and, 121; mixed messages in, 212–214; mutual participation in, 197–198; online sources of, 196; practicing, 195; preparing to use, 39; self-as-context, 42, 184, 190; therapist missteps with, 195–198; timing considerations for, 79, 201–203; underutilization of, 196–197; using what works, 214; winging it with, 194–195; wording changes to, 213–214. *See also* metaphors

experiential exercises (specific): anxiety machine demonstration, 201; box with stuff in it, 191; Child exercise, 100; Chinese finger trap exercise, 207–208;

Continuous You exercise, 121, 184, 190, 220; eyes-on exercise, 197; floating above the earth exercise, 210; label parade exercise, 42; leaves-on-a-stream exercise, 31–32, 210; lemon, lemon exercise, 119, 197, 208–209; Observer exercise, 184; physicalizing exercise, 42, 229; Stand and Commit exercise, 100–101; take-your-mind-for-a-walk exercise, 201

explicit vs. implicit work, 73–76

eyes-on exercise, 197

F

father/mother figure, 60

feelings: of being wronged, 159–163; depicting unwanted, 213. *See also* internal experiences

fidelity to ACT, 1, 2, 7, 25, 236

final sessions, 91–101; experiential finish in, 100–101; hallmarks of good, 97–101; next steps discussion in, 99–100; ongoing issues addressed in, 91–97; reviewing the client's journey in, 99; therapeutic relationship acknowledged in, 97–99

floating above the earth exercise, 210

fluid approach to ACT, 82–83, 91

fragility of clients, 132–133

functional analysis, 11–12

functional contextualism, 8, 10, 140, 181

fusion, 31, 35, 60, 132, 182

G

generalization, 13

getting present, 19, 68

Getting Unstuck in ACT (Harris), 241

glumness vs. honesty, 137

Goldberg, Jeremy, 213

group work, 90–91

guiding vs. yanking, 77–78

H

Harris, Russ, 239, 241

Hayes, Steven, 1, 9, 239, 243

hierarchical framing, 178, 185

hierarchy, inferred relation of, 16

homework problem, 164–172

honesty vs. glumness, 137

horizontal therapeutic relationship, 17, 56, 87, 98, 140

style of therapist, 45–66; authenticity and, 53, 54, 58; creative hopelessness and, 133–140; directive approach and, 46–49; individuality vs. fidelity and, 45–46; nurturing or enabling, 60; personal sharing and, 54–55; self-disclosure and, 50–51, 55; supportive vs. aligning, 60–66, 134; therapist/client equality and, 49–51; transparency and, 55–59

supporting vs. aligning, 60–66, 134

T

take-your-mind-for-a-walk exercise, 201

terminating ACT, 91–101; addressing ongoing issues, 91–97; elements in the process of, 97–101. *See also* wrap-up sessions

therapeutic relationship: clinical acumen used in, 226–229; difficult clients in, 229–234; equality in, 49–51; final session acknowledgment of, 97–99; handling curveballs in, 219–226; optimizing the potential of, 46; RFT for understanding, 17; self-disclosure in, 50–51; transparency in, 55–59

therapists: ACT competency in, 237–238; barriers to growth in, 236; getting in the room as, 51–54; personal sharing by, 54–55; self-disclosure by, 50–51, 55; style of, 45–66, 133–140

thinking: as learned behavior, 109; RFT theory of, 14

thoughts: defusing from, 18–19; depicting unwanted, 213; descriptive vs. evaluative, 112–120; evaluating during mindfulness, 210; exploring language and, 109–111; reluctance to defuse from, 120; thanking your mind for, 69–70; Thinker distinguished from, 111

timing, 67–80; ACT decisions about, 67, 76; active welcoming and, 69–70; barriers related to, 155; being present related to, 68–70; common missteps in, 76–80; creative hopelessness and, 125, 133, 143–144; exercise or metaphor use and, 79–80, 201–203; explicit vs. implicit work and, 73–76; guiding vs. yanking and, 77–78; listening process related to, 72; questions for therapists about, 79–80;

silence related to, 70–71; willingness and, 78

Tolle, Eckhart, 181

Törneke, Niklas, 242

trance-like states, 210

transcendent self, 20

transformation of stimulus functions, 16, 175, 199

transparency, 55–59, 172

trauma survivors, 159

two computers metaphor, 34, 202, 208

two scales metaphor, 212–213

U

uncompromising style, 137–138

unflinching style, 137

V

valued living, 20

values, clarification of, 20, 31

verbal learning, 78

victim role, 159–161

Villatte, Jennifer, 198, 243

Villatte, Matthieu, 198, 243

vulnerability, 51

W

Walser, Robyn, 22, 69, 133, 144, 173, 239

website for ACT, 91, 196, 238

welcoming, active, 69–70

willingness, 19, 31, 78, 212

Wilson, Kelly, 9, 242

word choice, 65–66, 105–107, 186, 213–214. *See also* language

workability, 9, 22

wrap-up sessions, 91–101; experiential finish in, 100–101; hallmarks of good, 97–101; next steps discussion in, 99–100; ongoing issues addressed in, 91–97; reviewing the client's journey in, 99; therapeutic relationship acknowledged in, 97–99

Y

yanking vs. guiding, 77–78

YouTube videos on ACT, 241

Z

Zurita, Patricia, 239

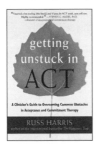